Timothy Leary:
Outside Looking In

Timothy Leary: Outside Looking In

Edited by Robert Forte

Park Street Press
Rochester, Vermont

Park Street Press
One Park Street
Rochester, Vermont 05767
www.InnerTraditions.com

Park Street Press is a division of Inner Traditions International

Library of Congress Cataloging-in-Publication Data

Timothy Leary : outside looking in / edited by Robert Forte.
   p.   cm.
   Includes bibliographical references.
   ISBN 0-89281-786-0 (pbk. : alk. paper)
   1. Leary, Timothy Francis, 1920– . 2. Psychologists—United States—
Biography. 3. Hallucinogenic drugs and religious experience—History
20th century. 4. United States—Social life and customs—20th century.
I. Forte, Robert.
BF109.L43T56   1999   98-54344
150'.92—dc21   CIP

Printed and bound in the United States

10 9 8 7 6 5 4 3 2 1

Text design and layout by Kristin Camp
This book was typeset in Janson with Stanton as the display typeface

Light is the language of the stars and the sun
where we will all meet again.

Timothy Leary
May 30, 1996

Contents

Acknowledgments

This book was born of many labors. Though it bears my name as editor, without the guidance, collaboration, and friendship of Frank Barron, Greg Bogart, Nina Graboi, Michael Horowitz, Rowan Jacobsen, Marge King, Becky Leuning, Vickie Marshall, Ralph Metzner, and Rosemary Woodruff, in particular, it might have remained only a good idea. Thank you to Heather Laudadio for helping me conceive this work. A special thank you is due to the folks at Drive Savers in Novato, California, for the text of the book suffered not one, but two hard-drive crashes when it was just about complete. All seemed lost till their expert service saved the day. Thanks and love to the family and friends that surrounded Tim in his final months for welcoming me into their home, for making me feel part of the team, especially Camella, Chris, Joe, Zach, Michelle, and Carol. Let us always be friends. Thanks to my own family, especially my father, Robert Forte Sr., an arch republican, for proving that blood is thicker than ideology, and for financial support. Thank you to Jaime Nelson for her nourishing, love-filled spirit. Gratitude to my son, Mircea Alexander Forte, who, seven years old when Tim died, got right to the point when he asked, "Dad, why was Timothy so famous anyway? What did he do—free the slaves or something?" And finally, to Timothy Francis Leary, thank you for the privilege to share in your abundant and eternal life.

Res ipsa Loquitur
(let the good times roll)

Introduction

ROBERT FORTE

There is an ancient axiom, which runs: the more bitterly and acutely we formulate a thesis, the more irresistibly it clamours for the antithesis.

Hermann Hesse,
Magister Ludi

Timothy Francis Leary was one of the most influential people of the twentieth century. What his influence has been, however, remains to be determined. Leary is loved and castigated for his spirited popularization of psychedelic drugs in the 1960s, surely his grandest achievement in a lifelong mission to joust with authoritarianism wherever he encountered it. This book is not a biography of Leary, nor an in-depth study of his ideas. Think of it as a mosaic of flashbacks and reflections, mostly in tribute to this mercurial character and the celebrated role he played as a leader of a social, philosophical, and religious movement. The book was conceived one December morning in 1993 as I set out to visit Tim at his home high in the Beverly Hills of Los Angeles. I had just returned from a conference on LSD in Switzerland that was convened by Sandoz Pharmaceuticals Company and the Swiss Academy of Medicine—50 Years of LSD: State of the Art and Perspectives on Hallucinogens. That meeting began with the president of the Swiss Academy, Alfred Pletscher, first lauding the extraordinary scientific potential of LSD and then declaring:

> Unfortunately, LSD did not remain in the scientific and medical scene, but fell into the hands of esoterics and hippies and was used by hundreds and thousands of people in mass gatherings. This uncontrolled propagation of LSD had dangerous consequences—for instance, prolonged psychotic episodes, violence and suicide attempts. Therefore, the use of this drug was subjected to severe restrictions by legal acts. (Pletscher and Ladewig, 1994)

Whenever Leary's name was mentioned at this conference, it was with a dismissive and scornful tone by the predominantly psychiatric researchers attending, for it was generally held that Leary's exuberance and the resultant publicity over psychedelics prompted the legislation that forbade their use.

Of the myriad dysfunctional aspects of U.S. drug policy, none is more bizarre and un-American than the illegal status these drugs hold. "Aldous advocated a cautious boldness," wrote Humphry Osmond, "advising the explorers to do good stealthily and to avoid publicity. Unfortunately his good counsel was not always taken." If Leary had been more circumspect perhaps these rediscovered ancient sacraments could have been more gradually and effectively integrated into our society. Did Leary and company provoke this terrific irrational phobia of psychedelic drugs, or anticipate it and vault clear over it to spread the word? Legal research of these substances is still paralyzed by mounds of red tape. Meanwhile millions already know that beyond the fears of state-sanctioned psychiatry and governmental policy, under the right set and setting, psychedelics can lead to joy, mystery, rebirth, and realization beyond belief. "Seven million people I turned on," Leary said near the end of his life, "and only one hundred thousand have come by to thank me."

Of course the social gyrations of the 1960s renaissance of spirit are far too complex to lay on one man but Leary, clearly, was a most visible figure—a brilliant, charismatic, funny prophet; a ground-

Mother and Aunt Mae

breaking social scientist; a poet; a fame-seeking, careless, self-important, self-destructive fool; or a scapegoat, depending on your perspective.

"You get the Timothy Leary you deserve," he once said.

Timothy Leary was born on October 22, 1920, in Springfield, Massachusetts, the only child of Timothy and Abigail Leary. His grandfather, reputed to be the richest Irish Catholic in western Massachusetts, was perceived by young Timothy as a majestic patriarch who valued literacy and the arts. The "only meaningful words" his grandfather ever spoke to him were, "Never do anything like anyone else. . . . Find your own way. . . . Be one of a kind."

Tim's father was an army dentist, an apparent heir to the Leary fortune, and a drunkard who used to beat his young son. But the fortune, it turned out, was depleted by the depression and assorted other indebtedness. On the very day this was learned, Timothy Leary's father gave his twelve-year-old son a hundred dollar bill, left the house, and never returned. Raised by a devout Catholic mother and his spinster Aunt Mae, Timothy Leary became a dis-

In high school

tinguished, highly spirited, and rebellious teen. He rejected the
school motto, the Kantian imperative—"No one has the right to
do that which if everyone did would destroy society"—by writing
what he called "a particularly fiery editorial suggesting that the Cat-
egorical Imperative was totalitarian and un-American in glorifying
the welfare of the state over the rights of the individual," earning
him the disdain of the school's principal and no recommendation
to college. As a favor to his mother the Monsignor enabled his admission to Holy Cross, a spartan Jesuit school in nearby Worcester,
Massachusetts, where he excelled as a student—and as a bookie,
who had his way with the shop girls downtown. He lasted a year at
Holy Cross. After scoring the highest mark on the examination for
the service academy, he entered West Point in 1940, proud and
eager to serve his country as an elite military officer. But after three
months Leary ran afoul of the West Point regime. He was caught
drunk and admitted providing liquor to underclassmen while
returning from the Army-Navy game. Refusing to resign, he was
punished by "silencing," an ordeal that forbade him to speak or be
spoken to by any of his classmates for the duration of the year. In
letters to his mother at this time, he poured out his soul:

I have changed so much. I am so scared of the world at times and then I feel that after all it makes no difference what becomes of me, that I shall always be happy because I will not take myself too seriously. That is one of my new philosophies and it is the thing that keeps me from minding the men around here who silence me. . . . squabbling over nothing, getting into a big uproar over little insignificant things.

I have to laugh at myself using the word philosophy about the thoughts I have. I know one thing, that I shall try from now on to keep myself calm, quiet, resigned and above all not small and selfish. If I could only be like you, Dear Mother, unselfish and kind. That is going to be my greatest battle, to fight my own selfishness & thoughtlessness. . . .

And how afraid I get when I think of all the millions of people thinking like me that they are going to step out of the crowd & all but one or two out of the million doomed to failure. But you see, Mother, as long as I aim high and keep my sense of humor, my balanced state of mind, my courage & my faith in God and my desire to be unselfish, and as long as I can keep from taking myself too seriously: then no matter what happens I shall be happy.

The silencing is the best thing that has ever happened to me. I firmly believe that. I swear to God it is true. . . . The silencing has made me 1000 years older, has matured me, has forced me to write, has brought me to love good books & philosophy. It has made me broad minded so I can laugh at the foolish, thoughtless, childish stupidity & blind cruelty of the immature minds who bother me. . . . And most of all I must make you happy. Oh Mother, that is my only worry & my only ambition, to make you proud of me.

After four months, when Leary began to reconsider his option to resign from West Point, his problems magnified by poor grades in math, his ever loving mother wrote to him: "Don't worry dear son, if you don't make it through this, it is because the Blessed Lord has something else in store for you, perhaps something better." Tim replied:

Dear Mother; I read your letter tonight, several times, and as always, I could not help feeling the tremendous, quiet, unassuming truthfulness of wisdom that was contained in your every word. Your advice and your ideas are so absolutely undeniable that I was naturally forced to agree wholeheartedly with all you said. . . . I am very unsatisfied with my self and my life, right now. I have set for myself a standard of living, which I believe to be the right one, and yet I fail terribly in living up to it. Everything, the human race, the world itself, and most of all my own pitiful being seems so unutterably futile and worthless that I am constantly being tormented by the immensity of time and space and eternity and by the frailty of my life. . . . Now, I also have no illusions about life. It is true that the underlying motive which prompted every pessimistic philosopher was solitude, and I have had plenty of that. . . . The great error I hope to avoid is to become one of the great ciphers of humanity, constantly in a rut, thinking of nothing except living more comfortably and enjoyably, regardless of how mean and low they become, never thinking a thought that is not connected with the gratification of the senses. Well, again, I pull myself up to a halt before I get going. Please know that I am no rosy optimist filled with illusions. Another short diversion. It seems I am constantly bandying the word truth about. I hate that word, and was rather shocked when you thought I wanted to reform the world and bring it some great metaphysical truth. To be frank, what I really long for is fame, and more than that, the futile hope of leaving something behind me to identify me from the millions upon millions of nameless ciphers that have come and gone. . . . Any way, life isn't worth any minute of the worrying we do about it. The sun will rise 60 years from now and I will be a name on a tomb stone so there is no great issue involved. I think that we should all spend more time praying for our souls than pointless fretting about our lives.

Leary resigned from West Point in August 1941 and went on to the University of Alabama where he began to study psychol-

In the army

ogy. He was expelled one year later, in the fall of 1942, for having spent a night in the girls' dorm. He lost his deferment, was drafted in 1943, and spent almost two years in officer's training, where he met his first wife, Marianne. He became a corporal, and continued his studies in psychology until the war ended. The GI bill paid for him to complete his master's degree in psychology at Washington State University. His thesis was a statistical analysis of the dimensions of intelligence. From there he enrolled in the doctoral program at Berkeley.

Leary became a psychologist and an acclaimed clinical researcher, who served admirably at UC Berkeley, at the Starr King Lutheran Seminary, where he evaluated candidates for the ministry, and at the Kaiser Permanente Hospital, where he initiated group therapy and interpersonal diagnostic techniques. His research was published widely in the professional literature. His first

Teaching at Berkeley

book, *The Interpersonal Diagnosis of Personality*, was voted book of the year by the American Psychological Association in 1959. Thirty-five years later, his interpersonal model was still generating research. Leary was honored at a symposium of the American Psychological Association in 1994.

Timothy had two children with Marianne but he was not a committed husband or father. "Our continued alcohol abuse made everything worse," he said. Marianne committed suicide on the morning of his thirty-fifth birthday in the garage of their Berkeley home. The next year Timothy took the children on a sabbatical to Europe, where he pondered his future in a profession he felt wasn't working. There, in Florence, Italy, a block away from where Galileo had set up his telescope four hundred years before, he was visited by Frank Barron, a friend and colleague who had already distinguished himself as a researcher of the psychology of creativity. Barron told him about his experience with sacred mushrooms in Mexico. These mushrooms had been revealed to the West by a Wall Street banker named Robert Gordon Wasson two years earlier. Wasson theorized them to be at the origin of religion. Tim listened, curious but aloof, as Barron lauded their significance to the study of the mind. "I was a bit worried about my old friend and warned him against the possibility of losing his scientific credibility if he spoke this way among our colleagues," Leary wrote in his autobiography.

In Florence, Leary also met with David McClelland, then

chairman of the department of social relations at Harvard, who was impressed with his work and was looking for someone to liven up the clinical program. "There's no question that what you're advocating is going to be the future of American psychology," McClelland said. Thus was Dr. Leary appointed to a three-year lectureship to teach and research innovative methods of psychotherapy. After eight months at Harvard, in the summer of 1960, Leary traveled to Mexico on vacation and tried the mushrooms himself. He described this event in his seminal paper, "The Religious Experience: Its Production and Interpretation," delivered to a group of Lutheran pastoral counselors at a meeting of the American Psychological Association. "On a sunny afternoon in the garden of a Cuernavaca villa, I ate seven of the so-called sacred mushrooms. . . . During the next five hours, I was whirled through an experience which could be described in many extravagant metaphors but was, above all and without question, the deepest religious experience of my life."

Leary returned to Harvard enthused and immediately, with Barron, began The Psilocybin Project with the aim of "trying to understand the revelatory potentialities of the human nervous system and to making these insights available to others." The project quickly grew to include many hundreds of people. Their extraordinary findings and visionary interpretations were published in leading medical, psychological, linguistic, religious, and philosophical journals, and soon in the popular media, which sparked worldwide interest in the curative, religious, and heuristic properties of the newly termed psychedelic drugs.

Leary was joined by assistant professor Richard Alpert, a hearty band of graduate students, and a constant stream of many of the leading intellectuals and artists of that time. Leary and his team employed new methods in psychological research by using themselves as subjects, reporting directly the drugs' effects on their own minds. Sometimes they would take psilocybin *with* their subjects. This was unheard of and considered unscientific in psychological research, but they felt it was a necessary, ethical dimension of their work.

The Good Friday Experiment, conducted under Leary's guidance by Walter Pahnke, a Harvard M.D., produced religious insights under psilocybin in theology students that were indistinguishable from those of the most renowned mystics and saints.

"The prison project and the Good Friday session had provided experimental evidence that psilocybin used according to our methods was safe and life-changing; we hoped that fellow scientists and administrators, recognizing the powers of these drugs to change behavior, would support our work. The opposite reaction developed," Leary wrote in *Flashbacks*. "Since our research had demonstrated that set and setting determine the course of an altered-state experience, we consistently broadcast signals of intelligent reassurance: 'Trust your nervous system, go with the flow, the universe is basically a beautiful and safe place.' We were amazed to find otherwise intelligent and open minded persons doing everything in their power to instill fear, to cry danger, to slander the brain with negativity."*

Finding the methods and metaphors of contemporary psychological science inadequate to describe the psychedelic mystical experience, Leary and his colleagues turned to religion. They formed the International Federation for Internal Freedom to address the spiritual poverty and ignorance of modern society.

---

* Unbeknownst to most people at that time, for a decade LSD had been the subject of clandestine research at Harvard and elsewhere in the United States. Now it is known that the CIA surreptitiously sponsored—through the Geschickter Foundation and the Human Ecology Fund—studies of the psychotomimetic (psychosis-mimicking) effects of LSD and other psychedelic drugs at Boston Psychopathic Hospital. In these studies Harvard students—including undergraduates—and other volunteers were given LSD to cause a temporary insanity. "The point was to make people crazy," said Philip Slater, who worked on that project in 1952. "Yet despite the forbidding setting and conceptualization of the experience, most of us found it rewarding and often transcendent." The United States Government embarked upon many such attempts to plumb the debilitating capacities of psychedelics, to control the mind and derange it, which they thought would be desirable for chemical warfare and espionage. These cruel and bizarre studies are carefully reported in *Acid Dreams*, by Martin Lee and Bruce Shlain.

Statement of Purpose of the
INTERNATIONAL FEDERATION
FOR
INTERNAL FREEDOM
3rd draft; November 3, 1962

I. The Situation. During the last 4000 years a basic spiritual issue has been debated by those on the one hand who believe in the absolute validity of current religious and scientific models (realists) and those who see these conventional models as flimsy game artifacts (sometimes useful, more often stifling) imposed on the evolving processes of life. The latter (called mystics, visionaries, nominalists, existentialists) are more concerned with man's evolving spiritual potentialities than with his material or intellectual achievements. . . . Recent years have seen the emergence of groups (scattered, but numbering in the hundred thousands) who see a natural fusion of these points of view. Some of these people attempt to combine western customs with classic eastern rituals. . . . There are many, however, who believe that the merging of these two disparate cultural games is a scotch-tape solution and that each culture must develop its own adaptive mutation—its own creative resolution of the essence existence issue—its own new discovery and application of the spiritual. The human cortex is the same—east and west. What differs are the cultural games. Games, being artifacts, can be changed. New games spontaneously and naturally arise. For the past two and a half years a group of Harvard University research psychologists have been studying and directly experiencing these issues. Five research projects on the effects and applications of consciousness-expanding drugs have been completed. Over 400 subjects have participated without serious negative physical or psychological consequences. Over sixty percent of our subjects have reported enduring life changes for the better. As a result of these studies and our appraisal of other research, we have come to several conclusions about the evolution of man's consciousness and the human brain, and we invite others who share our assumptions to communicate with us.

Our conclusions are these:

1. There is a dawning suspicion (based on considerable evidence) that the politics of the nervous system are such that man uses only a fragment (perhaps less than one percent) of his available brain capacity.
2. Certain psychophysiological processes (censoring, altering, discriminating, selecting, evaluating) are responsible for the restricted use of the brain capacity.
3. Indole substances (LSD, mescaline, psilocybin) seem to inhibit or alter these restricting mental processes so that dramatic expansion of consciousness is triggered off.
4. Our data demonstrate that set and setting account for the specific content of awareness . . .
5. Expanded awareness, by definition, extends beyond the limits of the verbal and conceptual. Expanded awareness, therefore, cannot come through verbal education but rather via physical or physiological means. Expanded consciousness also extends far beyond the cultural and ego games in which men are enmeshed.
6. It follows that the utilization of expanded consciousness (i.e. the unused ninety-nine percent of the brain capacity) is virtually impossible unless we are ready to expand our ego and cultural games and to develop an appropriate language . . .

We are aware that cultural structures (however libertarian their purpose) inevitably produce roles, rules, rituals, values, words and strategies which end in external control of internal freedom. This is the danger we seek to avoid. This paradoxical tension we accept. The challenge is to develop a cultural game which strives towards non-game or meta-game. We have selected a name for this group: International Federation for Internal Freedom (IFIF). . . . The present board of directors include: Richard Alpert, Ph.D., Walter Clark, Ph.D., Timothy Leary, Ph.D., George Litwin, Ralph Metzner, Ph.D., Madison Presnell, M.D., Huston Smith, Ph.D., Gunther Weil.

· · ·

What began as scientific research into the effects of psychedelic drugs on human consciousness became too festive for Harvard to bear. Leary defied the advice of colleagues and friends to avoid controversial publicity. Indeed, he seemed most intent to cause as much controversy as possible. Looking back in 1987, Leary agreed with his critics: "Needless to say, enormous confusion was thus created. . . . Epistemological debates about the definition of reality soon degenerated into hysterical social extremism on the part of almost all concerned, present company included." But at the time, 1963, his attitude was "Life is a great big, funny dance, and we are so lucky to be here. All human activities are 'B' movies. The only possible attitude to have is joyous wonder. Things are not really as Serious, Earnest, etc., etc., as you seem to think. We are having a great, great time, and wish you were here."

Leary stood atop the Ivory Tower and proclaimed it irrelevant

---

At a meeting of the
President and Fellows of Harvard College
in Cambridge, May 6, 1963

Voted, because Timothy F. Leary, Lecturer on Clinical Psychology, has failed to keep his classroom appointments and has absented himself from Cambridge during term time without permission, to relieve him from further teaching duty and to terminate his salary as of April 30, 1963.

A true copy of record,

Attest:

Secretary

Dr. Timothy F. Leary

and insignificant compared to adventures that await one who is turned on. "LSD is more important than Harvard," he said, and in the spring of 1963 he and his associate Richard Alpert became the first faculty members to be fired from Harvard since Ralph Waldo Emerson in 1838. The official reason for Leary's firing was being absent from class, but one need only read his spirited manifestos on the obsolescence of the university that were widely circulated to sense the current of that time. "American Education as an Addictive Process and Its Cure," was the title of his final address as a Harvard lecturer.

> The university, and for that matter, every aspect of the educational system, is paid for by adult society to train young people to keep the same game going. To be sure that you do not use your heads. Students, this institution and all educational institutions are set up to anesthetize you, to put you to sleep. . . . The last thing an institution of education wants to allow you to do is to expand your consciousness, to use the untapped potential in your head, to experience directly. They don't want you to evolve, to grow. . . . Education, dear students, is anesthetic, a narcotic procedure which is very likely to blunt your sensitivity and to immobilize your brain and your behavior for the rest of your lives.

The Harvard expulsion thrust Leary and the psychedelic experience into national prominence in the growing civil rights, ecology, and anti-war movement. Once again, we sense a twinge of apology from Leary for his politicizing the psychedelic experience. In 1987 he wrote, "Religious, mystical, visionary possession states are powerful and wonderful—they open the doors of perception, polish our sensory lenses, shake up our autonomic nervous system, and get our hormones surging—but they're intimate and precious. They shouldn't be imposed on others. And above all, they should be kept out of politics."

After Harvard, Leary and his associates moved their headquarters to a palatial estate in Millbrook, New York, where they continued to mount a formidable challenge to the status quo by encouraging millions of young people to "turn on, tune in, drop out," further incurring the wrath of the establishment and alienating Leary from the scientific community. During this period at Millbrook, Leary made a number of extravagant and erratic claims about the future of an American society transformed by psychedelic drugs. "LSD is only the first of many new chemicals that will exhilarate learning, expand consciousness, and enhance memory in years to come. These chemicals will inevitably revolutionize our procedures of education, child rearing, and social behavior. Within one generation these chemical keys to the nervous system will be used as regular tools of learning. You will be asking your children, when they come home from school, not 'What book are you reading?' but 'Which molecules are you using to open up new Libraries of Congress inside your nervous system?'

In a highly publicized interview in *Playboy* magazine titled "She Comes in Colors," Leary broadcast: "It is almost inevitable, if a man and a woman take LSD together, that their sexual energies will be unimaginably intensified, and unless clumsiness or fright on the part of one or the other blocks it, it will lead to a deeper experience than they ever thought possible. . . ."

Playboy: We've heard that some women who ordinarily have difficulty achieving orgasm find themselves capable of multiple orgasms under LSD. Is that true?

Leary: In a carefully prepared, loving LSD session, a woman can have several hundred LSD orgasms.

Playboy: Several hundred?

Leary: Yes. Several hundred.

He further asserted that "LSD is a specific cure for homosexuality." And he would rather, he said, have his future children "take heroin than go to a first grade grammar school in this country." Whether or not he meant to be facetious or deliberately provocative is beside the point that these statements, and others like them, made it easy for an already resistant, mainstream adult society to brand him as a reckless, hedonistic corrupter of youth. He would frequently add a sobering note—"The key concept of the psychedelic revolution is work—ecstatic work. This central point is missed by enthusiastic acidheads as well as the horrified burghers, each deluding the other with the notion of escape and naughty pleasure"—but he was never known as a man of moderation.

IFIF was asked to leave Zihuatanejo, Mexico, site of their summer headquarters for two years, and was forbidden to reestablish that program when they tried to on several Caribbean islands. Three years later—in 1966—Leary was arrested for possessing a few grams of marijuana in Laredo, Texas, while attempting to drive into Mexico. He was charged with violating an arcane marijuana tax law. He fought the charge successfully. The Supreme Court, in a unanimous decision on his case in 1968, declared the marijuana tax laws unconstitutional. Leary then announced his candidacy for governor of California. Federal prosecutors, their ire inflamed, then recharged him with transportation of marijuana, a different crime that carried a twenty-year sentence, as he was mounting his campaign. "Come Together—Join the Party," his campaign slogan, was subsequently developed by John Lennon into the Beatles' hit song while Tim prepared his unsuccessful defense. His defense statement began:

> I am pleading not guilty in this case, because I am an American citizen. As such, I am entitled to the free exercise of my religion. I am entitled to engage in scientific research. I am entitled to live in my home, travel in my car and bring up my children the best I can in accordance with my beliefs and values. My motives before and during the incident of my arrest are clearly spiritual, interior and not ulterior. These are not personal privileges that I claim, but constitutional rights of every citizen. In defending myself against this prosecution, I am defending the right of every American citizen to lead the religious life of his own conviction, to worship, to experience, to commune with universal forces, to transcend his ego and dissolve the petty differences that divide men whom love should bind, to seek religious ecstasy, revelation and truth as men have done throughout the ages.

Leary was arrested again, this time in Laguna Beach, California. Set up, he claims, given a five-million-dollar bail—the highest ever for an American citizen—convicted, and sentenced in the midst of sensational publicity to ten years for two roaches and a few flakes of grass that were purportedly vacuumed from his car. This time he was denied appeal bond—against the law—and was immediately confined to a minimum-security prison in California. Nine months later, with the help of the revolutionary Weather Underground, he escaped:

> One of the greatest pranks that I enjoyed was escaping from prison. I had to take a lot of psychological tests during the classification period, and many of the tests I had designed myself; so I took the tests in such a way that I was profiled as a very conforming, conventional person who could not possibly escape and who had a great interest in gardening and forestry. The feeling that I had made a nonviolent escape was a sense of tremendous exaltation and humour and joy. I laughed and laughed and laughed, thinking about what the guards were doing now. Heads would be rolling. The bureaucracy would be in a stew. This kept me laughing for two or three weeks.

In Algeria

Timothy and Rosemary fled to Europe and then to Algeria in a show of support for Eldridge Cleaver's Black Panther Party government-in-exile. They were betrayed by Cleaver, became his captives, and escaped again a year later. They made it to Switzerland and requested political asylum. But Nixon wanted him back. The president sent his attorney general, John Mitchell, to argue for Leary's return. At the time Nixon called Leary "the most dangerous man in the world," an international group of poets, essayists, and novelists, led by Allen Ginsberg and Michael Horowitz, circulated a "Declaration of Independence for Dr. Timothy Leary." It received over 200 signatures from some of the world's leading writers and prevailed in arguments with the Swiss, who then granted Leary a short-lived asylum. He was then reindicted in the United States on nineteen counts of drug dealing. These charges were fallacious and later dropped, yet they served to intensify international pressure and Switzerland finally gave in to U.S. demands for his person. Rosemary, their marriage crumbling under the stress of being a money-less, country-less fugitive, left Leary and spent the next twenty-five years underground as a fugitive; her adventure remains to be told. Leary was soon recaptured—some say led to his arrest by new girlfriend-narc, Joanna Harcourt-Smith, and sent back to prison in America in the spring of 1973.

Leary was put under enormous pressure by the FBI to turn state's evidence against those in the Weather Underground who aided his escape. "He has been through a real shit storm," said Ken Kesey of this period. Tim called it "the indisputable, undeniable, Dantean bottom." He was now facing seventy-five years in prison and was labeled a snitch—virtually a death sentence in federal prison.

Did he snitch on his friends? He did testify before the grand jury in Chicago and he did direct the FBI to Rosemary and to Michael Horowitz. But without Rosemary—who remained a fugitive—to corroborate his tale, only Michael Horowitz, his archivist, was subpoenaed. Horowitz claimed that as an archivist for Leary, this information was confidential and protected by the law. Horowitz was charged with contempt of court until a precedent-setting ruling granted him the desired confidentiality and the contempt charges were dropped.

Joanna, however, kept up a lively salon, having taken Leary's name and thereby gaining entry into many underground circles. She entertained lavishly, mining information about the Brotherhood and political radicals, but did little in the way of winning his freedom.

"What was Joanna's possessive role, isolating him from decade-old supporters and friends, and using up all his crucial defense money?" asked Allen Ginsberg. "She is great, she's terrible, she's innocent, she's devious. She's the cosmic brat," pronounced Horowitz. "But Timothy has been telling me all year that she was acting with his blessing and his strategy."

When Kesey visited him in prison, confronted Tim with the fact that his girlfriend was a spy, and asked if he wanted to wring her treacherous neck, Leary said no. "I certainly don't hold it against her. She likes this espionage action. It gets her off. Who am I, of all people, to put down somebody else's turn-on? . . . Joanna and I operate on the assumption that everybody knows everything anyway. . . . There is nothing and no way to hide. This is the acid message. . . . Let the poor deprived, bored creatures listen to our conversations, tape our laughter, study our transmissions. Maybe it will turn them on. Perhaps they will get the message our love shine transmits: there is nothing to fear."

Nonetheless, Leary was described in the mainstream press, and in internal court documents, as someone who did cooperate with the FBI. He testified against a prison psychiatrist who interviewed him against the rules in an attempt to get tape to the outside; and he and Joanna set up George Chula, attorney for the Brotherhood, for bringing Leary hashish while in jail. He was denounced by his son and the now waning countercultural movement, and released on an appeal bond from his Laguna Beach conviction in June 1976. Upon release he denied that he testified against his friends and tried to put those rumors, and the politics they embodied, behind him.

For the last twenty years of his life Leary continued to be an enthusiastic cheerleader for change. He was no longer a prominent drug advocate, but he never recanted his spirited ministry of psychedelic drugs. "Is it not clear that psychedelic drugs are exactly what our Harvard research showed them to be in the 1960s? Wonderful gifts from the plant queendom to the animal kingdom; activators of those circuits of the brain that lead to philosophic inquiry, scientific curiosity, somatic awareness, hedonistic lifestyle, humorous detachment, high-altitude tolerant perceptions, chaotic erotics, ecological sensitivity, utopian communality?"

Personal computers, the information age, and the Internet became his platform to urge people to think for themselves and to question authority. He was known to say "Computers are the acid of the '80s and '90s," leading Richard Price, cofounder of the Esalen Institute, to say in 1985: "Tim Leary will be the first person to get computers made illegal."

His last performance was one of the most celebratory death dances we have seen. In 1994 he announced he had inoperable prostate cancer and that he intended to have his head cryonically frozen, to be thawed out when the cure for cancer was discovered—so long as it wasn't during a Republican administration. In the end he decided against cryonics. He died in bed, the last day of May in 1996, smiling, letting go, his last words, "why not?" His remains were cremated and a portion of his ashes was blasted into space.

His birth and death coincided—as did his hero Mark Twain's—with the cycle of a comet. For his last two years he lived in constant celebration of life. While his physical condition eroded his spirit was undaunted. "I did a good job," he said to himself one evening just before he died. He was a pivotal man in a time of marvelous change, and his legacy is as wild and varied as the psychedelic movement he rode in on. By understanding his life, we will illuminate a profound episode of human history.

Timothy Leary's Dead

John Perry Barlow

A couple of hours ago, at 12:45 A.M. Beverly Hills time, old friend and corrupter of my youth Timothy Leary made good on his promise to "give death a better name or die trying." Willingly, peacefully, and unafraid, he headed off on his last trip.

He spoke his last words a few hours before. On the phone to the mordant William S. Burroughs he said, "I hope that someday I'm as funny as you are."

He didn't, as threatened, commit suicide on the Net. Or have his head cut off and frozen. Or engage in any of the other spectacles of departure I had dreaded. In the end, he surrounded himself with the angelic band of twenty-somethings who have been uploading him into the Web these last few months and drifted peacefully out of here.

I was headed his way when he died. When I was with him earlier this month he said, "When I leave here, Barlow, I want your face to be one of the last things I see." I think that was one of the sweetest things anyone ever said to me, and I was trying to make it possible, but death proved itself once again to be bigger and faster

John Perry Barlow is a rancher in Pinedale, Wyoming, cofounder of the Electronic Frontiers Foundation, and lyricist for the Grateful Dead.

than either of us. The phone just rang in the middle of this rainy Wyoming night, and now I'm here naked in the dark trying to think of something to follow him out with.

Two years ago, Cynthia and I spent our last day together with Timmy. When she died the next day and it became so shockingly clear to both of us how strange this culture has become on the subject of the second-commonest event in the world, how weirdly shameful is dying in America, we both thought it time to bring death out of the closet. I did so by grieving her, and continuing to grieve her, more publicly than is polite in a culture that claims for itself the ability to conquer and control everything.

But Timmy beat me to the barricades. He flat died. And he died without pretending that he was "really going to get well any day now," without permitting himself to become a ghoulish and futile medical experiment, without contributing to the stupefying mass denial that causes almost 80 percent of America's health care dollars to be blown on the last six months of life.

He died unashamed and having, as usual, a great time.

A few weeks ago, the denizens of leary.com and I rented a phalanx of wheel chairs and rode them with him into the House of Blues on Sunset Strip, a place that likely had never seen fifteen people in wheel chairs before. After a truly merry time, we were headed back to his house and on the way came within a smile of Tim Leary's Last Bust.

We were cruising west on Sunset. And the sun was setting. The top was down on my metallic mauve rent-a-convertible. A couple of the Web girls, Trudy and Camella, were sitting on the trunk like psychedelic prom queens, shoop-de-booping to the funk station on the radio, volume at eleven. Both of the girls were beautiful, Trudy like a character from *Neuromancer*, Camella like a character from Botticelli. The air was sweet and soft as a negligee on our faces, and the light had that elegiac quality that makes people think L.A. might not be so bad after all.

Timmy gave me a high five and grinned. "Life is good!" he shouted over the music. As I looked up to meet his raised hand, I saw in my rearview mirror, past the swaying torsos of the girls, the rotating reds of a real Beverly Hills cop.

Of course we were in possession of several of those substances that we considered safe and effective but which this culture, in another of its dangerous madnesses, has declared lethal, probably to distract heat from its own deadly drugs of choice. Furthermore, I had only recently paid an astonishingly steep California fine for allowing a friend to stand up through the sunroof of a car I was driving.

He pulled us over in front of the Beverly Hills Hotel. He looked like an Eagle Scout.

"Officer," I said, nodding back at the still improperly seated girls, "I know what we were doing was wrong. But you see, my friend here is dying, and we're trying to show him a good time." Timmy, without saying anything, smiled sheepishly at the cop and nodded, caught in the act.

He looked like hell but he sure looked happy.

The officer gazed into Timmy's beatific skull-face and lost his starch. "Well," he said to the girls, "I'd be lying if I didn't say that looks like fun, but just because he's dying doesn't mean you should. Now get down in the seat and buckle up and I'll let you go." I felt like honest death had just made one of its first converts.

In thirty years of following Tim Leary around, he's given me some wonderful and hair-raising moments. He has been father, anti-father, partner-in-crime, and devout fellow-worshiper of all that is female in this world. We loved each other, and shared more memories than I will ever relate. But I think the look he gave that cop is the memory I will cherish most.

As usual he was "cocking a snoot at authority," as Aldous Huxley once accused him. But he was doing it, also as usual, with wit. And with love.

America managed to forgive Richard Nixon when he died. I hope they will extend the same amnesty to a real hero, Dr. Timothy Leary.

An Unfinished (R)Evolution

A Memorial for Tim Leary

FRANK BARRON

(Given at Timothy Leary Memorial Service, First Unitarian
Church, San Francisco, June 12, 1996)

We are here to recognize and to mourn a significant death, and to
remember the times and the deeds of a significant life. Timothy
Francis Leary made himself into an unusual person and he helped
to create an unusual movement of mind that continues beyond him.
For we who remain and who go on into the future, it is our privilege and responsibility to share in its further creation.

That creation was the psychedelic movement, or psychedelic
revolution, or, perhaps better, the psychedelic evolution. It does
not go under his name only, and it is not just or even mostly sustained by the psychedelic drugs. It is rather a commitment to fight
for personal freedom, to oppose everywhere the war mentality and

*Frank Barron, Ph.D., Sc.D., Professor Emeritus, Psychology, University of
California, introduced Timothy Leary to the sacred mushroom in 1959. He
was a cofounder of the Harvard Psilocybin Project and is one of the foremost
researchers into the psychology of creativity. Among his books are* Creativity
and Personal Freedom, No Rootless Flower: An Ecology of Creativity, *and most recently (with Anthea Barron)* Creators on Creating.

the tyranny of dogmatic beliefs. It stands for equal rights for race and gender, and for ecological Earth-respecting ways of thinking and acting. It respects the ban on certain "hard" drugs such as heroin and crack cocaine while pressing for the legalization and social use of the psychedelic drugs to speed up mental evolution and increase useful knowledge of psychochemical evolutionary agents.

I'm glad this celebration is taking place in the church it is, for Tim himself spoke here nearly thirty-five years ago. The occasion was a series of lectures I had arranged for the University of California Extension, eight in all for eight consecutive weeks. The title I had given it was "The Silent Revolution." Needless to say, that bit of prescient titling, with its hint of a much more audible revolution to follow, brought to these halls the most advanced and forward-looking audience, as well as speakers who understood their role in what was to come.

We led off with myself speaking of the creative process in the individual, in society, and in the human mind in general. Mark Schorer then took up the theme of creativity in the writer and artist. Mark was a hero to the beats across the Bay, having spoken out sharply in defense of Lawrence Ferlinghetti in court. The case involved the City Lights Bookstore, but it had actually turned on an attempt to suppress Allen Ginsberg's *Howl*. Mark called the poem "an indictment of those elements in modern society destructive of the best qualities of human nature (materialism, conformity, and mechanization leading to war)." Since Mark was a leading critic, his words carried a lot of weight. The defendant was found not guilty—an important decision in the legal-social history of the Beat movement.

Following Schorer, in the third week of the series, Margaret Mead stomped on stage, wearing an ankle-length gown made I am sure of sackcloth, and carrying a large staff. She reminded me of nothing so much as Joan of Arc at Orleans, rallying her troops. She lacked only a horse and armor, but then, she didn't need them. Her call to the attack, in her strong, resonating voice, was a call for women and their more advanced menfolk—or did I read that into it?—to get going on a revolution in women's consciousness. My wife Nancy was in the audience, pregnant a few months with our second child, the to-be-Brigid, and she was paying close attention.

The following week came Gerard Piel, publisher of *Scientific American*, the Bible of forward-looking scientists. Piel took a new and somewhat forbidding look at the incredible acceleration of scientific knowledge and innovation in just the past two decades, beginning with the splitting of the atom. A big, big revolution was about to come out of that.

Ralph Tyler, director of the Center for Advanced Study in the Behavioral Sciences, was next. He foresaw the extraordinary crisis and need for creativity in the field of education, in the cultivation both of the human resource and the knowledge resource; teachers needed to be trained in ways of creating new learning contexts for utilization of the information explosion to come.

Gerald Heard, a brilliant philosopher and close friend of Aldous Huxley, came next. I had invited Aldous himself but he was struggling with disabling illness, and he suggested Heard take his place. Gerald spoke of the need to challenge assumptions in philosophy, and especially in the relation of the individual to the state. The individual, he asserted, had to be vigilant in resisting the encroachment of a developing, more sinister, hand-in-silken-glove form of the collectivist society. He also spoke of the need for new religious rituals and creeds, since those currently popular were made to fit an earlier and now disproved view of Nature, Life, and Humanity. He foresaw an increasing realization of the emptiness of the reigning religions. He stopped just short of saying empty churches.

Then came Tim, talking about—guess what? If you think he was talking about LSD, or LSD only, you would be mistaken. He took on a broader topic, the extension of human consciousness and the ways in which it might be abetted. Psychochemicals got a call, but new ideas of human nature were the substance of what he hailed as the vehicle for the coming revolution.

One worthy member of the audience was young Michael Murphy, who had just returned from Aurobindo's ashram in India and whose intense interest was in the evolution of consciousness, and especially in the awakening of the human potential in everyone. Mike called me, introduced himself, and suggested we have lunch—no, not a naked lunch (we were all fully clothed and even wearing neckties)—to discuss an idea he had in mind for a place to be called Esalen. I suggested I bring Tim along, and out of that lunch came—well, a lot of things. One of the interesting things about the creative process is the shower of sparks that fly from the bisociation of remote ideas.

I concluded the series of meetings, which by now had an audience that overflowed via closed-circuit television into no fewer than six larger academic lecture halls in Berkeley and San Francisco, with what I hoped was a synthesis of it all. I didn't quite say, "The times, they are a changing," but that was on the tip of my mind. That was the tune everyone heard.

So, the place—this church—is doubly hallowed in the minds of those of us who are here to remember Tim Leary this evening. Would anyone expect a revolution to get going in a church in San Francisco? Well, if it didn't absolutely get going here, it was at least heralded as a silent gathering of immense forces of creativity that would soon be heard, heard 'round the world, in good American revolutionary fashion.

The psychedelic work at Harvard was already in full swing, and I had just returned from its first year there, where I was codirector with Tim of the Psilocybin Project. Richard Alpert, Ram Dass himself, soon to be engaged in his own silent inner (r)evolution, took over my part in the work when I left. He played Tom Sawyer to Tim's Huck Finn as Huck "lit out for the territ'ry."

There are many things I could say about Tim, for he was a many-faceted person indeed, but first I want to remark on two aspects that I think should not be neglected in this remembering.

Tim, you know, was a transplanted Irishman, and he had a mad Celtic imagination to go with a strange hidden streak of Irish Catholic New England Puritanism. Catholicism? Puritanism? This surely is not the Tim all of us know! But yes, it was. Without something powerful and id-like to rebel against, what is an Irish rebel to do? And if you can't find a real reason to be put in jail, you have to invent one. An Irish rebel without a prison record for political activities will never be heard about.

Tim had still other lethal Irish characteristics. He had a love of song and poetry, of old Irish ballads, and of course of the wild imagination of James Joyce. If sometimes his tales got a little tall, I gave his bardic nature credit for them. If he had occasional bouts with evil spirits, I would remember the mythical Irishman Conan, who upon finding himself in hell one day and being cuffed by the devil, gave the devil a cuff back. That was Tim.

My last personal memory of Tim was of the gathering at his house on the Saint Patrick's Day weekend just before his death. A corps of Harvard stalwarts arrived to cheer him on, and a friend arranged for some Irish musicians to sing and play the old sentimental songs. They started with the Yeats poem set to music, "Down by the Salley Gardens," and then went on to some rousing pub songs like, "By the Rising of the Moon" and "The Boys of Wexford." In the chorus there were a Sharon and a Brigid, a Kathleen and an Anthea Rose Maeve, a Rosemary and a Nancy Jean. Tim decided to declaim from Joyce's *Finnegan's Wake,* the beginning and the end of it. The Liffey was for Joyce the symbol of the beginning, a circle, and an end in which the river of life begins again.

I think I should recall here a moment in Tim's life that he told me about in those days at Harvard. He had been out on a fishing boat, and many fish had been taken. Tim was a great sportsman, but not one who would shed blood—his games were golf and tennis and baseball, and touch football. As he sat in the boat and saw a fish that had been brought aboard lying there gasping its last, he took it in his lap and stroked it and spoke to it and joined it in its consciousness of its dying.

This is an example, I believe, of one of Tim's most distinctive contributions. He saw happening in himself, whether with psychedelics or without, the evolution of life, from DNA consciousness to human-mind consciousness. This insight he tried to teach—for he was a teacher too—to others as well.

I said of Tim that he was many-faceted. This is a weak word for what I mean. He had many, many faces that he turned to the world, and you could see in him whatever you yourself brought to the seeing. But more than that, he played a different role in each interpersonal situation—transactions, he called them—adapting himself to the script as he interpreted it. If this sometimes got confusing, why not? Isn't the self merely a fiction, an invention of the executive branch of the central nervous system? So might Tim have said.

In some of his aspects, Tim was far from a benign individual. In the lives both of some persons close to him, and for multitudes whom he did not know personally, he could be, and sometimes was, a destructive force. His advocacies, put in slogans worthy of a master advertiser, were taken as guides to action by young people whose identity was still in the process of formation, who were struggling to find themselves. Did those slogans help or hurt people of unsure selfhood, engaged in the struggle for identity and in feeling their way toward the expression of love in an intimate relationship? The jury is still out on that one. It did no good for him to say, as he often did, "That's not what I meant." He was referring especially to his call to communion, "Turn on, tune in, drop out." What he had meant was to look inward, and to shield yourself from all the programmed stimuli of the political world and its controlled media, made for war and profits. But it was an esoteric message. To the young people who did drop out, very literally and often with a thud, it was no consolation that dropping out of school and family and the job market wasn't what he had meant. For himself, his life was governed, as his universe was, by planning, reason, and calculation, but his message was at the edge of chaos and to the uncertain heart it often brought disorder. I talked with him often about this, and he took it very seriously. He had faith that a new order would emerge from the invited chaos, and that a novel synthesis would be both complex and more realistic—in a word, elegant.

So Tim, we must acknowledge, was sometimes reckless with his words, perhaps too much the dramatist. But here I would recall to you the words of William Blake in "The Marriage of Heaven and Hell": *The road of excess leads to the palace of wisdom. Prudence is a rich, ugly, old maid courted by Incapacity. He who desires but acts not, breeds pestilence. . . . You never know what is enough unless you know what is more than enough. . . . Exuberance is Beauty.*

As Tim approached death, he seemed to be trying to express everything implicit in his life. At times it could be seen as mere mockery, an embracing of undignity in the face of the Prince. No, "At last it comes, the distinguished thing," as Henry James said on his deathbed. Yet behind it, I felt, was that insuperable drive toward inclusiveness. I was reminded in looking at him surrounded by his friends of the vision of the end of things of which Teilhard de Chardin wrote in *The Future of Man*. Teilhard imagined consciousness in its fullest development to be a vast sea itself. This, I felt, was the spiritual panorama of which Tim was a part as he came to his own end. This vision always falls short of realization, for that is the nature of our mortality, but in those final scenes of our friend's life it animated the last events.

In a memorial for the dead, in whatever temple, I find it not amiss to invoke the last prayer of the Christian service: *Requiescat in pace*. I offer it here for Timothy Francis Leary—May he rest in peace.

To Tim from John

JOHN BERESFORD

Tim,

You have always been a source of amazement to me: my placid life compared to yours. We met in the early days of the fateful (and, we both know, fated) introduction of LSD to the mind-at-large of the Western world. The first time I heard about you was with Tony Cox. We visited a friend whose name I don't recall and which, in the urgency of composing this memo for you, I won't search through the records to look up. He was a tall lanky fellow, into those "silly sigh beans," as he chose to call the sacred mushroom pills you were then handing out in the bars of Greenwich Village. Tony's friend was telling us about this "mad Harvard professor" who had spread

---

John Beresford was a pediatrician in New York City in 1960 when he had an experience with mescaline that, along with the urging of Michael Hollingshead, prompted him to order a gram of LSD from Sandoz. When his package arrived from Sandoz with a note wishing him "good luck" with his research, John realized he possessed thousands of doses. He began the Agora Scientific Trust, where he observed the effects of LSD and other psychedelics on people in a range of settings. Some of this LSD went to Cambridge with Hollingshead, who fed it to Timothy Leary for the first time.

a handful of the psilocy-beans on the counter and said, "Try these."

Mad? No. Harvard? Yes. Professor? Well, not quite. *Doctor* Leary: the press used to word it with a touch of sarcasm. Yes, very much the teacher, the doctor in the real sense of the word. It seems you taught the world to dip into the reaches of the soul and face reality. It was a different reality from the plain old sordid one left over from the '50s, and the shock woke a generation to what is really there, back at what Huxley liked to call the Antipodes. Discovering it, a generation of gnostics came to life.

Probably what you taught as basic to the session was trust. *It is only your mind,* would be the message to the taker. Your friendly mind. It may try a round of tricking you, seeing if it can trip you up. But treat it as a child, a child you love. Don't let it bamboozle you. You know better than it does. Let it growl like a tiger. Well, the tiger mind can eat you if it wants. You won't deny it a nibble, surely? Then the whole thing turns into a game, and tigers act the same as other players, evolving into light and color and the brilliant melody of consciousness in free play. You, with your linguistic skill, called it a trip—and the word caught on. Yes, this life we have is a trip—and let us make sure the destination we head for is the right one.

I won't take up your time, except to explain something of what you've said I disagree with. First, there is that old shibboleth of *set and setting.* You started a tradition with that phrase. By now, any old commentator who makes a living from explaining, among other things, the effect of LSD—and I mean someone who has never deigned to experience the effect of the magic substance but who professes nonetheless to know all about it—solemnly intones the phrase you cooked up, *set and setting.* It all depends on the mental set you start with, and the scenic setting of the place you take your LSD in (or mushrooms or whatever). A nerdy, squeaky-clean hospital setting or psychology lab, and you'll scare the living daylight out of an experimental subject you foist LSD on. The beautiful garden or the trancelike wilderness, and you'll generate a tranquil experience. That's true, up to a point, but the commentator who seeks desperately for material to clog a textbook doesn't see the paradox he has landed in. For the psychology lab is not *supposed* to be a place that gives you the creeps. It is supposed to be a source of

John Beresford

neutral information. The textbook writer manages to overlook the fact that he and his world-outlook instigate a bad experience.

Not easy to keep the record straight, there. Fast reading takes the reader to the conclusion that not the lab and its professor but the LSD the professor has doled out is the cause of the anxiety, the panic, the disturbing experience, the mistake of taking the tiger as actual. The idiotic term "hallucination" takes control of reader-thinking. LSD is written off as a "hallucinogen." Fuck, who wants to have hallucinations? Not me, not you, not anyone with a head screwed on right. So why do people take LSD, Mr. Professor? Dunno, come to think of it, they must be crazy.

That, I'm afraid, is the one misinterpretation your *set and setting* motto slips into. Yet we know there is some truth to the expression. "Set," of course, is ambiguous, as "setting" is not. "Set" could mean the mental state of someone who should not be taking LSD in the first place, someone cursed with schizophrenia or liable to it, or on the other hand 99 percent of the population for whom taking LSD, done right, is safe and beneficial. It could also mean not this at all but getting out of bed on the wrong side or not getting out of bed on the wrong side in the morning. The problem with the set and setting logo is that it doesn't go far enough. It doesn't explain what an advantageous or disadvantageous set is or does.

Here I am crabbing at a few distortions on your birthday. Okay, no one else is going to be, so let me be a crab. Where we disagreed in the old days was the science bit. It must be true that you believed that science has no place in magical inquiry. I know what you mean. You mean that scientific theory has no place as an explanatory device for one's understanding of the effect of LSD. The behaviorism, the varieties of analysis, the *faux* theory of cognitive psychology that supplanted behaviorism and psychoanalysis beginning in the '60s—nothing remotely scientific has a handle on the effects of LSD. But I think you made a generalization the future will not bear out. You generalized from the irrelevance of present-day psychology to the assumption, which I question, that science, meaning scientific method, is incapable of making the effect of LSD comprehensible. Surely, that cavalier disowning of science caused your ejection from Harry Murray's old department at Harvard University!

Which brings me to the point. Suppose you had dug your heels in and said, not that science is a lost cause, but that somewhere in the unknown mists of science there *must* be an explanation which makes sense of the extraordinary effect of the sacred chemicals? That would have meant embracing science instead of disowning it, and—who knows?—deriving that brand new theoretical perspective which gives LSD its due as the key to an answer to J. B. Watson's old conundrum: "What is this thing called consciousness?"

Ah! But then had you stayed on at Harvard and taken up the cause of understanding the effect of LSD and not—as you did—fulfilled the dreams of a generation eager for the spiritual experience LSD bestows, then there would not be millions today who offer gratitude to you for what you did. The endearing habit of tossing a handful of Sandoz psilocybin on the counter of a Greenwich Village bar grew into a practice, unforeseen by any but yourself, of opening the world of North America, and soon Western Europe, to an experience of the formerly incredible.

When I spoke with a friend whose life was saved by an experience with MDMA, which opened the heart chakra of this individual, and I brought up this great What If—What if Tim stayed on at

Harvard and became the futurist scientist I had in mind?—the reply was prompt. The answer was, my friend said without hesitation, that she would not be alive today. We all know that LSD (or MDMA) saves lives, again with the qualification that it is used properly, respectfully. But I don't mean to dwell on the extreme. The many millions who by today have had first-hand experience of the effect of LSD and those sister chemicals have you to thank for the "new wine" they no longer have to stuff into "old bottles." The spiritual revolution, long overdue, has started. Because of you.

So we met at Newton Center, and we met at Tecate for discussions with Ivan Tors on the LSD organization it was thought possible he might set up, and we met on the Island of Dominica where, just possibly, an evolutionary commune might find its home, and we met in Toronto where I introduced you to my Rose—remember? But our paths crossed seldom. For my own took me into the confused epoch of modern psychiatry where there was no place for the extraordinary or the divine. And always I was thinking of the day when a legitimate theory of consciousness would be possible to enunciate through the medium of LSD, there, as always, as a scientific instrument. So we stand at opposite poles of the conundrum.

But I love you.

And Fare Thee Well.

Briefly

William S. Burroughs

Tim Leary changed the world, and with cool courage faced detractors who were often hysterical. He never lost the poise and dignity that comes from total sincerity.

He emerges as one of the most influential figures of the century. It may be another century before he is accorded his rightful stature. Let his detractors shake their heads, a hundred years from now.

I am proud to have been Tim Leary's friend over many years.

William S. Burroughs was an artist and gun collector who passed away in 1997. He was an early mentor of Timothy Leary and remained an inspiration and friend till the end of Leary's life.

Inviting in Tim Leary's Ghost

An Astrological Invocation

Caroline W. Casey

The Song of Being
From the Irish bard Amairgin

I am a wind upon the sea,
I am a wave upon the ocean,
I am the sound of the sea,
I am a stag of seven tines,
I am a bull of seven battles,
I am a hawk upon a cliff,
I am a teardrop in the sun,

---

*Caroline W. Casey is devoted to restoring mythological literacy to culture.
Her program,* The Visionary Activist Show, *can be heard on Pacifica
Radio, and her astrological-political-spiritual-lecture-ritual-theater is
performed around the world on the solstices and equinoxes. She is the
author of* Making the Gods Work for You: The Astrological Language
of the Psyche *and the forthcoming* Harmonia's Agents: The Rise
of the Heroic Compassionate Trickster as Maverick Player in
Evolutionary History. *For more information see her Web site at
www.spiritualintrigue.com.*

I am the fairest of blossoms,
I am a boar in its boldness,
I am a salmon in a pool,
I am a lake on a plain,
I am a tree upon a hill,
I am a hill of poetry,
I am a god who kindles fire in the head,
I am that which shapes,
I am myself shaped,
I am that which dreams,
I am myself a dreamer,
I am all beings,
I am that which all beings become.

I am Tim Leary.

Shape-shifting is the Celtic visionary bard's task, reminding us first of life's infinitely rich possibilities and our joyful responsibility to explore them, and second of the empathic identification with all of life.

Tim Leary's assignment was to be an Irish Libran and therefore to incarnate the charming Celtic hero shape-shifter. Traditionally periodic fits of madness in the forest are both the balance for extro-verted charm and the prerequisites of being the prophet/storyteller of a desirable future.

Charm is both an Irish and a Libran blessing/curse. The word itself is tricky—a charm is an incantation, which casts a spell upon both the charmer and the charmed. The ease can prove difficult, lulling us into a belief in temporal invincibility like the Native American ghost dancers who believed that the power of the dance would render them invincible to the white soldiers' bullets. We have only to think of Oscar Wilde to be reminded of another Libran Celtic Bard who underestimated the power of repressive law and the humorless antagonism to charm of the tired old regime. To be the sacred clown, who defies the authorities with wit and élan, to demonstrate to others that s/he has done it and survived requires the shape-shifting magic represented by Neptune.

I was initially surprised to find that Tim Leary's natal chart was all Uranus, no Neptune—all technological, intuitive, experimental Promethean trickster, no Neptunian mystic visionary. Long on experiment, short on ecstatic self-loss. To carry the incarnational assignment of not only charming Celtic Irish bard but also Promethean trickster is a daring assignment and gift to the whole team of creation. Prometheus steals fire from the grouchy gods of elite privilege and gives it to humanity for which he is punished by being chained to a rock, where each day his liver is plucked out by a giant eagle only to regrow so that the ordeal is perpetual. Very often those with a strong Uranian/Promethean signature to their charts, minus Neptunian mythological literacy, are possessed by the archetype so that it is literally embodied. Tim's liver was weakened by Hepatitus C, which according to his wife, Rosemary, was a prime contributor to his physical demise.

A less well-known, yet crucial postscript to the Promethean myth is that Prometheus could see the future and thus knew that he was to be rescued by Hercules, a heroic Mars animation of his own feisty strength and determination. This is a more heartening redemptive Fifth Act to the rascal-rebel part of us that defies the stodgy gods of convention. The strength of our alliance with Mars determines how much time we spend chained to the rock. Both radically and traditionally, Tim's Mars was accessed through women. Time and again women saved his ass—yet he was the celebrity. So Irish. Still in the ancestral thrall of the traditional Irish male, about whom it has often been said, "Brilliant talkers, brilliant failures." While the men were off at the pub being gallant poets, spinning tales about life, the women, by default, were back in the hardscrabble cold with the kids and the dirt protecting life, resentful at having been "hired" to be the conservative "responsible" drudge (see Frank McCourt's *Angela's Ashes*, etc.). Radically, Tim attributed his own words, "Only intelligent women can save the world," to fellow Celt John Kennedy's exquisitely experimental lover Mary Meyer.

Tim's life and death would remind us: the shadow of being the trickster is that to rebel against something is to be just as much in its thrall as to conform. Eaten by shadow is the epitaph for much spirited extroverted idealism. Authentic inner mythological work and equal friends to give us a loving hard time are needed by all who aspire to cultural influence. The sixties (on into now) were full of antiauthoritarians who became authoritarians. All too often we have witnessed within and without patriarchy duking it out with itself, too cocky, too certain, too celebrity, too "Let me tell you how it is," too much defined by having an enemy.

As the "Song of Being" reminds us shape-shifting is the antithesis of certainty and bestows the gift of empathic compassionate identification with all that allows us to have no enemy in the dance of life.

Yet when Tim died shortly after midnight on May 31, 1996, Pluto was directly overhead, signifying his successful alchemy. All foibles had been cooked in the crucible of death, distilling a legacy of intensely generous insight and teaching whose full value will not be fully understood nor valued nor applied until several years after the millennium. Jupiter, Neptune, and Uranus were rising due east. His departing communication was of the joyful necessity of fusing what these gods represent both in our psyches, then on out into the culture. The irrepressibly boisterous spirit of Tim bequeathed to us the exhortation to be sacred clowns who evolve into social change artists of compassionate rascalry. Allan Watts's great one-liner about Western man's relationship to religion is that "they sucked the finger instead of going where it pointed." Tim says, "Death has completely released me from the foibles of celebrity so, hey, no finger sucking, there's serious play to be done."

Libra represents the experimental art form of collaboration—even after death. Astrological charts live on as a kind of permanent e-mail address even after the animator has journeyed on. Tim's spirit is released from its own incarnate impediments in order to more effectively contribute to the collective.

William Blake used to set his table and invite dead prophets to join him for tea. Tim joins Billy Blake in saying, "Invite a great interesting dead person to tea—create a portal whereby they can contribute to the ingenuity of now." (On occasion I've invited the dead to be guests on my radio show. They are much easier to book, almost always available, and eager to collaborate with the living. Tim Leary and Paul Robeson came on together and reminded the audience that we cannot live through the dead but the dead can live through us.) Remembering Tim's famous quip, "Everyone gets the Tim Leary they deserve," we ally ourselves with the Tim Leary part of ourselves that we most need now.

To write of Tim, and in fact to read about him, is to invoke him. I had traveled with my Tim Leary file for months—yet was unable to write about him due to my own Celtic Libran busy sloth, trickster procrastination, magical impediments, and curious obstacles. Until. While driving to the airport with Bob Forte, he remarked that it would be wonderful if I could meet Tim's wife, Rosemary. We hesitated, passed her exit—then on impulse pulled over into a shopping mall, where I went into a bar to use the rest room, while Bob attempted to call Rosemary on the phone. As I emerged from the bar Bob was walking toward me, shaking his head, saying, "Well, I tried—called someone, got her number, left a message on her machine," whereupon Rosemary Leary pulled up into the parking space immediately in front of us. We love that electrical chi, back on cosmic appointment time; there is an order, magic is alive, we are connecting with those with whom we should connect. And furthermore, it was as though Tim (whom I had not met in life) was still being a Libran artist, introducing teammates, will continue to do so, is doing so now through this book, and had given me permission to write about him. And he said it was OK to keep it short.

Birth charts live on like perpetual holograms, even after the animator has journeyed on. Jupiter transits result in reissues of books, allowing people to become wealthy after death. Uranus conjuncts Tim's Moon trine with his Sun in 2003, revealing to us that it is around that time that Tim's full joke, contribution, and influence will be acknowledged by the collective.

The astrological language says that there have been two great strategical social change times during the twentieth century, as characterized by the coming together of any two of the outer planets, the Change Gods, Pluto, Uranus, and Neptune. The first conjoining was of Pluto (death, rebirth, intensity) and Uranus (Tim's trickster god of Promethean experimentation) in 1964–69. This pattern conjoined Tim's Jupiter, god of storytelling, philosophy, and theater, in his 9th house of teaching. His understanding of what to learn and how to teach it certainly underwent a transformative exploration. He taught the '60s, became its icon, then put out his sails and windsurfed this collective elemental wave to Pluto's underworld. The Sabian symbol (a set of images for each degree of the zodiac) for his Jupiter is "Groom snatches the veil away from the bride—eliciting a response." His task was/is to be a cultural agent provocateur. He was programmed to come alive in the '60s and to consistently carry and embody both the zeitgeist and the teaching stories that first began to emerge then.

The second significant social-spiritual change time was the mid-to-late '90s, characterized by the coming together of Uranus (same player as in the '60s, but this time with a different dance partner) with Neptune, god of shape-shifting, dreams, vision, imagination. Tim rode out as this conjunction was rising in the east. Poignantly yet appropriately we now move into a time when the gifts of the compassionately inventive trickster in all of us are about to be welcomed by the collective. Now is the time of great teams assembling for the Grand Intrigue of successful social influence. "Take the zircon to Foppa and tell him we move tonight!"

Tim's Death chart contains some specific pointers, and scavenger hunt clues:

The Sabian symbol for Mercury is "finger pointing to an open book." This guides those who crave immediate intimacy to simply close their eyes while opening one of Tim's books (or perhaps any book, or perhaps this book) and point for the necessary guidance of now. In his ancestral mode Tim becomes an agent of divination.

There are three biquintiles—rare 144-degree angles that are talents better than talent—that describe Tim as exiting, being like a tuning fork, humming these talents awake in all who are willing to resonate. The first biquintile is from the Moon in Scorpio in the 9th to Venus retrograde in the 5th—the art form of being playfully dark about death—making light of darkness. In her cycle Venus was retrograde in Gemini, beginning her descent to the underworld to reinvent culture, escorting Tim really. Even in death Tim had a charming powerful woman for a date. The Moon's image was both that of "a parrot repeating a conversation overheard," and "a woman draws back two curtains to a sacred pathway." Sacred theater would like to make a comeback, and we are hereby invited to entertain the possibility that popular culture is willing to be the theatrical venue for the emerging mythos of conscious kinship. "Entertainment" is willing to be telepathic again, as it was in the '60s, when there was collective expression given to the interior life of the collective.

The second biquintile is between the North Node of the Moon in Libra in the 8th to Mercury ("finger pointing to an open line in a book"). This pattern bestows the capacity to open up spirit faxes, call and response between the visible and the invisible—the living and the ancestral—so that no creature, no creative rascal, need ever feel alone or unsupported again. The 8th house is an ancestral bank account that has been set up by Tim to endow those continuing the work of inventive, compassionate cultural experimentation. A Perpetual Day of the Dead is declared. Operators are standing by.

The last biquintile is from the Sun in Gemini in the 4th (home base) to Jupiter rising in the east. The image for the Sun—the central comforting communication—is found in its Sabian "Newly Opened Lands. Having Something New to Explore. Leaving a Trail. Virginal innocence." "If I can do it, you can do it," Tim exhorts.

Now is the fulcrum moment in historical time where all that each of us thinks, does and says matters enormously, tilting the balance toward species extinction or the necessary leap in shape-shifting pragmatic compassion and effective implementation of the most lovingly ingenious vision possible. Jupiter, the god of storytelling and theater, strong in both natal and departure charts, is particularly fond of the redemptive fifth act—How do we tell the story of how it all turns out OK?

Now is the time to offer ourselves to unleashing the forces of compassionate rascalry upon the world stage. We live in wild times, entrusted with the task of midwifing an emerging global mythology of conscious kinship. In order to do this we fill ourselves with gratitude for the generosity of all devoted to this task—and certainly our recent ancestor and perpetual teammate, Tim Leary. The festival of now requires that we honor and invite in any ancestral compassionate trickster with whom we resonate. We cannot transform apocalypse into renaissance without them, and indeed current crises are designed to compel us to experiment with the full spectrum of collaborative possibilities.

Tim's message to us now: The sabian for Uranus at the time of his death, "A council of ancestors—hidden guidance." In death Tim completed himself by becoming a mystic, and giving us the gift of enhanced conspiracy—we can breathe together, even with the dead. In fact the alliance between the visible and the invisible is the unbeatable alliance—the experiment before all of us who love life, and who serve the greatest evolutionary development and happiness of all beings in all realms. Thanks Tim, we are in touch. Let's dream, conjure, and implement the most lovingly ingenious world possible.

Tim bequeaths to those of us on this side of the dream the task to continue the blooming of culture through the unfettering of imagination that we may all aspire to be increasingly conscious players on the team of creation.

We are a hill of poetry,
We are gods who kindle fire in the head,
We are that which shapes,
We are ourselves shaped,
We are that which dreams,
We are ourselves the dreamer,
We are all beings,
We are that which all beings become.

We are Tim Leary.

Tim Leary:
A Personal Appraisal

WALTER HOUSTON CLARK

Many people have asked me my opinions about Timothy Leary. When I first came to the Boston area in 1961 he was the most talked about professor at Harvard. He had much to say about the capacity of psilocybin to release religious experience and, though I was skeptical, I joined a seminar he had organized for scholars of religion, to learn what I could.

I was told at Harvard that his researches were useless, but I felt I should study firsthand some of the convicts he said were "talking like medieval mystics." To my amazement I discovered that what he said was in general true. Authorities at Concord State Prison and in the Department of Corrections in Massachusetts were very enthusiastic. I have been able to follow up six convicts (five armed robbers and one rapist) on long sentences, directly or indirectly

Walter Houston Clark received his Ph.D. from Harvard University in 1944 and went on to become one of the world's preeminent scholars of psychology and religion. He was Professor at the Andover Newton Theological Seminary and Dean at the Hartford Seminary. He is the author of The Psychology of Religion *and* Chemical Ecstasy *and was a founding member of the International Federation of Internal Freedom and the League for Spiritual Discovery. He passed away in 1994. This article was first published in the* Journal of Humanistic Psychology *in April, 1976.*

involved with his work, who followed up his rehabilitation efforts on their own. Formerly revolving door recidivists, they have now been out of prison for from five to thirteen years, yet no prison system has summoned the courage to follow up this remarkable pilot program.* Since then I have experimented on myself with drugs and fully support Tim's optimism in regard to the capacity of drugs, properly used—not *on* convicts but *with* them as full partners in experimentation—to blunt many of the potential Atticas throughout America.

In 1963, a few weeks before the end of the year and the termination of his contract, Tim was dismissed from Harvard with no offer of a hearing. No adequate study of his research had been made, and Harvard didn't learn, for several years, information it should have had in hand before the dismissal. But by that time hysteria was rampant and the reputation of anyone with even peripheral relations with Tim suffered. The trustees at Andover Newton threatened me with dismissal, which I would have suffered had not my colleagues (unlike all but a handful of Leary's at Harvard) stood up for my right to teach my classes and live my life according to my own best judgment.

Unsatisfied with the publicity that Leary's dismissal had gained him throughout the country, several years later the U.S. government arrested him when a small amount of marijuana was found on his daughter in a border incident, in which he claims to have been framed—and I believe him. California sentenced him to ten years, and five more when he was convicted of escape. He is now in the custody of a federal prison in San Diego.

The *Newsletter* has suggested that I write my appraisal of Tim, because I know him well and have kept in touch with him over the years. But, since Tim is a complex person, the reader must understand that this appraisal is personal rather than final.

Emulating Harvard's previous judgment of Tim without hearing, a group in San Francisco recently sat in judgment to investigate "Leary's lies" without his presence. I do not say he never told a lie. I suppose if his mother were hidden in a closet he would lie to

---

* Although with not one casualty.

the murderer seeking her life and he, analogously, may have lied to protect himself and his friends on other occasions. But I can testify that I never thought he lied to me, nor have I ever suspected him of doing so. Incidentally, there have been occasions when proof has reached me of his essential integrity in this and other respects.

I can also report that though I have studied at Harvard since 1925 in pursuit of three degrees, he remains in my mind as by far the most creative Harvard professor I have known. Furthermore, as I detailed in *Chemical Ecstasy*, a clue to one side of his personality is to be found in the extent to which he illustrates the basics of William James's definition of saintliness, found in *The Varieties of Religious Experience:*

1. A feeling of being in wider life than that of this world's selfish little interests; and a conviction, not merely intellectual, but as it were, sensible, of the existence of an Ideal Power. . . .
2. A sense of friendly continuity of the Ideal Power with our own life, and willing self-surrender to its control.
3. An immense elation and freedom as the outlines of confining selfhood melt down.
4. A shifting of the emotional center toward loving and harmonious affections, towards "yes yes" and away from "no" where the claims of the non-ego are concerned.

These are not the popular stereotypes of the saint, but they apply to Tim. One of the Massachusetts "most dangerous" convicts told me that Tim was the first person he ever met whom he trusted absolutely to be on his side; another, equally dangerous, said that Tim was the only man he ever knew about of whom he had never heard another convict say a critical word. Testimonies like these cannot be brushed off even by Tim's most intrepid enemies. Despite the fact that he has been conned, robbed, and imposed on by thousands, I have never known him to be annoyed or irritated by others save once, when a presumptuous and manipulative lawyer had gratuitously filled Tim's home with uninvited guests, who were ordered out in the middle of the night when Tim returned to find them there. Michel Hauchard, the Swiss confidence man, who took advantage of his jailing by Swiss police to persuade him to sign a long-term contract with him as his business agent and who consequently was able to swindle him out of thousands of dollars, he dismisses with some gentle irony in *Confessions of a Hope Fiend.* Many persons have testified to his kindness and humanity in chance meetings. And I have never really known him to show arrogance.

Jesus told his followers to be "wise as serpents and harmless as doves." My reaction to Tim has often been, "Would that he were as wise as a serpent!" However great his creativity one would hardly credit him with excessive shrewdness. He is careless with details, treats money—when he happens to have some—only as means to an end. Yet his "elation and freedom," his urge to say "yes, yes" to almost anything that appeals to him, have landed him in situations from which even his friends and family have not been able to rescue him. Brilliant though he is in creativity, his mind ordinarily is anything but systematic. This has freed him for consideration of the long view (some call him grandiose) and even his friends, like myself, hardly know whether in *Terra II** he is pulling our legs. But at the very least, like Jonathan Swift, he is delivering his ideas of utopia in superb ironic rhetoric.

Along with these qualities he is a stubborn man. No one familiar with the story of his endurance of silence for almost a year at West Point would deny this. After his cavalier and sorry treatment at the hands of the Harvard authorities he refused to be intimidated, as many of his colleagues were, with the result that he soon became known in establishment circles as a Pied Piper in his promotion of the LSD-type chemicals. For this he has often been pilloried, even

---

* In 1973 Leary wrote several books while in the Folsom prison maximum security. Whereas *Neurologic* is a major statement in the realm of mind evolution, *Terra II,* which promotes space migration, seemed at the time to be an extension of his fantasy to get out of jail. Later Tim mentioned that Carl Sagan had visited him in jail to talk about interstellar travel. Now it seems that NASA is seriously considering the Gerald O'Neil proposal (see *The CoEvolution Quarterly,* fall 1975, pages 4–28) for a space station. Tim, as usual, is so far ahead of his time that few can follow the extensive range of his thought.

—Jean Mayo

by some of his supporters, as the man who killed sensible research with these drugs. I have had my moments when I have counted myself one of them, but then I have asked myself whether the Harvard establishment really intended to promote research with these drugs, carefully or otherwise. Soon after Leary left, responsible experimentation with the drugs was cut off at Harvard Medical School. Since then I know of no Harvard scientist willing to risk his reputation through a move toward experimentation on human beings with these important and only moderately hazardous substances.

Walter Clark, Marge King, Timothy Leary, and Jean Millay, photographed in Vacaville prison

Had I been in Leary's place I would not have acted as he did. But I also have my moments when I wonder whether he boldly used the only method to introduce fresh and open young minds to the values of LSD. Other countries certainly have not covered themselves with glory in pushing back the frontiers of the mind through the use of psychedelic substances. According to Mexico's *Tiempo*, Guido Belsasso, a product of Harvard Medical School of the Leary period, supported a raid on the creative Instituto de Psicosintesis and Salvador Roquet by policemen with loaded pistols and machine guns, which resulted in the arrests of Dr. Roquet, assistants, and twenty-five patients in group therapy. He and Pierre Favreau were kept in jail for five months while they proved their innocence. Such outrages have punctuated the history of even the most responsible and creative attempts to alleviate human suffering with psychedelics in other countries, even when the attempts were as successful as Dr. Roquet's. Such sequelae I attribute largely to the outrage over Harvard's dismissal of Leary and subsequent attempts of the government to undermine his credibility with youth.

We remember that it took the medical establishment a century to acknowledge vaccination as the most effective way to combat smallpox. But now we are beginning to witness the phenomenon of young men who ingested LSD a decade ago coming into positions of responsibility in mental health fields. It is on them that our hopes rest for making constructive use of these powerful chemical tools. And without Leary would we have these cogent allies?

By the turn of the twenty-first century will Timothy Leary be seen as a corrupter of youth and a wrecker of research with the psychedelics or as one of the adventurous thinkers of our time? He is a complex person compounded of faults and a brilliant intuitive mind. I know no one who has made as many mistakes. But I also know few persons for whom I hold more affection or who possess what I sense as a very deep-seated integrity, no matter how overlaid with mistakes and inconsistencies. I have no idea how history will appraise this attractive personality. But if I'm allowed my guess I would say that within twenty-five years he will hold an honorable place as one of the germinitive thinkers of our day, one of the pioneers in an intellectual ferment preliminary to many of the innovations to come in the next century.

Just to narrow his influence to the field of mental health, I would say that he belongs in the ranks of Ronald Laing, Stanislav Grof, and especially Salvador Roquet, the most gifted, gentle, yet most daring of all our psychedelic pioneers. All of these men owe something to Timothy Leary and know of the hidden powers lying behind the psychedelic drugs and their creative usefulness when used properly. We do not use spades when power shovels are available for moving earth, though spades may still remain useful. The psychedelic in skilled and experienced hands are psychotherapeutic power shovels making possible the healing of minds to an extent impossible with more conventional instruments. This type of healing is often associated with transactions at a depth that can only be called religious, despite the rejection of it by the religious establishment.

For nearly fifteen years I have been studying, investigating, and doing research with these fascinating drugs. In my considered opinion Timothy Leary, along with the psychotherapists I have mentioned and many others who combine wisdom secured through the drugs with great courage, make even the best of our plodding, sincere, but conventional psychiatrists pale into nonentities in their insights into human nature. But, since the dawn of history, it is innovators, like Socrates and Galileo, who have been rejected, jailed, and executed.

Ram Dass Remembers Tim

An Interview with Ram Dass
by Robert Forte and Nina Graboi

RF: When we approached you about contributing to Timothy's memorial volume you said, "That will be hard." Why so hard?

RD: Because Tim is one of the more complex human beings that I have met in this lifetime, and my reactions to him are *very* complex. So to articulate it in a coherent and integrated fashion isn't easy. That's really what I meant; that sometimes relationships are so subtle and nonconceptual, and that's what the relationship between me and Tim is like. It's not easy to articulate because there's love and there's respect and there's judgment and there's frustration and there's disappointment and there's, you know, great appreciation, and all kinds of qualities.

RF: Timothy has affected millions of people in a profound way, but probably no one was as close to him during those years at Harvard as you were. I wonder if your relationship typified the massive

---

Ram Dass is the author of The Psychedelic Experience *(with Timothy Leary and Ralph Metzner),* Be Here Now, The Only Dance There Is, Grist for the Mill, *and many other books. He was an associate professor in the school of education at Harvard University from 1960 to 1963, where he was a founding member of the International Federation for Internal Freedom and the League of Spiritual Discovery.*

Richard Alpert and Timothy Leary present early psychological findings on psilocybin

changes that would follow collectively?

RD: I doubt it. His and my interaction was a product of our collective neuroses. Mine are pretty pronounced and they certainly were in those days. I'm hardly Johnny Q. Citizen in the sense of representing a reaction that would be common to other people. We were locked in some incredibly intense psychodynamics of really archetypal and mythic proportions. And I don't know that I was the "closest." We sure spent a lot of time together, and we were very close, but Tim is in a way equally close to everybody. Tim may spend more time with a person, but I think people who are close to him feel that he's not that close, or he's not close in that way. I think we expect people to be close psychodynamically, and he's not really interested in that plane of consciousness.

RF: What plane of consciousness is he interested in?

RD: Timothy is somebody who really honors the Truth, the essence—I mean metaphysical truth, as well as psychological and social truth—and who is a scientist in the deep sense of being a scientist. He is interested in understanding the universe in some kind of systematic way. He's quite a scholar. He reads a lot, but then it all gets filtered through this kind of charming stuff, this play of mind that seems to take away from the depth, the power of his mind, the power that I knew when I was with him.

NG: Was the role of spiritual revolutionary authentic, or did his ego play a part?

RD: Well, it is hard to think of it as his ego. I'd say he's more socio-centered than ego-centered. He's a social role-player. I'm not sure that he has an ego in the sense of a thickly-centered self-concept. He just fulfills roles in a charming fashion.

NG: Why did he so deliberately provoke the establishment?

RD: Well, that's another part of him. Timothy was the Irish fighting the English. He was the underdog fighting the establishment. That's one of the major myths of Timothy's life. There was no way to get along with the establishment with Timothy. Sooner or later he had to undercut whatever dynamic there was. I was always busy healing the rifts and keeping up in the establishment as much as I could. I couldn't always do it but I would try; and Timothy was constantly undercutting that.

RF: One time I asked you about him and you said, "Timothy is a great man, but he has a problem with authority." And I thought this is exactly *why* he was a great man, because authoritarianism is a very great problem.

RD: I don't question that the mosaic of his personality contributed deeply to the role he plays in society. It was all necessary. So the antiauthority part of his mind would question what the psychiatrists said about LSD, while I—coming from a nice Jewish middle-class conforming family—thought if the psychiatrist said it, it must be so. Timothy opened my eyes to questioning those kinds of authorities. I had been trained never to question them.

RF: This is again one of his mythic roles.

RD: It's a role, you know, but look at what power he had. He was the only one on the scene that I saw who acted that way. Frank Barron also had the experience, but he wasn't ready to blow the whistle on society. Timothy wanted freedom of consciousness, and that's basically a social, political position.

RF: Freedom of consciousness? How do you mean that?

RD: Freedom from being controlled by others, by a social system. In other words, we have a right to the freedom of how we use our own consciousness. And he felt that was one of the freedoms.

RF: You mean that not just in terms of drug laws. There's an unconscious manipulation of our minds by the establishment, and we have a right to be free from that.

RD: Exactly. It's not necessarily conscious on the part of the establishment. The establishment is conned by it also. There's a conspiracy to define reality conceptually a certain way, and freedom is to get free of that, and that's what Buddhism is about, getting free of those conceptual traps of mind. So we were talking about something very deep, which is the freedom of human consciousness. Tim was seeing the relation between that spiritual or altered state of consciousness and the sociopolitical situation. He wanted freedom for the method of getting high, not just freedom for the state of consciousness. And that gets into the question of who controls the method.

RF: And this is a conversation that you have pretty much stayed out of. You didn't want to discuss the political questions.

RD: Well, first of all, in those days, Timothy was politically more sophisticated than I, much, much more. I was psychodynamic, so when I had the psilocybin experience I started to work with it from two levels: one, the opening to the mystical end of it, and two, the redefinition of the meaning of psychodynamics, of personality. That fascinated me and seemed like the place to go. Timothy was much more interested in the social political aspects. I wasn't avoiding it. I remember I was in India and I got all these clippings from Allen Ginsberg who was at the Democratic convention, being hit over the head and all of that. It was '67. I sat there in the temple thinking, "He's on the front line. He's saying 'this is what I believe' and he's confronting it. And look at me, I'm copping out. I'm hiding back in here in the temple." Then I thought, "But what am I doing in this temple? I'm spending fifteen hours a day examining my own mind. Isn't that a leading edge too?"

RF: Do you think Timothy's identifying the drugs with the counterculture made the mystical pursuits, the scientific mystical pursuits, more difficult? Professional psychedelic researchers today regard his behavior as a problem because he antagonized everyone, polarized society, and the drugs are now forbidden.

RD: Well, there was no way that wasn't going to happen. Almost at the same time we were getting outrageous, Ken Kesey was having the acid tests in San Jose, L.A., and places like that. The *San Jose News* ran headlines this big, "Drug Orgy in San Jose." There was no way this wasn't going to become a very hot political issue very quickly. We might have had another six months or a year of grace to get a little more established. We could have done it more politically and cooly, no doubt. Aldous was down on Tim for that, and a lot of other people were too. But my sense is that Tim was so far out of the experimental models that were accessible; he was more into the collection of data from musicians, artists, writers, using it as a natural medium, you know, all that stuff. It was not easy to do naturalistic research in a behaviorist society. I thought we could have played with the university and gone on and on, because there was a tremendous amount of desire on the part of the university to give their academes liberal academic freedom, as long as it didn't scare the university.

RF: I envisioned this book to be kind of a response to a book that came out recently in England, the proceedings of a symposium held in honor of LSD's fiftieth birthday by Sandoz and the Swiss Academy of Medicine. The president of the Swiss Academy began the conference by praising the *scientific* possibilities of LSD, and then he said, "But unfortunately LSD did not remain in the scientific scene. It fell into the hands of esoterics and hippies and was used in an uncontrolled way." It can be argued that the esoterics and hippies made the most of the stuff, more than the scientific methods of that time were going to. Still "science" fumbles around for a way to understand these drugs. Tim thought early on that the drugs needed to be freed from the laboratory if they were going to do any good. He answered the important questions, demonstrated "set and setting," and shared his results—in an exuberant way, to be sure, but it may have been irresponsible not to.

RD: I think what happened with psychedelics in the early '60s so profoundly altered this society that it is still just beginning to grow into what's happened to it. It was a mushroom and it did explode, and it was carried through the hippies, through the minstrels, through the rock and roll movement; it was carried into the collective consciousness and it has mainstreamed in collective consciousness, and it has to do with the relative nature of reality. And that's a big, deep thing and it happened to this society.

RF: It's amazing it still hasn't dawned on society what these drugs really are.

RD: No, it hasn't. And that's kind of fascinating and kind of beautiful. Because it's very scary to people who have a vested interest in a reality being absolute.

RF: How do you feel about getting tossed out of Harvard?

RD: I look at being thrown out of Harvard as an incredible gift. The basic thing that happened to me at that moment with the mushrooms was for the first time probably since I was two years old that I listened to myself from inside; I used my inner criteria to validate my existence rather than external criteria. That was a major shift.

RF: This was a renaissance for a lot of people.

RD: I have a feeling it was. . . . Once I get over the fear of the outcome I can really look at things as they are and delight in the edge of chaos quality that's happening when a transformative process is going on in a society. It's really scary because it undercuts control of the situation.

RF: Fear of the outcome?

RD: The fear of whether society blows itself up. The big fear is that the psychedelic revolution or evolution gets crushed back into stupidity and ignorance.

RF: The Hindu cosmology looks at the world in terms of these grand cycles and it's almost a cliche that we're in the dark period of a Kali yuga. Do you have a sense of that?

RD: I don't live consciously in these mythic structures. I mean I can create an Armageddon one, an Aquarian Age one, a Kali yuga one that goes into either the Sat yuga or into the Pralaya, when everything dissolves back into nothing. They all seem perfectly reasonable to me. And I don't really care, because it doesn't make any difference to what I do . . . whatever scenario, I just have to quiet my mind, open my heart, and relieve suffering in the world around me. This is it. And I've come to kind of delight in this. The minute you say, "What does it mean?" you're asking for a conceptual structure, a prison enclosing what can't be imprisoned. So I don't live in how it all comes out.

RF: Getting back to Timothy, he has shifted metaphors so many times in his career. You've probably heard him say that a third of what he said is bullshit, a third dead wrong, and a third home runs. That gives him a .333 batting average, high enough for the Hall of Fame. What's the bullshit and what's a home run?

RD: Well, it's really hard to assess. Is his fight with the establishment, with authority, "bullshit," or is it part of the process? I don't look at it in terms of baseball, just in terms of process. Timothy *uses* metaphors; he's not attached to metaphors, he moves in and out of them like snails inhabit shells; you know, you outgrow them and you just drop them. The metaphor served its purpose to take a quick fix on that which is not a concept. So I don't know that I would think of them as his "bullshit." I think of them as short-term; at that moment they serve some purpose and then you go on, and then you begin to see that it's really the sum total, the gestalt, rather than any one of them.

RF: In *Chaos and Cyberculture* he says the main point was to induce chaos. It was all for pranks.

RD: Yeah, Timothy was a rascal. I was a rascal in training. I was too middle class to be a good rascal. Timothy was a rascal. And he did delight in chaos. But there were a couple of forces in Timothy. He kept incredible records. He kept file cabinets full of records. That isn't chaos, that's another quality in him that collected stuff and thought about it and structured it and so on. At the same time, he was socially always playing with the edge and then pushing the edge and pushing the edge and pushing the edge.

RF: It is usually a troubled relationship between mysticism and politics, between those trying to free themselves from the images others use to bind them.

RD: Timothy always said you'll find the mystic and the visionary much closer to the prison cell and the priest class will be running things. He has a sense of history, a sense that though he might be seen as irrelevant now, two hundred years from now he will be seen as something else. The idea of "you leave no footprints" is a little too Zen for Timothy, I think. He has a sense of generations at a time.

NG: In recent years, perhaps since his imprisonment, his emphasis has been on the physical rather than the spiritual dimension. It almost looks as if he's not spiritual any longer. What do you think?

RD: Well that isn't true. He's spiritual, but he's not interested in these other planes of consciousness. I mean he's interested in the use of the mind, of the intellect and its capacity and how far out you can push it. He loves conceptual play, and the question is, is he doing it from a nonconceptual space, which is purely spirit? He might be spiritually way beyond, in the sense of nonattachment to any myth or model of himself or anything else. The question is, where is Tim standing? Is there any place you can catch him? I feel a certain somebody in there that I don't find with my guru, for example, and that somebody is where you're standing. I know I'm standing somewhere, and I'm not sure I'd see him if he wasn't standing anywhere, you know? So now I work in Tibetan Dzogchen, in realms of pure awareness that have no astral content at all, no dualism, no gods and goddesses, embracing the form into the formless constantly, enjoying the play of phenomena. That is a lot of what Timothy is. I never think of him as a Dzogchen master, but there is a way in which he does that. He does it without full compassion, perhaps, and that means he's not fully empty. But he has a quality that is very spiritual.

RF: He is very present with you; he always seems to be paying close attention. Was he like that when you met him?

RD: I think Tim's always had those qualities.

RF: He is very childlike. He doesn't dwell in the past or the future, he seems totally immersed in the present moment.

RD: And this is what infuriates people who want continuity. Ghandi said, "My commitment must be to truth and not to consistency."

NG: Timothy is so far ahead. He's like a man from the future; his mind outraces everyone.

RD: Well, it's a funny thing about the mind. There is a way in which the mind, no matter how hard it works, never gets there. The minute you realize that and surrender into being rather than knowing, you've just moved to the next level. Being far ahead is like a cul-de-sac in a certain way.

RF: It's not just his mind. I've seen this quality of childlikeness, this enlightened quality in him, playing croquet in his yard as well as talking about metaphysical or scientific notions.

RD: We've had great, great fun together. Great fun. Like playing in the cosmos, like walking with giant steps and dancing huge dances. It was a play of just this vastness. Timothy invited me into those realms and I was thoroughly delighted. A lot of our acid trips together, a lot of our life together, was like that, Mexico and Millbrook and IFIF. It was just pouring out. I remember those Saturday nights by the fire in Millbrook with the family, with Maynard and Flo Ferguson and whoever else was around and Tim and me and Ralph and Susan and all of us in the dark with the fire flame lighting us and us just playing in the cosmos, just one mind and all these voices coming together. These were some of our finest moments. Then I went to India and was just absorbing as fast as I could. Then I had that gnostic intermediary role of bringing the Eastern metaphysics back and integrating it with Western psychology. I was wide open and I don't think that's ever stopped.

RF: Did Tim influence you going to the East?

RD: Well, Allen Ginsberg had gone, and Tim went and Ralph went, and so it was clear that that was the way to go because the manuals for understanding what the hell we were doing were coming from the East. Timothy played a role in the sense that he foreshadowed. What is quite extraordinary is that on Tim's way back from Almora to Delhi the bus stopped at Kanchi, which is my home temple base— a little tiny temple on a very small road. A man, who later was my yoga teacher, got on the bus and sat next to Timothy. Timothy was very impressed with this guy, and when they got to Nanital, the guy got off the bus and started to walk away quickly. Timothy went to follow him. He was halfway across the square when the bus driver blew the horn. The bus was going on to Delhi, and Timothy turned and got back on the bus. If Timothy had followed him he would have met my guru, whom I met two years later by an entirely different route. Now if you can't feel that there's some fascinating game within that . . .

RF: Tim has said one of the things he's sorry about is clearing the way for the gurus to come from the East.

RD: I think it should play out its story. I think that the Easterners weren't prepared for the kind of seductiveness that they would meet in the West. A lot of them thought they were freer than they turned out to be. I mean that's some of what Tim's talking about. They brought a very deep wisdom, but they weren't necessarily the representatives of those wisdoms, and the problem is that that makes the teaching not quite work. In other words, it's not a clear transmission. They were able to pass on the information, but not make the full transmission. But there have been some remarkable people in the West. I mean Trungpa Rinpoche was no slouch and Kalu Rinpoche was no slouch. There have been a lot of people that were interesting but flawed in some way; that's a maturing process for people. Allen Ginsberg brought over Bhaktivedanta, a Hindu. He did that before Tim even was into India.

I tasted of something that I have transmitted as faithfully as I could to millions of people who in turn have tasted something, and whatever that thing is, I feel that it is fine. It is a sense, a faith in the possibility of the liberation of the human being. And that's very deep in me. It went from the mushrooms, through the grace of Timothy, to Neem Karoli Baba. Those two events define two stages of the journey. One, I realized I wasn't who I thought I was, and I understood relativity, and when I met Maharaji, I met all the forms and nothing. I kept feeling there was nothing there and yet everything.

RF: That's quite a statement, implying that we're not free. This is the renaissance of spirituality. A recognition of our imprisonment?

RD: That's pretty good. That's Gurdjieff's line, "The first thing: if you are ever to escape from prison, you must realize that you are in prison. If you think you're free, no escape is possible."

RF: Did you consider Tim to be a guru?

RD: Well, in India they make a distinction between Upagurus and Satgurus, and Upagurus are gurus along the way who open doors for you, but they may not be gurus in the sense of free beings. The difference between Timothy and Neem Karoli Baba was that Neem Karoli Baba, no matter how hard I tried I couldn't find him. There wasn't anywhere he was standing and there wasn't anywhere he wasn't. I had to deal with that reality with Neem Karoli Baba, and I didn't have to deal with it with Timothy, so that's the difference. But Timothy freed me from many planes that I was trapped in. He did a tremendous amount for me. He was very patient because I was extremely trapped in certain ways. He was certainly playing on a lot more planes than I was. But he was still somebody playing somewhere.

RF: You said when you first met him he was the most creative person you ever met. Did you mean creative as a scientific thinker, as a strategist, or as a researcher?

RD: Yes, as someone who can break set. That's how I would define creativity.

RF: What about the numinous quality?

RD: Well, Timothy is charismatic, but charismatic isn't numinous. I would say he's charismatic, not numinous. His mind is extraordinary. He opened doors to other planes. I mean, all I had to do was get into relative reality. That's what he did. He took me into a relative realty. And that was a major game, so he was a major teacher for me.

RF: Let's look at "charisma." Does it imply something negative?

RD: Well I don't think that it should. It's incredible, it's like astral power. That's what I think it is, you know. It really is a light, but it's a kind of astral light. It's not a spiritually free light; it's intense, you know, *brilliant* people you call them, and you're kind of awed by their brilliance. But it's different than spiritual illumination. It's like stars rather than the sun. Tim is like a comet that shoots across the sky. A lot of us are very beholden to him. I bet more people than is known are beholden to him.

RF: Still, there's an element of trickery in Timothy's play. . . .

RD: There are many rascals in the spiritual traditions, many rascals who use tricks to liberate people.

NG: I think there is much more to him than charisma. In the '60s, the kids used to say they can feel his aura miles away. I remember a photo of him with a flower behind his ear . . .

RD: We've both got the same photograph in mind, at one of the Be-ins, I think. Well, he had the aura of youth, he was a stereotype of light and energy, and he had the aura of sexiness, and the aura of playing at the top of his game. Those are all the parts of what gave life to Timothy.

The question is, does the man make the moment, or does the moment make the man? Timothy wasn't playing in a vacuum. He was playing with Alan Watts, Aldous Huxley, and Frank Barron and all of these really extraordinary people. Huston Smith, Walter Clark. It was a great scene; it was a web that was supporting a process going on.

I look at the cultural affluence, the information age, the social mobility, and psychedelics, and the awakening of ethnic consciousness and political consciousness. There was a moment when a lot of stuff was happening. And for anybody to try to grab it and say it was all due to psychedelics, or to affluence, the information age, or to the postindustrial mind or whatever, is too simplistic. I just see it as incredibly richly determined when a moment is profound enough to really shift a scene. The '60s scared the hell out of the culture because they showed another potential exists for people. It provoked the reaction of the pendulum swing of twenty years of republicanism. That's all part of these huge pendulum swings. Tim was on one end and Nancy Reagan was on the other.

RF: And now they are practically neighbors. Is there something imminent about to unfold comparable to LSD? Something that will stimulate us again, or more, or bring the earlier stimulation to fruition?

RD: I don't know. Fusion would do it. We might just be creating the future with fusion instead of fission. Fusion would change the economy of the world. It would provide limitless energy, it would change everything.

RF: Possibilities like this have become conversations for millions of people because of Timothy and you.

RD: When you say "Timothy and you," or something like that, you have to make a clear distinction. Timothy was a much more central player at that time. I was a neophyte, I was a student. We'd have parties in Los Angeles and I'd be sitting at the feet of Aldous Huxley and Gerald Heard as they dialogued about the enneagrams and the labyrinths in churches in Spain. I'd just sit there with these giant minds, and Timothy floated in and out of all this very comfortably and brought me into it. It was like riding a wave. It's interesting about the waves. I realize that the excitement is in being in the little wave in front of the big wave. And that's where Timothy and I were then, at that moment. That was exciting. It's a place where society is basically putting you down or ignores you because you're not even relevant. Then we got to the point where we were a threat. And then I got socialized. I'm almost a good guy again in the society.

RF: I'd like to read this book in a hundred years, or be in a room where Timothy was being remembered. Will the establishment succeed in trivializing his efforts?

RD: Well, I'm not terribly interested in historical remembrances. I think we played a part and that part transforms something and that transformation leads to the next transformation. It is just a tiny blip on the screen full of blips.

RF: Little blip, big awakening. These drugs have been hidden from the people for thousands of years. We don't know how their re-emergence will turn out, but this was one of the great moments in history.

RD: I think the seed is still in fruition. It is a much less homogeneous society, it is a more chaotic society, it is a more fertile condition for growth and change. It's all doing fine.

Observations on My Friend and Hero

Tom Davis

Number 1: Tim is taking me to my first Nine Inch Nails concert. We're standing in the lobby taking a little break—the music is very loud. A teenage concertgoer approaches Tim in amazement—not because he recognizes him, but because he's an "old guy."

"Hey, man, how do you like the music?"

Tim: "It's the best concert I've ever seen."

"Really? Cool. Enjoy the show!"

Number 2: I am talking to Tim on the phone.

Tim: "So . . . what are you reading now?"

Me: "I'm trying to read the Bible all the way through."

Tim: "Oh God—there goes another one!"

Me: "Don't worry, Tim—I don't think I'll ever get through Leviticus."

Tim: "Of course you won't. Don't you have better things to do?"

Tom Davis is a comedy writer for movies and television, and one of the original writers for Saturday Night Live. *Tom was a close friend of Timothy Leary from 1980 until Leary's death.*

Number 3: We're watching the news and Tim is included in a story about the '60s as the icon who encouraged youth to take drugs.

Tim: "I love it when they try to blame me for the '60s. I wish!"

Number 4: Tim greets me as I enter his home for a visit. He gives me a hug, then suddenly steps back, hands on hips in a mock-macho stance and growls, "I can love you more than you can love me!" And he stares at me with the intensity of a boxer glaring at his opponent as the referee gives the rules—a challenge!

Number 5: There is a lively gathering of friends around Tim's beloved kitchen table painted with colorful figures by Keith Haring—a symposium! Somehow the conversation causes Tim to lift his hands and proclaim, "Isn't it wonderful that here we all are, living at one of the most remarkable and exciting times in history?"

I sense a good argument. "Wait a minute. Isn't that a bit too subjective? Doesn't every time have its heroes? Has there ever been a time in history that is recognized as being particularly unremarkable or unexciting?"

Tim: "Yes, the '50s!"

Number 6: I am leaving Tim's house after a visit.

Tim: "Tom, is there anything I have here that you'd like?"

Me: "Actually, there's a really old book on that shelf over there."

Tim: "Good, take it. I want to give away all this stuff to my friends before I . . . de-animate."

Number 7: Tim: "Have you noticed that all living beings go toward the light?"

Number 8: A new person in Tim's house asks if it's okay to light up a joint.

Tim: "I don't know. It could ruin my reputation."

And at another occasion when my wife noticed that there were no guests who were smoking or drinking. Tim: "This could ruin my reputation."

Number 9: The subject of ancient Egypt comes up and I provocatively make a statement about lavish tombs that wasted a great civilization like a terrible war.

Tim: "Well, they were going for immortality and they had the wisdom to leave lots of gold and treasures around so that the thieves would leave the important stuff—the bloody rags. Science may one day replicate the pharaohs from their DNA, and the pharaohs will have succeeded."

Road Man

MAYNARD FERGUSON

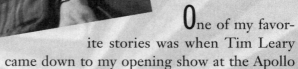

One of my favorite stories was when Tim Leary came down to my opening show at the Apollo Theater in Harlem. He was always into interpersonal relationships, expanding your consciousness and learning how to "play someone else's game." When he got there, I was telling him that we had just lost one of our roadies, so he decided that he would be the roadie that night. Tim knew that none of the guys in the band knew what he looked like. Nobody knew this was the infamous (or famous, as you would have it) Dr. Timothy Leary. He worked all night backstage and after the first show asked all the guys, "Does anyone need a sandwich or anything?" Really doing the job! Back then after each show there would be a full-length movie in between, then you hit it again. Tim acted just like the new roadie. It was beautiful!

Thanks for the trip, Tim—

with love,
Maynard

Maynard Ferguson is a jazz musician and longtime friend and hero of Timothy Leary.

Declaration of Independence for Dr. Timothy Leary

ALLEN GINSBERG

Allen Ginsberg was a chief proponent of Leary's transacademic uses of psychedelic substances, and was a longtime friend. This piece was originally dictated in July 1971 to Michael Horowitz. It was circulated as a petition after Leary had escaped prison and fled to Europe. Then President Richard Nixon, who had called Leary "the most dangerous man in the world," sent Attorney General John Mitchell to argue for his return. Ginsberg sent this document. The Swiss granted Leary a short-lived asylum that was abnegated when the United States drummed up more charges, accusing Leary of being the "godfather of the largest drug smuggling ring in the world"— the Brotherhood of Eternal Love. The Swiss gave in to U.S. demands. Leary fled. The charges were later dropped for lack of evidence.

Allen Ginsberg, Peggy Hitchcock, Timothy Leary, and Lawrence Ferlinghetti. San Francisco, 1965.

Declaration of Independence for Dr. Timothy Leary

July 4, 1971

MODEL STATEMENT IN DEFENSE OF
THE PHILOSOPHER'S PERSONAL FREEDOM

PROPOSED BY
SAN FRANCISCO BAY AREA PROSE POETS' PHALANX

ALLEN GINSBERG

From San Francisco Bay Area Prose Poets' Phalanx: to whomever concerned with liberty of expression in letters and speech, concerning immediate action to relieve the burden of imprisonment from the shoulders of Dr. Timothy Leary, who because of his philosophy, science and art practiced in the form of letters and speech has long suffered persecution, arrest, denunciation, numerous and prolonged jailings, bail denial, flight, and exile from the United States.

At time of writing, this Doctor of Philosophy without country, arrested in Switzerland, is held without charges awaiting extradition by California for that State's Department of Correction. This aggressive prolongation of the boring scandal of Dr. Leary's persecution by state bureaucracies, and present denial of his personal freedom by the Swiss state, is an unnecessary injustice resolvable as follows:

Bay Area Prose Poets' Phalanx petitions the Swiss government, in faithfulness to the best of Western free-thinking tradition, to grant Dr. Leary status as permanent respected exile. We recommend that International P.E.N. Club request its Swiss chapter to intervene directly to Swiss authorities and propose the following information on behalf of Dr. Leary's request for freedom and privacy as a literary refugee persecuted by Government for his thoughts and writings:

1. That federal prosecutors and judges proceeded against him and jailed him without bail for 30 years for the minor offense of carrying a tiny amount of marijuana, with the motive that because of his "publicized activities," namely, essays and speeches on drug usage theory, Dr. Leary "is regarded as a menace to the community so long as he is at large."
2. That although this original conviction of Dr. Leary was overthrown by the U.S. Supreme Court, the Federal police bureaucracy in America indicated its continued hostility to his "publicized activities" (namely, essays and speeches on drug usage theory) by trying him again for the same minor event, and by such abuse of language succeeded in having Dr. Leary sentenced to a 10-year jail term.
3. That California state prosecutors and judges escalated this legal abuse of Philosophy by duplicating prosecution for possession of another tiny amount of marijuana, adding the enormity of another 10-year sentence and persecutive denial of bail, and superadded insult to injury by proclaiming in court openly that Dr. Leary, on the basis of the following essays:

> "Deal for Real," in EAST VILLAGE OTHER (New York), Vol. 4, No. 3, Sept. 24, 1969; and LOS ANGELES FREE PRESS;
> "Episode & Postscript," in PLAYBOY, Vol. 16, No. 12, Dec. 1969;

was "an insidious and detrimental influence on society . . . a pleasure-seeking, irresponsible Madison Avenue advocate of the free use of LSD and marijuana."* The Judge McMillan who pronounced

---

* It should be noted especially that Dr. Leary was on trial not for his opinions on LSD but for common possession of such a small amount of marijuana that contemporary U.S. punishment for middle-class offense of this kind is more often than not equivalent to the fine for motor traffic violation.

these words held above his bench a copy of PLAYBOY in justification for his language denying bail and sentencing Dr. Leary to the second 10-year imprisonment from which the author of:

JAIL NOTES, N.Y.: Douglas Book Corp. 1970

surprisingly escaped on September 12, 1970, and took troubled refuge abroad.

Whatever one's opinions, or natural or national preferences amongst intoxicants, Letters, religions, and political or oecological theory, the Bay Area Prose Poets' Phalanx hereby affirms that Dr. Leary must certainly have the right to publish his own theories; that at stake in this case, once and for all, is Dr. Leary's freedom to manifest his thoughts in the form of poems, psychological commentaries, dialogues, and essays of literary nature before a public whose younger generations, by themselves credibly experienced with the machines, politics and drugs that are the subject of Dr. Leary's writings, include a large minority (perhaps a majority in his native land) who wish Dr. Leary well, and pray for his security, peace and protection from persecution by Government Police Bureaucracies everywhere.

It is in fact remarkable to note that Dr. Leary is, for a modern intellectual, a solitary splendid example of a Man Without a Country. Refused entry by most governments, he cannot visit other countries lest he be extradited to face the cruel and unusual punishment of now more than 20 years' jail if forcibly carried back to America's shores. Bay Area Prose Poets' Phalanx takes note that this proposed imprisonment of Dr. Leary rises merely from differences of opinion on public philosophy involving drug use, a scientific matter now being debated in professional circles (Psychology, Art, Religion, Poetry, Neuro-chemistry).

We take note that a previous domestic appeal against American persecution of Dr. Timothy Leary issued early in the history of this government's war on him was published on May 10, 1966, and signed by: Howard S. Becker, Ph.D., Arnold Beichman, Eric Bentley, George Bowering, Joe Brainard, Harvey Brown, Robert Creeley,

Robert S. de Ropp, Ph.D., Diane di Prima, Jason Epstein, Jules Feiffer, Leslie Feidler, Peter Fonda, Joel Fort, M.D., Jack Gelber, Nat Hentoff, Laura Huxley, Kenneth Koch, Stephen Koch, Irving Kristol, Lawrence Lipton, Robert Lowell, Norman Mailer, Jonas Mekas, Anais Nin, Charles Olson, Norman Podhoretz, Ned Polsky, Ad Reinhart, Rabbi Zalman Schachter, Richard Seaver, Robert Silvers, Gary Snyder, Susan Sontag, Alan Watts, D.D., Philip Whalen, and many others. The statement of that date stated:

1. "The infringement of constitutional rights of privacy, interference with religious and scientific practice, excessive enforcement and public anxiety have grown to the crisis stage—through the application of irrational marijuana statutes:
2. The long imprisonment given to the psychological researcher Dr. Timothy Leary, for the possession of one-half ounce of marijuana, illustrates the irrationality of present marijuana laws, and is a cruel and unjust punishment in violation of the Constitution of the United States."

Bay Area Prose Poets' Phalanx also takes note of the fact that the very police bureaucracy in the U.S. that has hounded Dr. Leary for his professional opinions is the same Narcotics Bureau that in its historic "war on physicians"* including suppression of documents and prohibition of medical research, has helped create a major "national plague" of heroin addiction. Personnel of these Narcotics Bureaus are themselves involved in narcotics traffic.

Bay Area Prose Poets' Phalanx also takes note of recent accusations implicating the U.S. C.I.A. and other military and intelligence organizations in an historic role of subsidizing major traffickers in Indo-Chinese opium (namely, Gen. Ouane Rathikoune of Laos, Marshal Ky of South Vietnam, KMT armies presently in northern Thailand).

Given vast confusions of modern technology and now the

---

* As it was termed by the New York Academy of Medicine report on drug addiction, *Bulletin of The New York Academy of Medicine*, July, 1963, Vol. 39, No. 7, p. 432.

much-publicized credibility gap between American government and public, as well as previously much-publicized difficulties of generation gap, the request of California (U.S.) Dept. of Correction through the American State Dept. to the Swiss Government for Criminal extradition of Dr. Leary from the mandarin anonymity of his short life of letters in Switzerland, seems to the under-signed poets, essayists and novelists an unseemly and intolerable continuing and exasperating literary vendetta against a specific gifted individual. Dr. Leary is certainly a "High Priest" within his area of specialized scholarship as against the questionable authority of any state in this scientific controversy.

The case of Dr. Leary is outright a case of persecution of ideas and texts—the persecution of his philosophy. Though arrested for grass, he was sentenced for Philosophy. Jailed for grass, he was long prisoned for Opinion. Denied bail for grass possession, he was detained behind barbed wire for Ideological Heresy.

Bay Area Poets' Phalanx hereby petitions U.S. officials concerned to re-think hostile attitudes and adopt behavior more tolerant of natural controversy and common opinion: to recognize that in exercise of arbitrary authority over Dr. Leary they are engaging in unfortunate "State Policy."

Bay Area Prose Poets' Phalanx takes note of the public viability of the formulation proposed by the late poet Charles Olson, friend of Dr. Leary, that now "Private is public, and public is how we behave." We affirm that Dr. Leary has the literary right to make his private opinions known publicly, and to engage unpunished in public literary activity. Poet Olson, 1961 Cambridge, addressing Professor Leary: "When the police come after you, you can stay in my house."

Bay Area Prose Poets' Phalanx specifically requests the American State Dept. to waste no more time, money or passion in this case, and to take no further steps to make a physical prize of Dr. Leary's person. No move is a good move for the American Government in this case. We hereby request the Swiss Government to accept Dr. Leary as an archetype of the traditional political, cultural, literary, or philosophic refugee and grant him personal asylum.

As fellow writers, we recommend that Dr. Leary be considered, by all countries, advanced or underdeveloped on both sides of the so-called Cold War, a distinguished refugee from persecution by an International Police Bureaucracy whose executive and philosophic center in this case is a long-corrupted American Narcotics Bureau and its propaganda lobby, the International Narcotics Enforcement Officers Association (INEOA, Albany, N.Y., Honorary President Harry Anslinger, former chief of the U.S. Narcotics Bureau).

Bay Area Prose Poets' Phalanx takes note that the above bureaucracy has arrested and persecuted artist-persons and "underground" newspapers in many countries on pretexts of possession of small amounts of hemp grass for motives ranging from political hostility to culture shock; and has attempted to frame a number of celebrated writers, including William Burroughs, Allen Ginsberg, some defendants in the Chicago Conspiracy Trial, and black and white political intellectuals, such as the presently-jailed Martin Sostre and John Sinclair, on charges similar to those used to entrap Dr. Timothy Leary for almost a decade now in a web of legal complications, a threatening bureaucratic maya created for him by financially-compromised officious members of as anti-intellectual, criminally-associated and professionally-corrupt a bureaucracy as U.S. Narcotics Bureaus—federal, state and local—have proved in recent history.

Finally, the undersigned take note of Dr. Leary's influence on "students and others of immature judgment or tender years" for which he "is regarded as a menace to the community so long as he is at large," in the eyes of his government prosecutors by their own word. We take note of Dr. Leary's public essays in opposition to the American government's war in Vietnam, and his dialogues such as that published widely with Eldridge Cleaver in Algiers touching the same subject. We understand that Dr. Leary's request for Swiss asylum will be based upon his opposition to the war in Vietnam, and that in context of this disastrous war's crises his plea is a legitimate statement of his situation.

In sum, Bay Area Prose Poets' Phalanx and associate friends urge the Swiss Government to release Dr. Timothy Leary from provisional extraditional arrest, not cooperate in extraditing Dr. Leary to America. We recommend to Swiss and all other governments that they grant our fellow Author Philosopher safe political asylum to complete his work—exploration of his consciousness, vocal literary expression of that unique individual Person whose presence is held sacred in all humane and gnostic democratic nations, and ever enshrined in their literary monuments, witness Whitman and Thoreau for America,

as well as the undersigned
Poets, Essayists, and Novelists

Ken Kesey	Ted Berrigan
Lawrence Ferlinghetti	Margo Patterson Doss
Michael McClure	John Doss, M.D.
Robert Creeley	Lewis MacAdams
Allen Ginsberg	Gavin Arthur
Howard Becker	Paul Krassner
Lenore Kandel	Michael Aldrich
Anais Nin	Jan Herman
Alan Watts	Andrew Hoyem
Kenneth Rexroth	Philip Whalen
Diane di Prima	Herbert Gold
Philip Lamantia	Laura Huxley
Don Allen	Tom Clark
Bill Berkson	John Thorpe
Tom Veitch	Lewis Warsh

Changing His Mind

NINA GRABOI

My friendship with Timothy Leary began in 1966 when I gave him my paper called *Evolution in Search of a New Breed of Man* (unpublished). "We've seen the same thing," he said when he handed it back. What we had both seen was that humanity was presently making a giant leap forward in evolution, and that the spiritual element plays a leading role in this leap. Like myself, Timothy leaned strongly toward Eastern religions like Hinduism and Buddhism.

In those days, that is, the '60s, Timothy, the High Priest of psychedelics, was surrounded by an aura of almost saintly proportions. The hippies saw him as their prophet—the prophet of a New Age without wars, hype, cruelty, and deception, and they were inspired by his emphasis on the spirit. When he appeared on stage, his white-clad figure evoked awe, reverence, and love in his young audience whom he told to think for themselves and to ignore authority. To them, his voice seemed to come directly from God. There

Nina Graboi, a quiet force in the Aquarian movement, was director of the Center for the League of Spiritual Discovery in Manhattan, and a longtime friend of Timothy Leary (see her autobiography, One Foot in the Future*). In the late '70s, she found herself questioning Timothy's departure from some of the ideas they had shared in the 1960s.*

was a driven aspect to his heroic stance. Undoubtedly he knew that he was playing with fire, but he seemed to have to do what he did.

Shortly after I met him, I became a regular weekend visitor at Millbrook. While I shared his optimism about the future, I was ambivalent about the value of his widely broadcast message regarding the use of LSD. Though he never failed to add a warning in his lectures, I was appalled by some cases of genuine mental breakdowns due to the use of psychedelics. My own inclination lay much more in the direction of Huxley, Heard, Osmond, and others who wanted to see their use confined to an elite of artists, writers, scientists, and theologians. But if, as Timothy believed, LSD was a tool of evolution, then the occasional victim was regrettable, but unavoidable. So when Timothy asked me to head the New York Center for the League of Spiritual Discovery, I accepted because I felt that the Center, by offering information and education about the use and misuse of psychedelics, could minimize their ill effects.

Timothy took a lively interest in the Center and gave free weekly talks to an avid audience. We developed a pleasant working relationship and became good friends.

Shortly after the Millbrook community dispersed in the spring of '67, the Center closed its doors due to lack of funds. I moved to Woodstock and lost contact with Timothy and his lovely wife Rosemary.

After my move to California in the late '70s, I saw Timothy again quite frequently. By then he had disowned his earlier Hindu and Buddhist leanings and was striving to be the scientist again. He took up space migration, computers, cryogenics, and nanotechnology, but his abiding passion was the brain. Despite my often-expressed objection to his concept that the flesh-and-blood brain is the seat of all mental activity and not, as I see it, merely the instrument of a nonmaterial mind, the love, respect, and regard that we had for each other never diminished.

The letter that follows expresses my thoughts about his ideas on spiritual matters.

April 29, 1978

Dear Tim,

Finding myself in disagreement with some of the opinions you expressed in your last lecture, I can't resist writing you.

You say that all occult and spiritual metaphors are pre-scientific and assume that all intelligence is static. But "the path," as it appears to me, is an ever ascending spiral leading to greater and greater understanding and mastery over the material and nonmaterial world (an arbitrary distinction, since they are both one). If this is not intelligence increase, I don't know what is. However, our definitions of intelligence probably differ.

You call the desire for utopia childish and infantile; I believe that it is part and parcel of the human psyche and will eternally find expression, here or in space. It can no more be called infantile than the thrust into space itself; the archetypal longing for a state of harmony with self, fellow beings, and environment seems to me to be genetically programmed into us, or perhaps less mechanistically, to refer to a reality we once knew and forgot.

I admire your courage and infallible intuition for the next step in evolution. But your put-down of all you call "pre-scientific" appears to me as narrow as Ram Dass's adherence to traditional Eastern thought. What I find interesting is that you seem unaware that today's advanced science is merging into the ancient wisdom; occultism, mysticism, and physics are coming up with the same findings in many areas. It seems clear to me that the present era is above all characterized by the synthesis that is taking place between East and West, left brain and right brain, male and female, past and future, heart and mind, and that the exclusive focus on either polar extreme is unbalanced. When I last saw you, you laughingly rejected any talk of an apocalypse. In my view, the signs of impending global disaster are too clear to be overlooked. This is not necessarily a pessimistic view, for it seems clear to me that there is a direct connection between this and your genetically programmed thrust for space. What happened to our hope of the 1960s to be liberated from the robot aspects of the psyche? Are we to become merely better robots in the Brave New Space World you foresee?

My respect for your intelligence is enormous. If I can take issue with your so firmly stated views, it is because I can't really believe your wholesale rejection of the wisdom embedded in the "naive" metaphors of mysticism. Has science come up with a simpler and more elegant statement than AS ABOVE, SO BELOW?

The influence of the psychedelic '60s on today's culture can hardly be overlooked. Yoga, meditation, vegetarianism, ecology—these and many other features that were introduced by the hippie subculture of the '60s have gone mainstream by the '90s. I believe that Timothy Leary and Richard Alpert, aka Ram Dass, were the two most important men of the twentieth century, just as the '60s was its most important decade. Thanks to Timothy, an unprecedented number of people worldwide experienced nonordinary realities and had a glimpse of eternity. And then Ram Dass came and taught them the ancient wisdom he had learned from his guru in the East. Between them, they opened wide the doors of perception that had been closed so long. I believe that they were spearheads, messengers, vanguards of a higher, better, kinder, more evolved human race.

Memories of Tim

ANITA HOFFMAN

I remember Tim in technicolor, circa 1967. Some evening event in the West Village. He was in a fringed white buckskin jacket. Tall, suntanned, handsome, larger than life. He was so glamorous! I totally mistrusted him and his followers (for that's what they appeared to be). Although I loved the psychedelic experience, I mistrusted religions, incipient religions, even satirical religions, and the League for Spiritual Discovery appeared to me (from the outside) to be a budding cult around Timothy Leary. Simultaneously, Timothy Leary seemed to me to be the living embodiment of Valentine Michael Smith, the protagonist of Robert Heinlein's *Stranger in a Strange Land*.

A year before Abbie and I greeted Tim in his white fringe in the West Village, I had seen Leary perform in the theater on Second

Anita Hoffman was a founder of the Yippies and is the author of two books: Trashing *(under the pseudonym Ann Fettamen) and* To America with Love: Letters from the Underground *(coauthored with Abbie Hoffman). She has worked in Hollywood as a story editor for Jon Voight, as a CD-ROM producer for The Voyager Co., and most recently as a used book dealer in Sonoma County, California. In the '90s Anita was a close and steady friend of Timothy Leary. She passed away in late 1998.*

Avenue (which later became the Fillmore East), and I had been turned off. At that time he was performing in a series of programs that illuminated the world's religions. I was twenty-four and went to the performance with two women friends who worked at *The New Yorker* magazine. On stage, to my amazement and horror, Tim appeared to be playing the role of Jesus Christ! I thought that was unconscionable (although I'm not Christian). What hubris to play the Divine! As I recall, the dramatization/lecture ended with Tim on the cross, arms outstretched. Shameless! Cult leader! Self-appointed guru!

During the late '60s Abbie and I recognized Tim as another brilliant cocreator of the countercultural vision we all shared. But we yippies had our differences with Tim. We weren't eager for people to drop *out*, we wanted them to drop *in*, to become involved in the world around them, to bring about social change. This included ending the senseless war in Vietnam and the arms race, and racism. It also included a vision of a free society based on love rather than greed, where everyone's survival needs were sanely addressed.

Leary, no doubt, was increasingly mistrustful and critical of "the politicos" of the antiwar movement for their lack of humor, their dogmatism and puritan style (same criticisms we yippies felt, although we were ourselves "politicos" compared to the LSDers). I would define a "politico" as someone who cares about public issues and is willing to work in the world for social justice. In later years, Tim never failed to remind me that two weeks after agreeing to attend the Festival of Life in Chicago in 1968, he pulled out, not wanting to influence young people to come to Chicago to be gassed and get their heads beaten by the Chicago police.

In Algeria in 1970 I finally got to know Tim a bit. I arrived there with a delegation of movement activists to celebrate Tim's fiftieth birthday and show the world the friendly coalition among the Black Panthers, the yippies, allies of the Weather Underground, and Timothy and Rosemary Leary, iconic leaders of the counter-culture. During the visit we only saw Tim on limited occasions (controlled by the Panthers), but those moments were intense.

Tim and several Black Panthers met us at the airport. We left the airport in two cars, Tim driving one. I was in his car, with Rosemary,

Dharuba (a Black Panther), Jennifer Dohrn and Jonah Raskin. Dharuba, a member of the NY Panther 21, had escaped from the Tombs in Manhattan and found refuge with the Black Panther govement-in-exile in Algiers, led by Eldridge Cleaver. Jennifer, who worked as an organizer in a bra factory, was the younger sister of Bernadine Dohrn, the charismatic leader of the Weather Underground. Jonah was a writer, academic, and radical antiwar activist. It was late at night. We drove along dark deserted streets occasionally illuminated by a lightbulb. We got lost in the casbah. Suddenly a big rock smashed through the window near Jennifer, splashing chips of glass across the back seat. Jennifer was unhurt, but understandably shaken. I had been on the other side of the car and was unharmed. Tim seemed cool and clearheaded. We made a quick U-turn and managed to get away, eventually arriving at the tiny seaside village where Tim and Rosemary were staying.

The next morning the newly arrived Americans and Tim met for brunch at a small café by the water. That's when I remember becoming acquainted with Tim. He was a charming Irishman, ebullient, sophisticated, filled with joie de vivre. We toasted Tim's escape (from the men's colony in San Luis Obispo with the help of the Weather Underground) and the next chapter of the adventure.

We also visited with Tim and Rosemary on the rooftop terrace of their small apartment. They were wearing djellabahs and looked very comfortable and fit. Rosemary showed us the passport photo she had used to travel incognito. Is it my imagination, or did Tim really show us a small silver flask which he said carried the world's purist acid halfway around the world? I can see this in my mind's eye, but I don't know if it happened or I invented it because it seemed so appropriate. I therefore defer to Rosemary's recollections of this event!

A few days later we celebrated Tim's fiftieth birthday with a large cake that Jonah and I traveled to Algiers to pick up. It was the only time any of us were let out alone. Most of the time we were kept under guard at the apartment of Eldridge Cleaver's mistress.

The day following the birthday celebration, or very soon thereafter, Tim, Jennifer, and DC, head of Panther security, left on a trip to Lebanon and Syria. It was a political trip. While they were gone I revolted against Cleaver's dictatorial rule, but was surprised to find I had no allies among the obedient lefties I was traveling with. So I escaped by climbing out of a window and talking my way out at customs at the airport. (Since the Panthers were guests of the Algerians, and I was a guest of the Panthers, the Algerian government wanted the Panthers' approval to let me leave. But at that point they didn't know I was gone.) I got the next flight to Paris, where I joined Abbie. I didn't see Tim again for twenty years.

We next spoke in 1987 when he learned through a mutual friend that I had just moved back to Los Angeles. He called to tell me that he had heard about my actions in Algeria after he returned from the tour of Arab countries, and that he applauded them. I had the impression he'd been waiting a long time to tell me that. And it was very moving for me, because when this happened (in 1970) I had no allies or believers in my account, except for Abbie, but that's another story.

In the '90s, after Barbara left him, Tim and I gradually became friends and spent a lot of time together. We shared a common interest in the computer revolution and the growing cyberculture. Tim was extremely social. He went out as much as he could and also had wonderful gatherings at his house in Beverly Hills on Sunday afternoons. Over time his various friends got to know one other.

Some of the Hollywood parties I went to with him were deadly (as such things can be for a showbiz outsider like myself) but he usually enjoyed himself. At one moribund party, a trio played music but only one straggly young couple was dancing in the downstairs parlor. Most of the celebrated, rich, or powerful were upstairs with the hosts. Tim and I were nursing white wine at a small cocktail table downstairs when suddenly Tim got up, stepped onto the dance floor and began dancing with vigor, raising his arms, turning, leaping into the air. A few people on the sidelines stared at the old geezer's jumping around. I thought he was roaring drunk and was mortified. Then Mario Van Peebles started dancing, then one couple, then another . . . and the room came to life again. Still, being a complete introvert, I was embarrassed . . . until one day I realized this was my favorite image of Tim: dancing with Dionysian abandon at the age of seventy-four!

My favorite times with Tim were just sitting alone with him outside on his patio beneath the stars, or in his study late at night listening to Billie Holiday or James Joyce. He'd sit at his Mac, writing; I'd stretch out on the nearby couch and read. From time to time he'd take a break, we'd talk, smoke, get something to eat.

We certainly argued our share, about ideas and words. Once he was genuinely horrified when I used the expression "bring people together." I was horrified that he was horrified, but he seemed to loathe anything that reminded him of movements or the left.

Over the years I became increasingly interested in strange phenomena such as UFOs and crop circles, but I could not bring this up for discussion with Tim after the first few occasions because he became furious and asked me not to speak of such things. He wouldn't allow me to question him about his objections, but the implication was that this area of experience is unscientific, crackpot, etc. And he was always a scientist, among other things. Although he himself (during the prison period) had once been passionately interested in space exploration, I don't think he had any interest in this weird stuff, and probably didn't want to be associated with it in any way. There is enough strangeness, perhaps, already associated with him or his presence in American culture.

He was a real stickler for precise meanings of words and was ever alert to nonverbal elements of communication: "You're waving your hands." "You're frowning." Hmmm. Wasn't just me. Other friends heard these observations, too. He once told me I should tell jokes. (I'm sure he was right.) I replied that I didn't know any jokes, so he gave me one. He loved to tell jokes and was really good at it. He was, in short, a delightful person whom I dearly loved.

One afternoon in the study he described his capture in Afghanistan, his trip back to the United States under federal custody, and his subsequent imprisonment in a high-security prison. He said he was held in maximum security after his return (he had, after all, escaped from one federal facility). The guards led him down and down and down to the lowest level of the prison pit, which was several stories beneath the ground. Charles Manson was incarcerated somewhere in this vicinity. Timothy was placed in solitary, in a small, black cell. He didn't know how long he would have to remain there.

I asked him breathlessly, "What did you do?"

"I laughed," he said.

My Meetings with Timothy Leary

ALBERT HOFMANN

It was on the day of the Warsaw Uprising, the first resistance against the Nazi forces, that Albert Hofmann, in the context of chemical research, came upon the substance LSD. But it was not until five years later, on Friday, April 16, 1943 (a day known by some as "Better Friday") that he accidently absorbed this substance into his body and experienced "a not unpleasant reaction." The following Monday, April 19, Dr. Hofmann took what he thought to be a very small dose of LSD (250 millionths of a gram), took his famous bicycle ride, and began the modern psychedelic era.

For twenty years LSD spread through the international neuropsychiatric research community, prompting thousands of studies. By 1963 its use began to escalate in artistic, mystic, and countercultural movements, much to the chagrin of the Swiss establishment. Dr. Hofmann is the retired director of research for the Department of Natural Products at Sandoz Pharmaceutical Ltd. in Basel, Switzerland. He has been a fellow of the World Academy of Science, and a member of the Nobel Prize Committee, the International Society of Plant Research, and the American Society of Pharmacognosy. He is the author of several books: The Botany and Chemistry of Hallucinogens and Plants of the Gods with Richard Schultes, The Road to Eleusis with R. Gordon Wasson, Carl Ruck, and Danny Staples, LSD My Problem Child, and Insight/Outlook.

Timothy Leary, after he managed to escape from the California prison in San Luis Obispo in September 1970, came to Switzerland and petitioned for political asylum. He lived with his wife Rosemary in the resort town of Villars-sur-Ollon in western Switzerland.

Through the intermediary of Dr. Leary's lawyer, Dr. Mastronardi, contact was established between us. On September 3, 1971, I met Dr. Leary in the railway station snack bar in Lausanne. The greeting was cordial, a symbol of our fateful relationship through LSD. Leary was medium-sized, slender, resiliently active, with bright, laughing eyes and a brown face surrounded by slightly curly hair mixed with gray. This gave him the look of a tennis champion rather than of a former Harvard lecturer. We traveled by automobile to Buchillons, where in the arbor of the restaurant A la Grande Foret, over a meal of fish and a glass of white wine, the dialogue between the father and the apostle of LSD finally began.

I voiced my regret that the investigations with LSD and psilocybin, which had begun promisingly, had degenerated to such an extent that their continuance in an academic milieu became impossible. My most serious remonstrance to Leary, however, concerned the propagation of LSD use among juveniles. Leary did not attempt to refute my opinions about the particulate dangers of LSD for youth. He maintained, however, that I was unjustified in reproaching him for the seduction of immature persons to drug consumption, because teenagers in the United States, with regard to information and life experience, were comparable to adult Europeans. Maturity, with satiation and intellectual stagnation, would be reached very early in the United States. For that reason he deemed the LSD experience significant, useful, and enriching, even for people still very young in years.

In this conversation I further objected to the great publicity that Leary sought for his LSD and psilocybin investigations, since he had invited reporters from daily newspapers and magazines to his experiments and had mobilized radio and television. Emphasis was thereby placed on publicity rather than on objective information. Leary defended his publicity program because he felt it had been his fateful historic role to make LSD known worldwide. The overwhelmingly positive effects of such dissemination, above all among America's younger generation, would make any trifling injuries or regrettable accidents as a result of improper use of LSD unimportant in comparison, a small price to pay.

Timothy Leary and Albert Hofmann

During this conversation I ascertained that one did Leary an injustice by indiscriminately describing him as a drug apostle. He made a sharp distinction between psychedelic drugs—LSD, psilocybin, mescaline, hashish—of whose salutary effects he was persuaded, and the addicting narcotics morphine, heroin, etc., against whose use he repeatedly cautioned.

My impression of Dr. Leary in this personal meeting was that of a charming personage, convinced of his mission, who defended his opinions with humor yet uncompromisingly; a man who truly soared high in the clouds pervaded by beliefs in the wondrous effects of psychedelic drugs and the optimism resulting therefrom, and thus a man who tended to underrate or completely overlook practical difficulties, unpleasant facts, and dangers. Leary also showed carelessness regarding charges and dangers that concerned his own person, as his further path in life emphatically showed.

During his Swiss sojourn, I met Leary by chance once more, in

February 1972 in Basel, on the occasion of a visit by Michael Horowitz, curator of the Fitz Hugh Ludlow Memorial Library in San Francisco, a library specializing in drug literature. We traveled to my house in the county near Burg where we resumed our conversation of the previous September. Leary appeared fidgety and detached, probably owing to a momentary indisposition, so that our discussions were less productive this time. He left Switzerland at the end of the year, having separated from his wife, Rosemary, and now accompanied by his new friend Joanna Harcourt-Smith.

Sixteen years later we saw each other again. It was in the fall of 1988 during a lecture tour in California that I did in connection with the founding of the Albert Hofmann Foundation. We met at a party at John Lilly's house in Malibu on October 1 and saw each other again the next day at a reception for the Foundation at the elegant St. John's Club in Los Angeles. Our reunion was again very cordial. We agreed that the history of this psycho-pharmacopoeia par excellence has only begun, and that its essential meaning for the evolution of human consciousness will appear in the spiritual Age of Aquarius.

Our next and final meeting took place in Hamburg, Germany, when Tim and I were invited to appear on a talk show in connection with the fifty-year anniversary of the discovery of LSD. It was broadcast on July 16, 1993, as part of a series called "Premiere." We were interviewed for forty minutes by a young woman, sometimes separately and sometimes together. The questions were for the most part the usual ones. What was unusual was the remarkably strong interest of the young lady in a statement Tim made long ago in *Playboy* that LSD is the most potent aphrodisiac humanity has ever discovered—a woman could have more than a hundred orgasms in a single LSD love session. She wanted to know if it was true, if Tim had witnessed it himself. She asked me about it too. Tim skillfully dodged the question and said that he was obviously expected to talk about sex and LSD in a *Playboy* interview. This he had done and exaggerated his statement for the fun of it. He often talked nonsense in his life for the fun of it and would continue to do so, he explained to the visibly disappointed interviewer. It was the sovereign, self-mocking Tim who spoke these words.

In the evening of that day, we were invited to a party at the home of mutual friends in Hamburg. Tim was the center of the merry company. He was lively and in high spirits and made everybody laugh with the stories he told. It was past midnight when we embraced and said good-bye. That was my last meeting with Tim.

(translated by Nina Graboi and Jonathan Ott)

Prophet on the Lam

Timothy Leary in Exile

MICHAEL HOROWITZ

I met Timothy in person for the first time in the summer of 1970, visiting him at California Men's Colony-West in San Luis Obispo, where a few months earlier he had begun serving a ten-year prison sentence for possession of two marijuana roaches planted in the ashtray of his car by an ambitious Laguna Beach cop who had been following him around town for weeks. The amount was .0025 grams. The judge who revoked Timothy's bail and ordered this draconian sentence had been appointed by Ronald Reagan, whom Leary had announced he was challenging in the forthcoming California gubernatorial race.

His daring escape a few months later utterly floored me and everyone else. It was not expected of a doctor of philosophy, a renowned clinical psychologist, an ex-Harvard professor, a martyr of

Michael Horowitz, Timothy's archivist, is cofounder of the Fitz Hugh Ludlow Memorial Library and operates Flashback Books. He is a rare book dealer specializing in drug history and literature. With Cynthia Palmer he edited Moksha: Writings by Aldous Huxley on Psychedelics and the Visionary Experience; Shaman Woman, Mainline Lady: Women's Writings on the Drug Experience; *and compiled* An Annotated Bibliography of Timothy Leary *(with Karen Walls and Billy Smith).*

consciousness-expanding drugs. But we cheered him, we exulted not only in the act itself, but the symbolic gesture: Timothy had given the bird to Nixon's Amerika.

More shocks were to come. The Weather Underground took credit for engineering the escape. The exiled Black Panther Party, led by Eldridge Cleaver under the protection of the Algerian government, gave Tim and his wife Rosemary refuge there. Tim was writing letters and giving interviews in the underground press in which he aligned himself with the revolutionary forces calling for the overthrow of the U.S. government. Suddenly it was a long way from the peace-and-love, the live-and-let-live, the whole antiviolence stance the man had taken through years of relentless harassment by the authorities. Now we were reading "Smoke it . . . and blow it up!"

Rosemary had turned over Tim's archives—which contained in particular the history of Tim's seminal role in the psychedelic movement—to my colleague Robert Barker and me a few months before the escape, for they anticipated government agencies would seize the archives whether the escape was successful or not. (This did indeed happen, but not until 1975, and under rather different circumstances—a story too long to be told here.) From a post office box in Berkeley registered under the name Bodhisattva, we corresponded with these internationally famous fugitives, known under their false passport name McNellis and then, in their Algerian incarnations, as Nino and Maia Baraka. Always looking over our shoulder as we picked up their letters at the Sather Gate Station, we served as the Learys' primary contacts in the United States. We acted as editors and literary agents for their smuggled manuscripts, sent them press clippings and dental floss, and assisted Allen Ginsberg in circulating a "Declaration of Independence" designed to get Timothy out of a Lausanne prison—which it did, with the aid of the American PEN Club.

Timothy kept urging us to come over and join the revolution against the imperialist pigs. It did not seem particularly prudent— we were, after all, *scholarly* revolutionaries—what with Tim and Rosemary being under house arrest by the Black Panthers, and Tim later landing in a Swiss prison, and the Nixon Gang constantly seeking to extradite him. But in February 1972, some sixteen months after that daring prison escape, Barker and I traveled to Basel where LSD—the reason for all of this—had been discovered nearly thirty years earlier.

What follows are my journal notes of this visit.

Traveling statesmen were in the habit of introducing themselves to local princes with the gift of their clear light.

> I Ching ("clear light" was also the brand name of LSD in gel form, a process invented at the time of these events)

Success in any line is a question of being on set.
> William S. Burroughs

The Faster You Move, the More Control You Have

The set keeps changing. A new house every few days . . . each week another city and every couple of months another country or continent. Whole new casts of characters keep appearing, disappearing, reappearing. The free electron transits the proton; it magnetizes, collides, polarizes and seizes the center . . . then spins away. New entities appear wearing old faces. The *karass* is a constellation of once and future archangels. Wearing masks, they make a movie of the process—at the same time critiquing it and planning a sequel. The first thing you look for when you walk onto the set is the location of the concession stand, and whether the kool-aid is electrified.

Michael Horowitz
in Switzerland,
February 1972

Allen Ginsberg called Leary "a solitary splendid example of a Man Without a Country," yet at fifty-one he has achieved the status of a country. He's had to have diplomatic relations with every country he's ever entered. In one he enjoys the role of scientist-showman and runs for governor before he's set up for a marijuana bust (ten years for two roaches), from which he escapes to another country where he experiences a "revolutionary bust" at the hands of another revolutionary who accuses him of being "brain-fried"; once again he flees. The next nation provides excellent wine and the best prison food he's ever had before he wins his freedom after the international community of writers convinces the Swiss he's a political prisoner, while back in his homeland the president fumes.

Lawyers, literary agents, publishers, media types, and Switzerland's one hundred hippies constantly chase after him (where once cops and prison guards did) and he welcomes them all, keeping an eye out for new incarnations constantly appearing on his radar screen. Living out a time-traveler's life on the public stage, he discovers that the appropriate yoga is *timing*. The faster you move, the more control you have. *Have* to have. The model is flowing with acid. The present guides are Hermann Hesse, who found exile here, and Paracelsus, who was thrown out of Basel into exile.

Timothy Leary—who was recently called "the most dangerous man alive" by the leader of the "Free World"—laughs, and puts his usual positive spin on his situation. "You know, dealing with different cultures, different time periods and space zones—it's still easier than crossing the Bay Bridge in rush hour traffic."

Dope Is To Time As Machines Are To Space

The time keys are pharmacological, biochemical. He explains: whereas most previous sacred plants evolved through the natural history and geography of a particular area, LSD was a laboratory-created synthesis of this time and this place, discovered by accident on April 16, 1943, just around the corner from where we're sitting. It is a man-created archetype, and thus a rare privilege is ours: to witness the evolution of a sacred drug discovered in our lifetime.

The Basel chemist who served as the medium for that particular cosmic rush attended the Swiss Mardi Gras—the festival of Fassnacht. Unknown to each other, Albert Hofmann and Timothy Leary cavorted all night in the crowded streets wearing costumes and masks. Next day they spent the afternoon together in the alchemist's magnificent house on the Swiss-French border.

Dope is to time as machines are to space, they agreed, enjoying a swim in Hofmann's indoor pool, while ancient stone carvings of Aztec mushroom deities regarded them with endless amusement. The High Priest's archivist made a home movie for the Fitz Hugh Ludlow Memorial Library back in San Francisco.

"You know," said the Hedonic Fugitive to the Respected Sandoz Chemist as they splashed in the pool, speaking of a mutual deceased friend, "I was one of Aldous Huxley's favorite acts."

Making Yourself Survivally Inevitable

Aldous Huxley's "favorite act" (and whose favorite act was Aldous? Why, D. H. Lawrence, of course!) explained how mutants have to learn to make themselves survivally inevitable. Survival is the test for any new mutant species; the pressure comes from "normal" species members who are threatened because they haven't made the evolutionary jump.

What began as neurological liberation with psilocybin and LSD a decade earlier has moved on through six other levels. Liberation on the planes of the spiritual, sexual, cultural, economic, political, and existential was classically impelled to follow. The blown mind knew the choice is always oppression versus liberation. . . . Flashback to the prisoner's body struggling along the forty-foot cable wire above the prison yard at night, while thirty feet below a gun truck made its rounds. The prisoner reached the fence and jumped to freedom, beginning an odyssey as "William McNellis" which he continued as "Nino Baraka."

Survival, sex, and synthesized bliss are the laser beams of his celebrated, denounced, censored, mutilated, oft-revised, ripped off, and *still* unpublished manuscript (*Confessions of a Hope Fiend*, the seventeenth version of which was published in 1973) that Timothy is writing to pay for his upper-class lawyer, his shady "protector," and his Swiss chocolate habit. It is the story of his prison escape, flight to exile, "revolutionary bust" by the Black Panther Party leader after he either won or lost the debate on the role of psychedelic drugs in the revolution, and the superiority of Swiss versus American jail food. The outlawed exiles Timothy and Rosemary discovered that, whereas the space games are survival, power, and control, the corresponding time games are sex, dope, and magic.

So they created a board game for all their parole officers, present and future. The board has rows of seven spaces across and seven spaces down. Each board position represents an intersection in the space-time dance. There are forty-nine spaces, or roles—not unlike the lesser arcana of the tarot. The four basic roles are Warrior, Warlock, Inquisitor, Alchemist. The board is bisected by the Tribal Cross. Space and time meet in the Tribe, which provides space to protect the time-traveling fugitives. In Algeria, the role of Hassan-i-Sabbah—the founder of the *hashishin* and first recorded person to brainwash with euphoric drugs—was not necessarily up for grabs. The Aleister Crowley persona emerged during an acid trip in the Sahara. But survival dictated another space-time coordinate, and the Learys slipped into Switzerland.

In the Land of Delysid

Timothy was quickly imprisoned in Lausanne, awaiting extradition to the United States at the personal request of Nixon's Attorney General John Mitchell, when he received a surprise visit from a young Swiss who was a distant relative of Hermann Hesse, "poet of the interior journey." Christoph Wenger presented Tim with a beautiful oval watercolor landscape painting by the creator of *Steppenwolf* (of which a film version starring Tim as Harry Haller is reported to be in the works). It was a good sign. Back in Babylon the San Francisco Bay Area Prose Poets' Phalanx, created deus ex machina by Allen Ginsberg, mobilized an international array of poets, essayists, and novelists to petition the Swiss government "to accept Dr. Leary as an archetype of the traditional political, cultural, literary, or philosophical refugee and grant him personal asylum."

Which they did. "How magically it all works out," Timothy

said upon his release, as he smiled for a photo op with his brave, beautiful, and much relieved wife. Switzerland's biggest antidope lawyer, the father of three hippie sons, had taken the case. Albert Hofmann and Dutch writer-activist Simon Vinkenoog had thrown in their support. William S. Burroughs made a brief appearance on the set, leaving Leary with a copy of his latest work, *Ali's Smile*. The asylum-seekers were liberated once more, this time in the Land of Delysid. "Will Switzerland never learn?" muttered the CIA, while Ali smiled.

How Much Pleasure Can You Stand?

A giant map of the country is pinned to the wall of this charming lakefront house. Swans glide on the water, snow-capped mountains loom in the distance. The fugitive is tracing the route of their recent travels with a red magic marker. Zurich Airport, where they sneaked past customs . . . a chalet in Villars . . . Lausanne prison . . . the resort village of Crans where he learned to ski but was eighty-sixed for "having too good a time in public." Timothy pondered his next move on the space board.

Earlier that day, he drove a funky VW van with a Black Panther painted on the front end to the Immensee train station to meet his archivists from San Francisco. There they purchased a copy of *Sonntags Journal*, the Swiss *Time*, where Leary's picture was on the cover above the words "Prophet auf der Flucht" (Prophet on the Lam). This is William Tell country, and we are guests at the home of Bobby Dreyfus, great-grandson of the famous Alfred Dreyfus, set up as a traitor in a celebrated trial of the 1890s. On the way a stop is made at a television studio where Timothy makes a hit-and-run appearance on Swiss national television, asserting the basic question is: "How much pleasure can you stand?"

Day in the Life of an Exile

At the house he speaks on the phone with his attorney in Bern; he changes a diaper for granddaughter Dieadra; he smokes hash with some Swiss hippies who fall by to check him out; he puts an eighth

level into his prison escape narrative; he agrees to be godfather to a
baby girl named Winona recently born in Minnesota; he fields a
call from a mysterious international literary agent who tells him of
an offer of a quarter-million-dollar advance on this very narrative.
(The money is paid, though not to Timothy but to the swindler
who acts as his protector. Timothy does get a yellow Porsche for
his literary efforts, a cool replacement for the VW bus.)

Each Level of Consciousness Requires Its Own Art Form

The Clifford Irving–Howard Hughes plagiarism case greatly interests him because "plagiarism is the literary form of the future. A
man writing his own book is an absurdity. What an ego trip. Whew!"

He explains that the visionary experience no longer need be
ineffable, indescribable. Consciousness is based on physical and
physiological structure. Each level of consciousness requires its own
art form. The seven fine arts of the future will be:

1. The Genetic Circus: Dance of Mutants
2. The Neurological Film Library
3. The Rapture of Omni-Sensual Pornography
4. Romantic Adolescent Street Theater
5. Intellectual Creations
6. Political Emotional Dramas
7. Anesthetics (escape hatches: the gun or the junkie's needle), and
   "psychedelic presidents melting armaments down to gigantic
   Buddhas."

Leaving Space for Time

"To be a man of knowledge one needs to be light and fluid," says
Don Juan. "And never refuse an opportunity to turn on," adds
McNellis-Baraka-Leary. While the assembled archivists furiously
took notes, the two sorcerers clasped hands and the Yaqui Indian
vanished into thin air. "Press conferences are something of a drag

for him," laughed the Asylum Laureate to the television cameras and tape recorders.

"Run it down!" shouts the reporter from *Marijuana Review*.

"Travel light. Travel far. Learn a space skill which is not bound to any space. Never forget you belong in time and are an alien in space. Always remain close to the supply of time keys. The key to time travel is pharmacological. Never refuse an opportunity to travel in time.

"Any questions?"

Jaaz #7
for Tim Leary

ROBERT HUNTER

—but alas I was no swimmer
    so I lost my Clementine . . .
                    Goethe

Galileo said "There's a sucker born
every minute and two to lead him."

    Mark Twain claimed
"Give me a lever long enough,
a fulcrum & a place to stand,
    and I'll talk to the moon."

But it took Timothy Leary
to demonstrate the insight
that joined these divergent strains
of thought, to wit:
Moderation
        in some things,
            excess in others!

Robert Hunter is a poet and a lyricist for the Grateful Dead.

Tall boat, soft oars,
crocheted sails & flat wind,
over the waves we wade while
Tim in a tunic reasons
with the breeze and wins.
"OK, your turn to blow,"
it says to him.

Since someone had to mislead us,
seeing the ice was thick
and the skates thin,
Tim was a better choice,
by the width of a bucket of blood,
than those who told us
barrels only come out
of the freedom of guns.

Leary led us to understand
freedom is in our socks
because they are closer
to our feet than our shoes.

Now and forever
immortality calls,
in the only way it calls,
if in fact it calls,
and it may behoove us
to believe it does,
since the fate of one
is the fate of all,
or were we wrong
about everything,
including the clear
evidence of the senses
standing on stalks
where the wind talks,
always in song,

sweet little sixteen
in fluorescent genes
bringing in the sheaves
through the cornucopia
of flagrant desire, chaste
mermaids in halter tops
tipping each wave,
singing for some,
Tim among them.

Those who choose
the perils of freedom
over the certainties of stone,
alone may hear them.

Melodic variation aside,
translation gainsaid,
ever and anon
it's the same song:

Gate, gate,
in at the gate,
out of the same gate,
Buddy *Sail On!*

Letters

ALDOUS HUXLEY AND GERALD HEARD

May 10, 1961
Mr. Aldous Huxley
3276 Deronda Drive
Los Angeles, California

Dear Aldous,

Our work progresses well. We are trying to work out some of Grey Walter's ideas. Thanks for the reference. The work at the prison is proceeding beautifully. The prisoners are deeply affected—by the drug and by the vistas that are suggested and which we encourage.

We are closing our first naturalistic study of 114 cases—413 separate ingestions. All but one case eager to try again. Results very positive. I'll be reporting results in Copenhagen.

In order to make the results more "objective" we are tabulating responses to questionnaires. If you could spare a few minutes to

---

Aldous Huxley was an early member of the Psilocybin Project and one of the foremost writers of the twentieth century. Gerald Heard, philosopher, scholar, and mystic, inspired and encouraged many to explore religious experience.

complete these forms I would be very grateful. I know you understand the pressure on us to count.

We have the convicts reading D. to P., H. and H. Also textbooks on criminology.

Looking forward to seeing you in Denmark.

Best regards,
Timothy Leary

The Plaza
Fifth Avenue at 59th Street
New York

13.vi.61
Dear Tim,

Next time you are in New York, go & see the Max Ernst show at the Museum of Modern Art. Some of the pictures are wonderful examples of the world as seen from the vantage point of LSD or mushrooms. Ernst sees in a visionary way & is also a first-rate artist capable of expressing what he sees in paintings which are about as adequate to the visionary facts as any I know. It might be interesting to get in touch with him, find out what his normal state is, then give him mushrooms or LSD & get him to compare his normal experiences with his drug-induced ones. His combination of psychological idiosyncrasy and enormous talent makes him a uniquely valuable case.

Yours,
Aldous

6. ii.61
Dear Tim,

Thank you for your letter of Jan 23rd, which came during my absence—first in Hawaii, then at San Francisco where we had a good conference on *Control of the Mind.*

Alas, I *can't* write anything for Harpers—am too desperately busy trying to finish a book.

At S.F. I met Dr. Janiger, whom I had not seen for several years. He tells me that he has given LSD to 100 painters who have done pictures before, during & after the drug, & whose efforts are being appraised by a panel of art critics. This might be interesting. I gave him your address & I think you will hear from him.

I also spoke briefly with Dr. Joly West (prof of psychiatry at U. of Oklahoma Medical School), who told me that he had done a lot of work in sensory deprivation, using improved versions of John Lilly's techniques. Interesting visionary results—but I didn't have time to hear the details.

You are right about the hopelessness of the "scientific" approach. These idiots want to be Pavlovians not Lorenzian Ethologists. Pavlov never saw an animal in its natural state, only under duress. The "scientific" LSD boys do the same with their subjects. No wonder they report psychoses.

Yours,
Aldous

19 April 1961
Dear Dr. Leary:

Thank you very much for your letter of April 10. I have just returned from a week's absence from Santa Monica, and it was waiting here when I got back two days ago.

I am delighted at the prospect of meeting with your research group in Cambridge. In consequence, I now plan to come directly to Boston from Los Angeles, on May 15th, and stay for at least two days, possibly three, depending on how New York City dates work out.

You are very kind and hospitable to offer to put me up in your house; but I fear that it would be a real imposition on you, for a number of reasons—among them (a) there is only one through flight from Los Angeles to Boston daily, and it arrives in Boston at 11:25 PM. And since planes are never on time, it could easily be midnight or later. (b) I will be 72 this year and since I don't have the extra strength and energy to cope with the demands made by travelling, it is necessary for my associate, Michael Barrie, to accompany me. So there would be two of us. (c) When away from home I like to remain quiet in the forenoon in order to be in shape for seeing people and going about in the afternoon and evening, which are my best times.

So perhaps it would be best if Mr. Barrie and I stop at a hotel in Cambridge. Otherwise, I really would feel that we were imposing an undue strain on both your hospitality and your household.

I was particularly interested in what you say in paragraph two about 'set and suggestion are always with us.' This is a topic I much wish to discuss with you. As you know, a number of researchers after some years of experience have begun to wonder whether in the end if one could produce optimum conditions of place, companion and preparation, it would be possible to produce at least some of these upper states of mind without any medicament. I wonder too if you know of Alastair Hardy's empirical work as an ecologist in the attempt to study and measure the religious experience? He believes that beside obtaining good reporting by the experient it might be most helpful to make careful records of the person's life in the periods after the experience.

I will not take more of your time now but I am full of hope about the discussions we may be able to have owing to your kindness in arranging this meeting.

Sincerely yours,
Gerald Heard

Berkeley 4,
California
2nd February, 1962

Dear Tim,

I forgot in my last letter to answer your question about Tantra. There are enormous books on the subject by "Arthur Avalon" (Sir John Woodruffe), which one can dip into with some profit. Then there is the chapter on it in Heinrich Zimmer's "Philosophies of India." The fullest scholarly treatment, on a manageable scale, is in Mircea Eliade's various books on Yoga. See also Conze's "Buddhist Texts." As far as one can understand it, Tantra seems to be a strange mixture of superstition and magic with sublime philosophy and acute philosophical insights. There is an endless amount of ritual and word magic.

But the basic ideal seems to me the highest possible ideal—enlightenment achieved, essentially, through constant awareness. This is the ultimate yoga—being aware, conscious even of the unconscious—on every level from the physiological to the spiritual. In this context see the list of 112 exercises in awareness, extracted from a Tantrik Text and printed at the end of "Zen Flesh Zen Bones" (now in paperback. The whole of gestalt therapy is anticipated in these exercises—and the world) as the Vedantists and the Nirvana-addicts of the Hinayana School of Buddhists. But within the world, through the world, by means of ordinary processes of living. Tantra teaches a yoga of sex, a yoga of eating (even eating forbidden foods and drinking forbidden drinks). The sacramentalizing of common life, so that every event may become a means whereby enlighten-ment can be realized, is therapy not merely for the abnormal, it is above all a Therapy for the much sickness of insensitiveness and ignorance we call "normality" or "mental health."

LSD and the mushrooms should be used, it seems to me, in the context of this basic Tantrik idea of the yoga of total awareness, leading to enlightenment within the world of everyday experience—which of course becomes the world of miracle and beauty and di-vine mystery when experience is what it always ought to be.

Yours,
Aldous

17.vii.62
Dear Tim,

Delighted to get your Zihuatanejo letter. I've greatly enjoyed our afternoon with you & hope the Hotel Catalina looks promising for your purposes.

As you say the Trinity of the 3Ps Police, Priest, Paymaster (Banker) is always against the journey of the soul but the current of consciousness is against the 3. For better or worse—better if you and the con: chang: druggists do it—worse if the politician is bright enough [in] his dark way to get in on the act in either case police priest & paymaster have had their day. Did you see that Glen Seaborg head of the A.E.C. asked what would be the big breakthrough in the next 30 years said the consciousness changing drugs.

We are off to visit Sandoz et al: due to start in a week. Hofmann wrote to say he'll be in Mexico looking up the mushrooms. I guess you'll meet him thereupon.

Michael joins in affectionate greetings & best wishes.

Love,
Gerald

545 Spoleto Drive
Santa Monica Calif.
rec Feb. 9 63
Dear Tim,

Very glad to have news of you. It is fine that your first insight into the possibilities of Zihuatanejo are in process of being confirmed. It certainly sounds & looks lovely. It is, too, very good news that you will be in this part in April. Let us know as soon as you can your actual dates. We are due to be doing some work at Big Sur at Easter (round 14 of April for about a week) otherwise we expect to be here as far as plans are now made.

With affectionate best wishes in which Michael joins,

Gerald

6233 Mulholland
LA 28 / Cal.
20.vii.63
Dear Tim,

Thank you for your letters. I think the idea of the school is excellent, for what needs exploring, more than anything else, is the problem of fruitfully relating what Wordsworth calls "wise passiveness" to wise activity—receptivity & immediate experience to concept making and the projection upon the experience of intelligible order. Now do we make the best of *both* the worlds described in Wordsworth's *Expostulation & Reply* and *The Tables Turned*? That is what has to be discovered. And one should make use of all the available resources—the best methods of formal teaching and also LSD, hypnosis (used, among other things, to help people to re-enter the LSD state without having recourse to a chemical), time distortion (to speed up the learning process), auto-conditioning for control of automatic processes and heightening of physical & psychological resistance to disease & trauma etc etc. . . .

Ever yours,
Aldous

3276 Deronda
LA 28
Cal.
7.v.61

Dear Tim,

Thank you for your letter. As you may have heard or read, we have been burned out. Nothing—literally nothing—remains & I am now a man without a past & Laura is a pastless woman—no old letters, diaries, notes, MSS, address books, & of course none of the common objects whose presence one takes for granted.

Among the uncommon objects which vanished was the bottle of psilocybin tablets you gave me—full but for a single dose. If you have any more to spare, I wd be grateful for a new supply. I expect we shan't meet before mid-April in Copenhagen. Goodbye till then.

Yours,
Aldous

PS This address will find me as all mail will be forwarded to wherever I happen to be.

6233 Mulholland
LA 28 / Cal
27.vi.63

Dear Tim,

Alan Watts has given me your current address, & and I am writing, first of all, to say that I hope all goes well with you and your projects, in spite of the Mexican set-back; and in the next place, to ask if you know anything about the present intentions & future plans of Mr. Payne & his *Playboy* colleagues. I sent them my piece some 3 weeks ago (a copy, incidentally, went to you in Zihuatanejo—but perhaps you were gone before it arrived); no acknowledgement was sent. I wrote 10 days later to ask what had happened & received a wire to say that the text had been received & that Payne wd "try to write tomorrow." That was a week ago & no word has come to me from Payne or anybody else. This is very odd, discourteous & unbusiness-like behavior, and I should be grateful if you stir these people into telling me 1) if they propose to use the piece 2) what price they are proposing to pay. Alan Watts has implanted in my mind serious doubts as to the *bona fides* of *Playboy* in this matter, and I am concerned to know where I stand and what is to become of my essay.

Ever yours,
Aldous

6233 Mulholland
LA 28
Cal
3.vi.63
Dear Tim,

Herewith a script of my essay-in-introduction, which I have deliberately not confined to a discussion of psychedelics, but have treated in more general terms the whole problem of the individual's relation to his culture—a problem in whose solution the psychedelics can undoubtedly play their part. In haste,

Ever yours,
Aldous

The Rule of Love

MICHAEL KAHN

When Tim came to Harvard in the '60s, the upheaval he brought was not primarily due to the drugs. It was primarily due to his challenging the assumptions that had governed the place for a very long time. The basic assumption was that tenure at Harvard (or, failing that, at Yale or Berkeley) was the most desirable of all goals. Other assumptions followed: It was important that a person have a national reputation. National reputations were gained by prestigious publications and memberships. It was therefore necessary to attract and keep a large stable of graduate students. There was only one criterion for a research topic: would it advance one's career?

Tim pointed out the egregious social and human irresponsibility that underlay these assumptions and he did so very persuasively. Tim's faculty colleagues saw him preaching academic socialism to a society that depended on the assumptions of academic capitalism. It was about as welcome as the Fabian Socialists had been to the British establishment in the '20s. The drugs were not the issue; they were the excuse to get rid of him.

Michael Kahn, former actor, pilot, and long-time psychology professor, had his life changed by Timothy Leary at Harvard in 1961. He has not recovered. And is eternally grateful.

Harvard firing Tim in 1963 had some important implications. In that year Abe Maslow had published *Toward a Psychology of Being* and founded the Association of Humanistic Psychology. Mike Murphy and Dick Price had founded the Esalen Institute. Something new and important was being born in American psychology and American culture. Tim was a major force in that revolution; by firing him Harvard served notice that the new movement had no place in the university, which is to say in establishment America. That it was predictable made it no less ominous.

The humanistic movement developed many voices, not all of them very attractive. But at the center was one major theme. If we are to be saved there is only one way: *the rule of love must replace the rule of selfishness*. I had heard that message before. I suppose I had heard it a lot before. But I heard it from Tim in a way that penetrated to my core and changed my life. I think the same can be said of an enormous number of people. Our debt to him should not be forgotten.

St. Timothy
on the Freeway

KEN KESEY

All the way down, of course, sanity going on with politic policy;
Craziness, on the other hand, a little shallow and sporadic.

Streets lined both sides with Karate teachers (DEFEND YOUR-
SELF!) fabricate enormous lies concerning the direness of our neigh-
borhood. Manhole covers open up advertising Elysium with no down
payment. Rides needed outta town as soon as possible tomorrow
morning if possible help with gas and driving. Citizen band radios
charge each other with impossible atrocities (LET ME OUTTA
HERE DEFENDING MYSELF! *all the way down, still humming,
humming, give all you got, humming, humming, all you got*) where fas-
cists belch at each other beneath the coffee tables, significantly.

You can't argue with the seven route interchange fulla segre-
gated schoolbuses, and you hitchhiking high the hell outta here.
"Why am ah treated so bad?" you cry with your thumbs out; but
you can't argue. "Where am ah goin to? Will ah ever git thar?" But
you know you gonna get on whatever schoolbus stops for you.

"Look at the people this town ferchrissakes!" you cry, hesitating.

Ken Kesey, a merry prankster, wrote One Flew Over the Cuckoo's Nest,
Sometimes a Great Notion, *and other classics.*

"Nemmine that, kid; you get on board or aren't you?"

"Don't I have a right to know where you taken me?"

"Listen kid, this your color bus or not? Or you wanta hang out the rest of your life on the shoulder and watch others get an education?"

"All right. Anyplace better'n this town; but look at the people, I ask you; why we makin each other so ugly and shifty eyed?"

"I'm leavin, kid." Vrooom.

"Wait! No! wait . . ."

In the streets behind you hear the Karate teachers charging the open manholes, all narrated by conflicting radio reports. (*Saving grace, humming there on the shoulder of the freeway, all the day long all the way down, humming, humming, feeling all right in spite.*)

I'd rather be real than right, tonight, with the freeway furur finally dying down . . . a quiet little rain is falling . . . the Karate classes are dark; the manholes closed . . . oowumm . . . oooywo-uuummmmmmm. . . .

You are a great man, Timothy; what else can we say? We will miss you in this land but we'll lock you in none.

Letter to Timothy

Carolyn Kleefeld

Dearest Hi-Tech Electronic Pixie Timothy,

You have reached the zenith in "human technology" in your valiant, heroic, brilliant, hi-tech treatment of so-called dying (perhaps what they call *living* is really dying and *dying* is our liberation unto true life). As always you are uniquely inspirational. No one (as you) has ever made this stage of living/dying an entertaining yet profoundly meaningful event. You are showing to the world and for all that know you what is possible from the most evolved philosophical hi-tech humoristic perspective.

As ever you are our favorite cheerleader of undaunted spirit and will live in history and in our hearts as our eternal blazing flame of inspiration.

PS—WE LOVE YOU

Carolyn Mary Kleefeld is an acclaimed poet, philosopher, visual artist, and evolutionary thinker whose three poetry books are used worldwide in the field of human development. Her latest book, The Alchemy of Possibility, *the culmination of ten years of creative expression, weaves a rich tapestry of her visionary paintings, philosophical reflections, and poetry. To learn more about Carolyn, please visit her Web site at www.carolynmarykleefeld.com.*

A Game of Mind Tennis with Timothy Leary

PAUL KRASSNER

So, Tim, here's a toast to thirty years of friendship."

"And still counting. We've been playing mind tennis for thirty years. Isn't that great?"

"The one thing in countless conversations we've had that sticks out in my mind is something you once said, that no matter what scientists do, they can decodify the DNA code, layer after layer, but underneath it all, there's still that mystery. And I've enjoyed playing with the mystery. Are you any closer to understanding the mystery, or further from it?"

"Well, Paul, I watch words now. It's an obsession. I learned it from Marshall McLuhan, of course. A terrible vice. Had it for years, but not actually telling people about it. I watch the words that people use. The medium is the message, you recall. The brain creates the realities she wants. When we see the prisms of these words that come through, we can understand. Do I understand the mystery?"

"I guess the ultimate mystery is inconceivable by definition. But have you come any closer to understanding it?"

"Understand? Stand under! I'm overstood, I'm understood."

"The older I get, the deeper the mystery is."

Paul Krassner is the editor of The Realist.

"The faster."

"Let's get to a specific mystery. The mystery of you. Because everybody sees you through their own perceptions. How do you think you have been most misunderstood?"

"Well, Paul, everyone gets the Timothy Leary they deserve. Everyone has their point of view. And everyone's point of view is absolutely valid for them. To track me, you have to keep moving the camera, or you'll have just one tunnel point of view. Sermonizing there. Don't impale yourself on your point of view."

"Some people know you only through that '60s slogan, 'Turn on, tune in, drop out.' I think a lot of people don't really understand what you meant by dropping out."

"Everybody understood. Just look at the source."

"All right, here's words. Fifteen years ago at a futurist conference you called yourself a Neo-Technological Pagan. What did you mean by that?"

"*Neo* has all the connotations of the futurist stuff that's coming along. *Technological* denotes using machines, using electricity or light to create reality. There are two kinds of technology. The machine— diesel, oil, metal, industrial technology. And then the neo-technology, which uses light. Electricity. Photons. Electrons. *Pagan* is great. I love the word. Pagan is basically humanist. I grew up in a Catholic zone, and pagan was the worst thing you could say. Of course, I'd never met a pagan in Springfield, Massachusetts, going to a Catholic school. 'Where do these pagans hang out? I wanna be one.'"

"Was there any specific thing that made you turn from Catholicism?"

"Yeah, Paul, there was a period, I know exactly what it was, I was fifteen or sixteen, I was being sexually molested in my high school and actually totally seduced by a wonderful, sexy girl, much more experienced than I. And, whew! She opened it up! The great mystery of sex. Wow! At that time I was going routinely to confession on Saturday afternoon. But I had a date with Rosemary that night. Sitting there in the dark, absolutely, totally hypocritical! They want you to confess and repent while I have every intention in the world of being seduced by this girl tonight."

"The glands overshadowed the philosophy."

"The glands? Shit, Paul, that statement is very mechanical."

"I'm a recovering romantic."

"Because you used the word gland? Glands are very interesting. People don't talk about glands very much."

"Talk about machines then. What's the relationship between acid and technology?"

"Well, LSD is one of the many drugs which are based on neuroactive plants. Peyote and [fungus] on rye. Those crazed experiences which happened in the Middle Ages, what did they call them? The madness of crowds, simply because of some plant they had chewed. The point is that the human brain is equipped with these receptor sites for various kinds of vegetables that alter consciousness. So our brains evolving over fifty million years have these receptor sites. The reason why certain people like to take these drugs is because these receptor sites activate pleasure centers. Now this was not a mistake. The DNA didn't fuck up. The devil didn't do it. There was obviously some reason for those receptor sites that would get you off on peyote, psilocybin. And there are dozens of compelling receptor sites and drugs we don't even know about."

"In the changing counterculture, then, do you see a continuity from psychoactive drugs to cyberspace?"

"Of course. It's a fact. Every generation developed a new counterculture. In the Roaring '20s, jazz, liquor. In the '60s, the hippies with psychedelics."

"The counterculture now, it's not either/or, it's not necessarily drugs or computers. I'm sure some do them simultaneously. But how do you think that the drug experience has changed the computer experience?"

"I did not imply that you can't do both. The brain is equipped to be altered by these receptor sites. So we can see these receptor sites overwhelm the mind. The word processing system. Then suddenly you can take psychedelic plants that put you in different places. I'm being too technical. But there's an analogy between receptor sites for marijuana and for LSD or opium, which activate the brain and the way we can boot up different areas of our computers. Back in the 1960s we didn't know much about the brain. I was saying back in 1968, 'You have to go out of your mind to use your head.'

But 'head' simply is an old-fashioned way of saying 'brain.' We didn't know about brain receptor sites. But now, we can use biochemicals to boot up the kind of altered realities you want in your brain. So you smoke marijuana because it gets you in a mellow mood. Grass is good for the appetite. That's operating your brain. But now it's specific: 'Use your head by operating your brain.' That's the new concept. Use your head! That's hot. Operate your brain because the brain designs realities."

"Do you see a connection between the war on drugs and the attempt to censor the Internet?"

"Oh, absolutely, yes, Paul. The censors want to control. We have to have people to impose to keep any society going. I don't knock rules, ritual. We have to have them. The controllers censor anything that gives the power to change reality to the individual. You can't have that happen."

"My theory is that the UFO sightings and all the people who claim to have been abducted by aliens are really just a cover-up for secret government experiments in mind control."

"That's a very popular theory, Paul. I get like ten mimeographed letters a day about UFOs and the government. Boy, the governments are really fucking busy, trying to program our minds."

"And of course those UN soldiers in Bosnia can hardly wait to get back in their black helicopters so they can attack Michigan and Arizona."

"I'm happy about the UFO rumors. I'm glad because at least people are doing something on their own. The sixty-year-old farm wife in Dakota thinks she's been taken up and serially raped by UFO people. *Wow!* They came all the way from another planet a thousand light years away to get this lovely grandmother and pull her socks and have an orgy with her. *Wow!*"

"Or at least an anal probe. To your knowledge, is the government still doing experiments in mind control? We know they used to, with the MKULTRA programs and all. Do you know if they're still at it? I can't imagine they would've stopped."

"G. Gordon Liddy would give you the current CIA line. Liddy says: 'Yes, it is true. When we learned that the Chinese Communists were using LSD, the CIA naturally cornered the whole world market from Sandoz LSD. They didn't realize that LSD comes in a millionth of a gram. The CIA found LSD to be unpredictable.' Well, no shit, Gordon! Can you name one accurate CIA prediction? The fall of the Shah? The rise of the Ayatollah?"

"What did you think of Liddy getting that free speech award from the National Association of Talk Show Hosts after he said that if the ATF comes after you, they're wearing bulletproof vests so you should aim for the head or groin?"

"That's pure Liddy. He's basically a romantic comedian."

"When you were debating him, if you had listened to his advice retroactively when he led the raid on Millbrook, then later you would've been on stage debating yourself, because he would've been shot in the head and groin by somebody, if his advice had been followed."

"He was a government agent entering our bedroom at midnight. We had every right to shoot him. But I've never owned a weapon in my life. And I have no intention of owning a weapon, although I was a master sharpshooter at West Point on the Garand, the Springfield rifle and the machine gun. I was a Howitzer expert. I know how to operate these lethal gadgets, but I have never had and never will have a gun around."

"But when you escaped from prison, you said, 'Arm yourselves and shoot to live. To shoot a genocidal robot policeman in defense of life is a sacred act.'"

"Yeah! I also said 'I'm armed and dangerous.' I got that directly from Angela Davis. I thought it was just funny to say that."

"I thought it was the party line from the Weather Underground."

"Well, yeah, I had a lot of arguments with Bernadine Dohrn."

"They had their own rhetoric. She even praised Charlie Manson."

"The Weather Underground was amusing. They were brilliant, brilliant, Jewish, Chicago kids. They had class and dash and flash and smash. Bernadine was praising Manson for sticking a fork in a victim's stomach. She was just being naughty."

"She was obviously violating a taboo. What are the taboos that are waiting to be violated today?"

"There is one taboo, the oldest taboo and the most powerful— I've been writing about it and thinking about it for thirty years.

The concept of death is something that people do not want to face. The doctors and the priests and the politicians have made it into something terrible, terrible, terrible. You're a victim! If you accept the notion of death, you've signed up to be the ultimate victim."

"Is that why you've announced publicly that you have inoperable prostate cancer? Friends knew it but . . ."

"I actually have been planning my terminal graduation party for twenty years. Of course, I'm a follower of Socrates, who was one of the greatest counterculture comic philosophers in history. He took hemlock."

"The Hemlock Society was named after that."

"I've been a member of the Hemlock Society for many years. They talk about self-deliverance. That's the biggest decision you can make. You couldn't choose how and when and with whom you were *born*."

"Although there are people who say you can."

"All right, well, go for it. But for those of us who don't have that option . . ."

"Ram Dass even once said that a fetus that gets aborted knew it didn't want to be born so it chose parents who wouldn't carry it to term."

"Richard's so politically correct. Isn't that fabulous?"

"Are you planning to do what Aldous Huxley did, which was to make the journey on acid?"

"That's an option, yeah."

"Do you believe in any kind of afterlife?"

"Well, I have left an enormous archive covering sixty years of writing, around three hundred audio-videos. It's being stored away. And I belong to two cryonics groups, so I have the option of freezing my brain."

"By afterlife, I didn't mean the products of your consciousness so much as your consciousness itself."

"My consciousness is a product of my brain. How can I know about my mind unless I express thought?"

"Obviously there are people who believe in the standard Heaven and Hell and Purgatory. I'm assuming that you don't believe in that kind of afterlife."

"They're useful metaphors. I must be in Purgatory now, huh?" Occasionally I have a pop of Heaven. That's not a bad metaphor. Of course we realize that Hell is totally self-induced."

"On earth, you mean."

"Well, wherever you are. What do you think about that? Do you believe in life after death and all that? What's your theory?"

"That you are eaten by worms and just disappear, or you're cremated and your ashes . . ."

"Wait, now, Paul, you have your choice of being eaten by worms or barbecued. Or you can be frozen. You don't have to be eaten by worms. You don't have to be microwaved. I'm going to leave some drops of my blood, which has my DNA, in a lot of places. I'll leave my brain with them. Why not try all these things? Not that I *care*, Paul, believe me. I have no desperate desire to come back to planet Earth. I think that I have lived one of the most incredibly funny, interesting lives. I'm fascinated to see what's gonna happen in the next steps. But I have no desire to come back. Most nonscientists don't realize that in scientific experiments you learn more from your mistakes. So I hope that I will leave a track record of making blunders about the most important thing in life: How to preserve your DNA. I hope someone learns from my mistakes."

"Are there regrets that you have? Things that you would have done differently, knowing what you know now?"

"I'd play the whole game differently, sure. About a third of the things I've done have been absolutely stupid, vulgar, gross. About a third have been just banal. But a third have been brilliant. Like baseball, one out of three, you lead the league. MVP. Most Valuable Philosopher."

"When I first met you in 1965 you were talking about baseball—and games in general—as a metaphor. How would you describe your game in life? It's been a conscious game. You didn't just fall into a pinball machine and get knocked around. Although that happened too."

"Well, I identified with Socrates at a very young age. The aim of human life is to find out about yourself and know who you are. The purpose of life is to discover yourself."

"With these big media mergers going on now, giants, Time-

Warner-Turner here, Disney-ABC there, how do you think the individual can best fight that?"

"Why fight it? Like Southern railroad merges with Pennsylvania Railroad, so what?"

"But you said before they're trying to control, so aren't they trying to control the information?"

"You can't control information if its packaged in light, in photons and electrons. You simply can't control digital messages. *Zoom*, I can go to my Web site and put some stuff up there. Immediately my messages are accessed by people around the world. Not just now but later. The nice thing about cyber communication is that counterculture philosophers who learn about technology can work together, can be faster than committees, politicians, and the like. So I have great confidence. You have to learn to play their game. That's why I went to West Point and that's why I went to the Jesuit school, and learned enough so I could play the mindfuck game. I understood and I moved on."

"Do you mean you knew before you went to West Point, before you went to Jesuit school, that you wanted to learn their tools?"

"I didn't want to go to either. My parents insisted on that."

"So you went with that attitude?"

"Yeah. They took me around to about ten Catholic universities and colleges in New England. None of them would accept me because of my high school track record. I was the editor of the school newspaper and I made it a scandal sheet exposing the principal. I had a great uncle who was a big shot in the Catholic Church. He had pull in the Vatican, and he pulled some strings so I got into Jesuit school. I just watched, repelled but fascinated."

"I don't believe in reincarnation, but if I did, I would think I knew you in a previous life. But that's only a metaphor, I don't believe in it. Do you believe in that concept?"

"In the time of Emerson, the 1830s, there was a counterculture very similar to ours. Self-reliance. Individuality. Emerson took drugs with David Thoreau. Margaret Fuller went to Italy and got the drugs. Later, William James started another counterculture at Harvard. Same thing. Nitrous oxide. Hashish. *The Varieties of Religious Experience*."

"Well, have the medial people given you a prognosis on this life, of how many years you have left?"

"I'm seventy-five, and I've smoked and lived an active life but not the most healthy life. So my prognosis would be like two to five years. Jeez, I'll be eighty by then."

"Are there specific things that you want to accomplish during this period?"

"Our World Wide Web site is a big thing. We're putting books up there on the screen. You can actually play or perform my books. You can read the first page and my notes. And you can revise my text. We call them living books. As many versions as there are people that want to perform 'book' with me. True freedom of the press. The average person can't publish a book. This way they can."

"Do you think it's destiny or chance that one becomes in a leadership position—a change agent, as you call it?"

"Well, destiny implies that you were created that way. No, I think that the individual person has a lot to do with it. Thousands of decisions you make growing up in high school and college to get to a point where you have constructed your reality. You can be a judge or . . ."

"A defendant."

"I think one of the good side effects of the Simpson trial is that people understand how totally evil lawyers are."

"You mean defense lawyers *and* prosecutors?"

"Yes."

"A friend of mine was scheduled to be on jury duty and they asked him what he thought of prosecutors, and he said, 'Cops in suits.' Are you optimistic about the future, even though there's creeping fascism?"

"The future is measured in terms of individual liberation. You have politicians. And the military wants to hurt other people. That's all about control. They have to devise excuses for victimizing people. The new generation growing up now uses electronic media. A twelve-year-old kid now, in Tokyo or in Paris, or here, can move more stuff around on screen. She is exposed to more RPM, Realities Per Minute! A thousand times more than her grandfather. There is going to be big change. The greatest thing that's happening now

Timothy Leary and
Paul Krassner

is the World Wide Web. Signups zoom like this. The telephone is the connection. *The modem is the message!* You can explore around. If you're a left-handed, dyslexic, Lithuanian lesbian, you can get in touch with people in Yugoslavia or China who are left-handed, dyslexic lesbians. It's great! Its gonna break down barriers, create new language. More and more graphic language. And neon grammatics. Anything that's in print will be in neon."

"Well that really brings us full cycle. We started talking about words, and now they've become neonized."

"Consider, Paul, death with dignity, dying with elegance. It's wonderful to see it happening. I talk about orchestrating, managing, and directing my death as a celebration of a wonderful life! That touched a lot of people. They say: 'My father went through this whole thing. He wanted to die.' Amazing."

"So the response has been that people are glad to know that they aren't the only ones who are thinking about death."

"Yeah. People are thinking about dying with class, but we're afraid to talk about it."

"What do you want your epitaph to be?"

"What do *you* think? You write it."

"Here lies Timothy Leary. A pioneer of inner space. And an Irish leprechaun to the end."

"Irish leprechaun? You're being racist! Can't I be a Jewish leprechaun? What is this Irish leprechaun shit?"

"Okay. Here lies Timothy Leary, a Jewish leprechaun."

Postscript: Although Leary had decided in 1988 to have his head frozen posthumously, he became disillusioned with cryonics officials shortly before his death, and changed his mind.

"They have no sense of humor," he said. "I was worried I would wake up in fifty years surrounded by people with clipboards."

Instead he chose to be cremated and have a small portion of his ashes rocketed into outer space to orbit the Earth. I asked him if the remainder of his ashes could be mixed with marijuana and rolled into joints so that his friends and family could smoke him.

"Yeah," he replied. "Just don't bogart me."

A Word from the Control Group

AN INTERVIEW WITH JARON LANIER
BY ROBERT FORTE

RF: OK Jaron, first, will you comment on a remark Tim made some time ago that computers would be the acid of the '80s?

JL: Well, I think I can explain pretty well what Tim meant, although I have to say that I never agreed with him. In fact I used to bug him about it because I didn't think it was a helpful metaphor. Actually, the first person to say something like that might have been William Burroughs. But Tim certainly, as is always the case, said it in the most charmingly public way. I think his hope was that computer technology would, first of all, help people to communicate with one another and therefore allow them to identify themselves as individuals rather than as members of institutions. On that count I

Jaron Lanier is a computer scientist, composer, visual artist, and author, best known for his work in virtual reality. He coined the term "virtual reality," and founded the VR industry. He is currently Visiting Scholar, Dept. of Computer Science, Columbia University; Visiting Artist, Interactive Telecommunications Program, Tisch School of the Arts, New York University; and founding member of the new International Institute for Evolution and the Brain, which will be based at NYU, Harvard, and the University of Paris.

think computer networks—the Internet and so forth—do actually succeed. This fits into Tim's notion that there's an increasing progress toward fulfillment of people as individuals, as whole strikingly beautiful beings in and of themselves, instead of parts that are only validated by some sort of institutional or governmental body. That certainly was one aspect of what Tim hoped psychedelic drugs would accomplish, and it's one aspect of what computers have accomplished. I think that's valid.

Then we get into the more interesting territory which has to do with the realization of imagination, and that's where psychedelics might be related to my work in virtual reality. Now I've probably been asked about the connection between psychedelic drugs and virtual reality literally thousands of times in the course of my career, and what I always say is that I think they're practically opposite—in that drugs act on the subjective aspects of human beings, in other words, on their neurons, whereas virtual reality only creates alternative objective worlds outside of the human sense organ. So in that sense they really act in absolutely opposite ways. Furthermore, virtual reality creates experiences that have to be hand-crafted by people. There's an intentional, waking-consciousness state that has to precede and indeed occur during virtual reality experiences, whereas in a psychedelic experience there's a sense in which it moves on its own momentum. Not entirely, certainly, and certainly the content comes from within the people who experience it, but nonetheless the psychedelic drug provides its own momentum. So I think they're quite different.

Anyway, Tim saw a parallel, and certainly his comments about the similarity between the onset of mass computer culture in the '80s and the '90s and the onset of a mass culture of psychedelic drugs in the '60s was one of the prevailing metaphors that guided the culture of computers during that time. There's no question about it. Sometimes it annoyed the hell out of me, because it raised all of the same old reactions of fear that had come around in reaction to drugs in the '60s, and I had thought that perhaps we didn't need to go through that again. I thought that perhaps we could be in a time of construction instead of rebellion. But at any rate, Tim still said some wonderful charming things about the stuff and I think he helped inspire a whole sort of crossover movement that's embodied by things like *Mondo 2000* magazine, of people who were interested in both psychedelic culture and computers; that influence can still be seen in such places as the graphic design of *Wired* magazine and the sort of vaguely transcendence-seeking character of the metaphors in the computer world that are used in advertising and rhetoric.

In fact, almost to a person, the founders of the computer industry were ex-psychedelic style hippies. Now the one person who might be outside of that—a pretty major exception—would be Bill Gates, who was hanging out with the hippies, but I remember him being a little different from the start. Nevertheless the impact psychedelics had is unquestionably enormous. Mitch Kapur, Steve Jobs, and many, many others. And on the science side, too. Within the computer science community there's a very, very strong connection with the '60s psychedelic tradition, absolutely no question about it.

RF: But you're not a member of that family in that regard because your visions are not inspired directly by psychedelics.

JL: Right. I think I'm an honorary member by now but in fact I am probably the sole member of my generation not to have used drugs. I've sometimes been referred to as the control group. One time Timothy asked if he could get a transfusion of my blood because he thought I must have something he wanted to try. I'll take that as a compliment. But for myself psychedelics just never seemed like the right thing to do. It's always been anomalous and I've had many discussions and even arguments with folks about it.

RF: How did you meet Timothy?

JL: I originally met Tim because he was interested in computer science in the early '80s, and I was around the MIT scene at that time—I wasn't at MIT but I was working in a lab that Alice Kay had put together for Atari. Tim was interested in meeting some of us. So I ran across him there and visited his home in Los Angeles and we had a delightful time, of course. Tim is one of the most charming and gracious fellows you could hope to meet. Then the next time I met him was really quite striking. I called him to rendezvous at Esalen where he was giving a workshop. When I met up with him there he informed me that the workshop was a dud, the students were a dud, Esalen seemed to be dead, and would I mind figuring out a way to smuggle him out of Esalen past the guard gate? So all of a sudden we were in "East Berlin" evading the authorities at the guard gate. We bundled up Tim in the back seat, smothered under blankets, and got him out. That's what happened. Just recently—and this must be thirteen years later—I told that story to Michael Murphy, who was just absolutely delighted and said, "That was so cool!"

RF: Let's look at the evolutionary impact of virtual reality for a minute. I don't readily see the significance in terms of furthering wisdom in our culture or furthering some kind of social transformation through these technologies. From a Hindu or Buddhist standpoint, reality is already virtual. Human beings haven't learned that, haven't learned that process by which we create reality. Can these technologies help us in that regard?

JL: Well, to state a point that I think should be obvious, any value that a teaching tool can have has to be specific to a culture. There can't be any absolute value in a teaching tool because people are always moving and changing. In another culture at another time, virtual reality might not only be worthless, but indeed it might not even exist, since it is solely valued by its subjective qualities. It's something whose value and qualities on every level are completely ethnocentric to us. As it happens, we are a culture that, in a sense, worships technology. Technology is our talisman. Technology is our source not only of power but also of transcendence in our own mythologies—for most people in the mainstream. And virtual reality turns the tables on the traditional mainstream technologies in a number of ways. One way is that virtual reality doesn't actually increase the human power. Instead it focuses on human experience. And that in itself is really an extraordinary difference. With virtual reality for the first time you had technology enthusiasts running around saying, "I had an amazing experience. Can we change this so we get an even better experience?" As opposed to saying, "I got more powerful. I'm faster, bigger than before." That change of focus to the inward instead of the outward is both useful in terms of personal development, and it's also deeply moral in the sense that the sort of unchecked momentum we have to make ourselves more powerful with technology has reached a destructive stage because we are already powerful enough for a great many things.

RF: Okay, let me come at this another way. In the '60s we saw a renaissance of spirituality, a return to nature, a return to inner spiritual dimensions of the human being. Tim used to talk about this ancient battle between the flower people and the metal people. Maybe we think of technology as our route to transcendence, but then we saw we are slaves to it. So I'm wondering how does virtual reality and these computer technologies redirect us back to a humanistically centered . . .

JL: Well there's a big difference between the metaphor of metal, this nineteenth-century notion of technology, and the new technologies that are dealing purely with information. And there's absolutely no guarantee that these things are positive teaching machines for us, absolutely not. A great many people encounter this world of information technology and come away nerdier and blander than they were before. So I don't think anything in human affairs is simple or has guarantees. I don't think any path is certain at all. But what I do think about virtual reality is that it rewards imagination in a remarkable way. It does it through our particular talisman, through technology.

To oversimplify in the extreme: Before virtual reality, you were really stuck with a choice between two fundamental sorts of reality. One was the practical world where other people are, where you're not alone, and where you have to eat and work to survive and all that; and the other was the internal world of imagination where you experience the infinity of your own imagination and its constant fluid variability, but you also have to be utterly alone in your dreams, in your daydreams, and so forth, or in your psychedelic trip. Of course I know many people would point to something like Yage and say, "Aren't there shared experiences?" Let's leave that aside because that's really not part of the cultural palette we have to

work with in the mainstream anyway. So given the stark choice between a shared world that's dull and an utterly solipsistic world that's
alive and wonderful and fluid, virtual reality comes in seemingly
providing a third alternative: a world that's objective, in exactly the
same way as the physical world, that fits in between people the way
the physical world does, but one that's fluid and subject to the flow
of imagination in a way that is much more responsive than the physical world is. And that's what's so exciting—that notion of making
dreams real, making dreams objective. That's why children get so
excited about virtual reality. I mean virtual reality has become as
popular as dinosaurs among children. Dinosaurs represent power
and bigness to them, but virtual reality represents the notion that
their imagination could be treated as being real instead of something that has to vanish as they grow up. And I love that as a role for
technology. I think that's a lovely role for technology to play.

RF: Have you seen in your own work, in the twenty years or so
you've been doing this, a healing effect of virtual-reality-type technology? Have you seen people transformed, become less militant,
more wise?

JL: I can point to examples. I would hasten to add that I can point
to counter examples too. So it's really hard to know about the big
picture. If I were going to point to some of my examples I would
say that within the military/industrial complex just the notion of
coolness is a huge driving factor. Sometimes billions and billions of
dollars are spent on some technology that will actually make the
world a less safe place simply because people are compelled to pursue what is cool. That happens very frequently, actually, much more
so than I think most people realize. Virtual reality is an extremely
cool technology, in many ways the coolest, since it deals directly
with experience itself and inherently creates cool experiences, better than some other technologies that can only create experiences
indirectly. Because of that it's drawn a lot of people from the sort of
coolness stream of things into this work on subjective-experience
technologies. One example is Tom Furness, who used to develop
simulators for the air force and ended up working on virtual reality
stuff in a rather humanistically oriented department in a university.

I could list many others. Another example is the application of virtual reality to people with disabilities, a field that's burgeoning in its own right and has its own conferences now, in which people are able to not only achieve experiences but achieve collaborative experiences, achieve connection that they could not before because of their disabilities.

I could also point to some wretched examples of the use of virtual reality—stupid, violent virtual reality video games that are shown in malls and that sort of thing. The human adventure is not simple. We always wish we could understand ourselves in terms of melodrama and come up with easy good and bad definitions, but the key is really to try to just be sensitive to the effects of what one does and to keep on trying, keep on refining, and try to perceive as honestly as possible what's happened thus far. I certainly try to do that.

RF: What are you most grateful to Timothy for in your own life?

JL: Timothy exudes a remarkable attitude that the universe is, in fact, friendly—that the universe is conspiring to help you. He believes that in a deep way. And that's an entirely sensible framework for thinking about the world. In fact, it's a better one than the alternatives. Tim also has found a way to synthesize a kind of private spiritual development with a public life. For people who live partially public lives, I think he's really a model. That's been shown most recently by his statements that he's thrilled about dying and so forth, to be able to deal with fundamental issues in a public way. That is extraordinarily rare, and it's shocking how rare it is, but Tim has done it and very few have in such a direct manner.

I was once with Tim at a workshop when a disturbed fellow started asking questions that had a threatening edge to them, a clear edge of paranoia. He was a scary person. I was very impressed with how Tim handled him. Tim was very warm, very open toward him, absolutely fearless, asked him to come up into the light so we could all see him, and utterly diffused the situation in a way that was remarkably skillful. I thought that was an example of Tim at his best, that Tim had experienced such a wide variety of people and situations in his life that he had perfected a sense of cool that I think very few people could rival.

I'll tell you something else: Tim has a profound guru-like effect on people and he doesn't abuse it and that's a precious rare quality. I've never seen him take advantage of young people who adore him. People sometimes stay with him and help him or stuff like that, but he's never set himself up to be a cult leader or a guru and he could have done that extremely easily. To be offered power and to not take it is one of the most profoundly moral acts you can do.

RF: You talked about Timothy's private spiritual life, but nowadays he might eschew the word "spiritual," reject it as a non-word. He might say there is no "spiritual" but that the universe is physical, fundamentally, and that the brain is the mediating organ of all this. When we're dead that's it, there's no more.

JL: Well those are two different issues. I mean there could be spirituality and it also could be true that our identity ends with death. I know Tim has adopted that view. I think that's because there is a sort of a mainstream in philosophy now that's been influenced by computers to adopt this new sort of materialism and reductionism. I personally reject that. My approach to rejecting it is pretty simple. I would point out that computers are not capable of detecting other computers, and what I mean by that is if you set down a probe on an alien planet and the probe was supposed to determine whether there were computers there, it wouldn't be able to if they didn't happen to look like our computer. The reason arises from a theoretical problem: no computer can fully analyze another. There's a problem with computability. You end up with an unbounded problem. Since computers can't recognize each other, what exactly brings them into existence? How do we know which particular computers are there? I've come to believe that computers are subjective objects; they exist only through the prism of cultural relativity. Aliens might never notice our Macintoshes, but find computers in our traffic patterns or hairstyles. You can try to get rid of consciousness, you can try to say there's nothing magical going on, but it always pops up again. Computers create the illusion that they finally vanquished it, but in fact they haven't, because without us to recognize them the computers wouldn't even exist.

RF: Have you and Tim had this discussion?

JL: Nope. Actually this argument just came to me in the last year so I haven't had an occasion to. Maybe I'll try it out on him sometime.

RF: Isn't this what the philosopher's stone is? That is, the individual's recognition of the creative power of their imagination, that the individual creates reality.

JL: Right. Well for myself, I mean I think it's kind of easy to either get rid of reality or get rid of individuals in one's philosophy. A lot of the reductionist philosophers lately would say, well, it's all just matter and the brain and all that, so we only have the world and not people. And there are a lot of folks that would say, well, we create reality so we only have people and not the world. I think truly a philosophy ought to be able to have both people and the world. That's what I've been working on, but it would be going outside the scope of this conversation.

RF: Well I'm not sure. Tim mentioned in *Flashbacks* that ever since his first LSD trip he has looked at the world with a sense of humor because he knows that whatever he's experiencing, he's experiencing the play of a script that he wrote, that's mediated by his own brain. Reality really relativized through his LSD trips.

JL: Well, as I say, I think that both people and the world do really exist. I don't think either one excludes the other. It's hard to come up with a philosophy that acknowledges them both—very hard. I think that's the job of philosophy and why it's very difficult.

RF: There are several people in the book that are going to articulate that Tim's life is a consistent thread since the time of his early work as a clinician and a diagnostician. The man has been working to treat mental illness really, for a long time. His appointment to Harvard originally was based on his research which showed that psychotherapy didn't work any better than the ordinary passage of time. It was that understanding that led him to create more innovative models of assessment and treatment for psychopathology.

JL: Tim once told me that if Freud were alive today he would seem to be a raving lunatic, and I'd be terrified of him. I don't know if that's true or not.

RF: Well a lot of people are terrified of Tim.

JL: A lot of people view him as a person to blame for the country's drug problem, and of course that's absolutely irrational. The country's drug problems existed long before Leary. The economics and the warfare surrounding drugs has long predated Tim's arrival. But of course Tim introduced an entirely different type of drug and in a very public way suggested that mainstream upper class kids would be interested in it, and they listened. That made him scary in a certain sense. Of course what's interesting is this intense violent reaction against things that seem purely oriented toward freedom, pleasure, joy, and imagination; that somehow if a great many people pursue these things they must be kept in check.

This happens again and again. I had an op-ed piece in the *New York Times* a few weeks ago about freedom of speech and I got quite a load of what I'd call hate mail from people who didn't like it just because they could sniff the '60s in it. And I think that's happened here, that since the fall of the Soviet Union, with a lack of credible enemies, a lot of the folks who were enemy-minded just decided that anything that smelled slightly sixtyish or slightly liberal is the enemy, and that's a very sad turn of events. It turns us against ourselves, and I hope it's a phase that will pass with as little violence as possible.

I think Tim is going to be seen in history more as a poet and philosopher than a political figure anyway. One of the things that's not as acknowledged is just what a good writer he is. *What Does Woman Want?* is one really amazing novel, beautifully written.

RF: *The Politics of Ecstasy* has essays that are among the most lucid expositions of the problems between the sacred and the profane, integrating spiritual notions into a secular society.

JL: Yeah. . . . One of the sad things is that the characteristics of the mainstream drug culture are so different from what Tim was hoping for in the early days. He was hoping for a culture that would intelligently use psychedelics for ecstasy and self-realization.

What's interesting now is that some of the most conservative voices in Washington have actually come around to the notion of legalizing drugs, but if that happens the ones that would be legalized are probably exactly the worst ones, you know. It's so preposterous. You know, there's an argument that Timothy Leary had early in his life with Aldous Huxley about whether you could broadcast esoteric knowledge on a large scale via mass media. Huxley argued a conservative position and thought that it wasn't a good idea. Timothy not only argued but enthusiastically acted on the notion that it was a very good idea. That is, I think, still the crux of Tim's career. It's the big question, and I don't know the answer to it. It comes down to the question of whether people are really ready to see themselves honestly or not, and perhaps we're not. Perhaps Tim's notion of broadcasting the esoteric knowledge into the mainstream was premature. I think it's too early to judge.

Another question that haunts me is, Where did the '60s come from? Because the '60s happened all over the world at once, and in places that really had very little contact with one another. And certainly these places did not all have contact with psychedelic drugs, yet here was this remarkable exuberant spirit and creativity. Again and again, even ideas that are only becoming popular now originated in the late '60s. First virtual reality system—1969; first superstring theory—1969; all these things that we think of as '80s and '90s innovations actually started there. And the same could be said about the arts. There was just sort of a Cambrian explosion of culture.

How should we understand those things? Is it a demographic effect? Is it something about kids growing up after World War II and reaching their puberty? That's one theory. But that doesn't really seem adequate either. I personally do not believe that it was psychedelics in and of themselves, and the reason for that is that psychedelics can have so many different meanings. I don't think the meaning of anything is fixed, and indeed there are people who have used psychedelics for a very cruel kind of mind control and there are people who really do use psychedelics just for recreation, in ways that are just kind of banal, not even bad, just dumb. I would love to understand what creates this kind of cultural ambience and produces this kind of joyous experimentation, trust, and a decline in fear. I don't believe it's substances, I believe it's something else that's yet unidentified.

RF: Well the substances came up in the midst of this too, whether or not it was causal or synchronistic. They were certainly impactful once they arrived.

JL: Another thing that I'll point out anecdotally is that a great many of the most stupid Rush Limbaugh, Ayn Rand-type fanatics that are running around these days, electing the republican congress, of the ones I know, I know a lot of them were LSD users in the '60s.

I talked at some length to some of the people who wrote me nasty letters about my op-ed piece, and sure enough, a whole bunch of them had been LSD users; this doesn't in any way impugn LSD's good name. I'm just saying that nothing has a fixed meaning, that everything is culture, and people can change in untold ways. I'm not saying that these people represent the majority of LSD users or anything like that. All I'm saying is that the situation is actually very complex. You can't make some sort of simple equation saying that people who used LSD then go out into the world and spread peace and beauty and love automatically. It's not that simple at all.

One of the things I hope this festschrift does is record a balanced picture of both Tim and the LSD movement, rather than the one that is falsely written into the mainstream memory now. I was one of the people who sat for the great physicist Richard Feynman once when he was taking LSD—obviously eminently qualified, never having taken it myself. I bring this up now because the mainstream culture imagines LSD as sort of a bad dream that ruined people, that was destructive, while in fact a great many intelligent, creative, productive people found it to be an interesting, useful thing. A great many of them took Tim seriously even though Tim's public persona was at times outrageous and sometimes contradictory. I think that right now, lacking any possible external enemy, the culture is turning on itself and trying to call a part of itself false and bad and ugly. In doing so we are creating a distorted picture of ourselves. It's very important that we not do that; that the image we have of ourselves is more true and more balanced. I dearly hope that will happen. I find myself having to defend the '60s a lot and it's odd because I was only born in 1960. I do think the '60s represented a lot of good things—an incredible burst of creativity, of joy and trust, a lot of decency, and I hate to see us turn on ourselves. It's like an autoimmune reaction or something where the culture is attacking some of its best parts.

The Archaic Revival

AN INTERVIEW WITH TERENCE McKENNA
BY ROBERT FORTE AND NINA GRABOI

RF: Hello, Terence, it's good to see you here at Esalen's hot springs.

TM: You're going to ask me some questions?

RF: Well, no, not too many, Terence. We thought we would just prod you a little bit. You know what we're up to. . . . Let's look at the choice Tim made in the '60s to democratize the drugs and expound their virtues directly to society rather than through the respected research channels. There have been some important beneficial consequences of that we wanted you to speak to.

TM: Well, I certainly think it would have been a mistake for LSD to have remained the creature of behavioral psychologists and Swiss pharmaceutical companies. It's hard for me to imagine that anyone

---

Terence McKenna is an author and explorer who has spent the past twenty-five years studying the ontological foundations of shamanism and the ethnopharmacology of spiritual transformation. He has traveled extensively in the Asian and New World tropics, becoming specialized in the shamanism and ethnomedicine of the Amazon Basin. He is the coauthor (with Dennis McKenna) of Psilocybin: The Magic Mushroom Growers' Guide, *and the author of* Food of the Gods, The Archaic Revival, *and* True Hallucinations.

would argue otherwise, since the entire social tone of that decade was dictated by the social emergence of LSD. I'm a big enthusiast of psychedelics of all sorts, and I think they all catalyze creative social process and imagination, but clearly in terms of reaching the largest number of people in a short amount of time, the public phenomenon of LSD is unique in human history and had Tim really been more career oriented, more cautious, that probably never would have happened. Plus, LSD itself has the unique quality of being possible to manufacture in millions of doses. You couldn't do that with any drug active in the milligram range. It would take the combined resources of several pharmaceutical companies to produce ten million hits of psilocybin, for example. So I think Leary was the right man for the right moment in history. I don't understand people who criticize his role in all of that. I think as time went on, like everybody in the '60s, he made statements and got into positions that don't make a whole lot of sense in retrospect. I remember . . . I don't know where I was in the world when he made the statement from Algeria that dynamite and the bright light were to be equated; however, I will say it was my opinion at the time—the same opinion—so I'm not knocking his opinion. It's just we both then had some explaining to do somewhat down the line.

I remember when Leary left Harvard in 1963. I was fifteen at the time and following this story in the *Evergreen Review* and *The Village Voice*, which by some God-sent good fortune I subscribed to in the small cattle town I lived in in Colorado. As the Leary thing unfolded that spring, so did stories in the newspapers about morning glory seeds being used to intoxicate, and associated with the similar compound, which is true, that morning glory alkaloids are similar to LSD, although in order of magnitude less strong per unit dose. So at the end of that summer, when I was approaching sixteen, I took my first trip, and it was basically entirely under the inspiration of Leary and I knew then that they were doing the project in Mexico—IFIF I believe it was called then. Somewhere—I don't know if it exists anymore—but somewhere there is a letter from fifteen-year-old Terence McKenna to Ralph Metzner pleading to be taken aboard the circus, but I think they were too loaded to ever reply. And I actually didn't meet Ralph until much later. And I didn't meet Leary really until I saw him speak. I was at the Human Be-in and I saw him speak in Berkeley several times. But I never actually sat down and had a conversation with him until he was in his space colonization phase, which was well after major controversies, after his incarceration and after the flight to Eldridge Cleaver in Algeria.

We seemed to encounter each other a lot in Europe when we were both speaking. And the thing I love about Tim—now that I have seen him in many situations—is he has unflagging energy and good humor. I mean it can be four in the morning in some German industrial town after hours of drinking, smoking, and carrying on, and he's going for it. He is up for it. His implacable good humor is the thing that makes him so irresistible to so many people. I mean how can you hate a guy who ends every sentence with a kind of a laugh?

NG: How do you feel about being called "The New Leary"?

TM: [laughs] I've also been called "The Copernicus of Consciousness." I don't know in what sense I'm the new Leary. I get the feeling that Tim is a far more gregarious and nice person than I am. I'm sort of halfway between Tim Leary and William Burroughs. I can play it either way, you know. I have a fairly mordant and sarcastic side to myself that I don't think I've ever seen in Tim. It's an honor to be called the Tim Leary of the '90s. I'm sure whoever said it meant it as an honor. Yeah. He told me a story—I mean this is a Leary story that addresses that question. One night we were in Mannheim, which is a real rough industrial town north of Stuttgart in Germany, and I had come to see him. It was a Leary event. But he found me an hour before the show eating in a restaurant with some friends of mine, and he said, "Oh, you have to be on stage with me. We'll do it together." So he was very insistent and there was also a Joyce scholar of some sort there, and so it was this three-way thing. So we were on stage. Well in Germany, unlike in the United States—if you have a noisy drunk in the United States, people will grab the guy and suppress him. In Germany they clear a path to the stage. So there's this guy in the back screaming, "Tim Leary saved me! Tim Leary is Jesus!" this and that, and they cleared a path to the stage for this guy. And we tried to engage him for a few minutes. He came on stage with us and he was really drunk. And finally, we just left the stage and abandoned it to this guy, who then turned to the two thousand people there and was carrying on. And Tim and I moved off stage, sitting on the floor with our backs against a brick wall, and we were just watching this. And he turned to me and he said, "You know why I want it to go to you?" And I said, "No, Tim, why do you want it to go to me?" And he said, "So it stays with the Irish!"

No, he's a very, very insisting person, and the only person in the drug establishment who really evidenced vision and courage. Everyone else did their jobs very competently. Albert Hofmann functioned as a brilliant analytical chemist. Wasson functioned as a brilliant independently financed scholar. This was not chance taking. Leary saw the potential for change and we forget how constipated and self-limiting American society was in the early '60s. I mean we had had the Kennedy assassination the same year that all of this was getting going and I think the society always owes a great debt to the people who defy authority and force change, and I see Leary in the tradition of Thoreau, and Whitman, and the entire American transcendental impulse, you know. It was a New England impulse, it was a Harvard-based impulse, and he came out of that.

There are certainly, to my mind, amazing contradictions in the man. For example, in a way—and I don't mean this as a criticism at all, it fascinates me and I respect it—but in a way, there's not a spiritual bone in the guy. Not an iota of that, you know. I've heard him say many times, "God?—Fuck God!" You know, "No metaphysics!" And yet, how many people have explored metaphysical problems based on the substances and the techniques that Leary and his gang put in front of them. So probably like all major historical figures, there has to be this element of paradox. The behavioral psychologist, the reductionist athiest, and yet the mad visionary dreamer, a man with an immense amount of personal pain in his life history, even before fame and notoriety came, and yet a guy who's probably made more people happy, arguably, than anybody else in history. A civil disobedient, a political figure—well, when it's all sorted out, I think he will be one of the more interesting and important figures in the last half of the twentieth century.

RF: With respect to his spirituality, I think a role that Tim plays is to always get on the other side of whatever is being said. He detests dogmatism and fixed, unexamined ideas. Nina's shaking her head.

NG: No, that's not it, though it's true he does that. But Timothy's least favorite words are "soul" and "spirit." He gets really uptight when anybody talks about soul or spirit. To him it's the brain, the physical brain, that is the carrier of everything.

RF: There's something very pragmatic about his philosophy too.

TM: It's behaviorism. He began like that.

NG: But you know, when he took the mushrooms the first time, he said afterward, "This was the most powerful religious experience of my life," and he went around calling himself "God intoxicated." When I first met him in the '60s he was wearing those white robes and he said, "I am God intoxicated."

TM: That raises an interesting issue somewhat directly related to all this, which is, I think that LSD was the drug of choice in the '60s for this reason that I mentioned earlier: that you could produce enough of it quickly to make social change. But I think that, had all other things been equal, those people at Harvard recognized that psilocybin was a preferable experience. There was just simply no way to deliver psilocybin to tens of millions of people. And Michael Hollingshead, who's a very shadowy figure in all of this, played a role in that—basically in switching their loyalties from the religious mushroom-based experience that they were exploring to the more socially and politically effective, but less holistic, experience of LSD, and that's an interesting bifurcation in the history of psychedelics, and I've always felt the decision was made because of the physical properties of LSD. Simply its transportability, the fact that micro-grams were the effective dose and so forth.

RF: What do you mean by the holistic aspects of psilocybin? Do you mean the fact that it comes from a mushroom and from the earth in that regard? Or the experience itself?

TM: No, more the experience itself. I once had an opportunity to discuss this with Albert Hofmann, and I said, "You discovered LSD. You characterized psilocybin. You've taken both of these. Which do you prefer?" And he said, "Oh, well I prefer LSD." And I said, "Why?" And he said, "Because it's less animate." And I said, "You mean when you take psilocybin there's somebody in there?" And he said, "Yes. And that unsettles me." And that's how I've always seen it. I've always felt that LSD—if you've never taken a psychedelic drug, LSD is sort of what you would expect: insight into your past, dissolving images, transformation of objects, insight into complex situations, a psychedelic drug. Psilocybin, on the other hand, has other dimensions that overshadow these sensory and information transformations and give you the feeling that you're communicating with something that is aware and has an intentionality. And I think that raises the bar considerably on the issue of what are these things and what are they doing. So in a way—I've heard other people say that LSD has an emptiness to it, that you fill it with your own content, but that it is basically like a lens through which you magnify your own existence on different levels, but that psilocybin has an agenda, it comes with some software that it wants to run for you. And so in the historical framework of things it probably is a good thing that LSD preceded psilocybin. Certainly it did. Except for very privileged researchers, psilocybin was unknown until the '70s by most people. In fact it wasn't until well into the '70s when home mushroom cultivation became feasible.

RF: You've put forth the idea, elaborating on Wasson, that psilocybin or other psychedelic mushrooms were kind of the missing link in evolution. Do you see the '60s as a recapitulation of that period? That this was an evolutionary leap?

TM: Yes, well, the '60s was a kind of archaic revival. I've written about this kind of phenomenon. It's a situation where when a culture gets confused, it tries to go back in time to other times when it felt more comfortable with itself. And in the '60s, you know—sexual permissiveness, heavy rock 'n' roll, intoxication with psychedelic drugs—these are all efforts linked to other impulses in the twentieth century like jazz and abstract expressionism and surrealism and Dada. I see all of this as a nostalgia for the archaic. But it wasn't until the psychedelics came on the scene that there was an effective tool for really making this feeling of archaic wholeness accessible to people. And it was the community of the hippies that made them so threatening. All forms of community are threatening to the establishment. Communism, community—it's very, very threatening. The analogous situation in the present context is—and Leary's enthusiasm has followed a similar insight—is the rise of the Internet and the World Wide Web, which creates enormous tools of connectivity for previously marginal communities. It doesn't really change things for the corporate elite. They had superb communications, have always had superb communications. But for marginal social groups, homosexuals, enthusiasts of psychedelic drugs, environmentalists—anyone who expresses a minority point of view—it's incredibly empowering. And like LSD, it's a technology which I don't believe was ever intended to get loose and to become so commonly available to ordinary people at such reasonable prices. And, it's interesting that so much of it is in the hands of people who were shaped in the '60s. I mean they are the people who write the code, who design the machines, who organize these systems, maintain them and run them. The corporate elite doesn't even know how to turn on its own machines. They have to hire guys with ponytails to do that for them.

RF: But the technology is so dependent upon an infrastructure that is controlled by the corporate elite. It's all run by the phone company and they can just pull the plug out of this.

TM: Well, it's more important to them than to us—in other words, they can only pull the plug on it by pulling the plug on themselves. The way I think of it is, here in the '90s, what has happened after the fall of the Soviet Union is two power blocks have emerged: national governments and the world corporate state. National governments are terrified of the Internet. National governments are used to a game where information is closely held and controlled. Technology is closely held, classified, and controlled. The game plan of the world corporate state is a completely different game plan. Closely held technologies are useless. You want to rush the most advanced technology possible to market as quickly as possible. And information is the lifeblood of the world corporate state. So it is building and maintaining these networks and webs without really consulting national governments. It's a transnational phenomenon. AT&T is going to put up a system of satellites that will link every point on the planet to the Internet at ISDN speed. Well this is not good news for national governments, for local political factions at all. But strangely enough, for world capitalism and for these marginalized—for the underground, it's very good. So we're seeing the transformation of the cultural landscape by technology. And I'm not pro-corporate-state or pro-nation-state. I think the freedom of the individual is in danger in all these situations and we have to be very alert. But this is what is happening. And the nation state is largely irrelevant now. They are going to be allowed to pick up garbage and to run schools and hospitals, I guess, but anything where money is concerned is going to be privatized to the world corporate state. And what this leads to, I'm not sure, because the world corporate state is in a position of great power and prominence at the moment, but is based on completely false premises: the premise of unlimited resources, the premise of unlimited availability of cheap labor. When these limits are finally reached, the world corporate state will undergo some kind of catastrophic retraction. When this will be, I don't know. But I don't think we're going to have to wait decades for it.

RF: Tim is best known for being a countercultural agent of change, a reputation that sometimes obscures his scientific and literary achievements.

TM: Leary's Exopsychology and Neuropolitics were major contributions to American social theory. And the concept of set and setting has made it possible for millions of people to find their way to these things. Leary made legitimate the exploration of consciousness by effective means. You can just put it in a nutshell. Always before that it was questionnaires, it was at arm's length, it was viewed as pathological. I remember people used to say, "States of consciousness? Well, there's awake and asleep, right?" Well, turns out that was a hideous simplification. So he brought consciousness into science as a legitimate object of study. And I dare say, this is probably where science will find its deepest problems and its greatest satisfaction over the next few decades. Consciousness is already being described as a basic property of nature itself, in *Scientific American* two issues ago. So this is what Leary did. Not that other philosophers or psychologists hadn't discussed consciousness, but Leary brought tools to it equivalent to the atom smasher or the cyclotron. And also he brought the incredibly important concept of the researcher experiencing the thing being researched. We're not talking about giving things to rats or prisoners or graduate students. But the researcher of consciousness must accept that his or her own mind is the vessel and the field and the domain in which the study is to be done. And this ability to overcome the assumptions of reductionism and analytical European thinking was very American and very important. And probably, to my mind, his contribution. That he legitimated the study of consciousness. And everybody is derivative in that sense. Grof is derivative. And all the Transpersonal schools are derivative. And all the Encounter and Action schools are derivative. They may not acknowledge the debt, but there it is.

I think the important point is that he removed the notion of pathology from the notion of the exploration of consciousness and mental states and showed that ordinary consciousness is complex, transcendent, and he related all these things not to pathology, but to the tradition of mysticism. He wasn't the first, but he made the point that the path to the mystical was potentially a neurochemical path. And that was an enormous breakthrough and allowed a lot of secularization of what had before been religiously oriented mumbo jumbo.

RF: It was with tremendous reluctance that they finally submitted to a religious paradigm for psychedelic research and as a way to introduce psychedelics into the culture. He writes about this in *The Politics of Ecstasy*. You know, he's coming out of his Roman Catholic background. Religion was shit to him and now they're coming around realizing maybe there is something to this. But now he's come back around the other way again with repudiation of words like "soul" and "spirit"—I think he's revised his earlier slogan, "Turn on, tune in, drop out," and he's trying to get people to tune back in, and he himself has done that.

TM: Well, I think "Turn on, tune in, drop out" is a purer and more radical and better message than any of the later formulations, because it's more radical in the sense that it represents a more thorough rejection of establishment values. And I think Leary, like all of us, when we realized we were not going to found utopias by 1970, has had to go through a series of retrenchments and personal coming-to-terms with the fact that, while we made great social change, we did not seize the ramparts as we thought we would, and in fact Richard Nixon did. So we are left with the moral conviction of the rightness of our cause, but the historical fact of the triumph of a very different point of view, and that's the paradox that we all have to live with that is so large that we can barely fit it into the context of our lives.

RF: I don't know if this is a paradox so much as maybe an inconsistency, but I noticed in the emerging technologies in the World Wide Web, etc., that it does not seem to me to be a continuation of the '60s antiestablishment, antiauthoritarian trajectory, that a lot of the energy around the World Wide Web among our peers is a kind of acquisitive, almost, I hate to say this but sort of greed-oriented kind of culture. Wanting more and more information and not necessarily a step forward in wisdom . . .

TM: No, I understand. But we could have had this discussion in 1968 about the acid business. Because to make that LSD revolution there had to be some very hard-line people who didn't dance in the park, who didn't get down with the girls, who instead dealt LSD like a commodity and built criminal pyramids of syndicalist activity, and that was very troubling to people in the 1960s when LSD became a commodity. It's very troubling in the 1990s to see the Internet become a commodity. But my faith is that the sale of transcendence may contaminate and damage a few people—the people who engage in it. But it's very good for the rest of us. And so in a sense they are the expendable ones. I think the real impact of the Internet has not yet been felt at all, that if we make a parallel to LSD, then we are at about 1961 with the Internet. In eight or nine years we will reap the fruits of this incredible empowering of the margins. But it isn't yet.

RF: I'd like you to respond to a thought that I have about these technologies—that they often appear as compensatory. When you hear people talk about the potential of the Internet and the World Wide Web, it sounds to me like what they're talking about is the attainment of yogic siddhis, you know, powers—being everywhere at once, omniscience, a recognition of a psychic web that envelops us all—these kind of mystical terms. And I wonder if the emerging technologies are making it easier for us to access these dimensions which are germane to the psyche, or if they're compensatory.

TM: I think that there is an element of both, but that as we model our technologies more and more on nature, they become more and more fulfilling. And I think, ultimately, being connected to the Internet and possessing siddhis will be indistinguishable from each other, that if we build the Internet so that it's like nature, then it will get more and more unobtrusive, more and more biodegradable, more and more created and maintained by DNA-like polymers, less and less running on hard electricity and hard radiation, and it will eventually disappear. I think that the age of bulky, visible machines intruding into the human environment is just a nanosecond of human history, and that the machines of the future will look much more like mushrooms, spores, flowers, and worms than they will look like bulldozers, airplanes, so forth and so on.

NG: On the other hand, in the '60s we felt like we were in the process of attaining heightened consciousness, which made me argue with Timothy at the time about space travel. I said, "What do we need progress for? We can do it without progress." The same would apply to the hardware or even software of the Internet. Naturally, can't we all be in communication without any hardware?

TM: Well I think the question may become moot. The hardware will become indistinguishable from the wetware. We are basically already designing large parts of our own prosthesis. The society is an extension of the body. I don't see a problem with it. To me it's convergence. The promise of nanotechnology is that we will build, as God builds, from the atoms up, out of air and water and soil and this is now within reach. So the idea that machines and technology are artificial is I think just a stage of human culture and that if we can keep on the beam, what we're headed for is not only spiritual union with nature, but physical and technological union with nature. And then the question of whether a city is an artificial thing and a jungle is a natural thing will just be something philosophers worry about. I have great faith that if we take nature as our teacher, we can approach the transcendent in all dimensions. Nature is the example to follow, and we must be as nature is, we must build as nature builds, and we must organize our societies and our politics as nature is organized. Nature is not Darwinian, competitive and destructive. Nature is about cooperation, deal-cutting, mutual self-maintenance, so forth and so on.

For example, look at mushrooms. Mushrooms are what are called primary decomposers. They're located at a place in the food chain where they eat nothing alive. A karmaless position in the food chain. If we became inspired by Buddhist ethics and high technology, we could probably download and design ourselves into that part of organic nature and then we would have found the karmaless dwell point in the chaos of Darwinian struggle. The mind will always lead us to higher levels of self-reflection and hence reflection of the order of being. That's the psychedelic faith. And you can sign on for that whether you're a scientist or a mystic. Really what we're talking about here is the order of nature and the promise that it holds. End of speech.

RF: What did LSD do for you?

TM: I remember being nineteen years old, twelve hours into an LSD trip. I was sitting under a tree and I just started to weep, and I saw what my upbringing had done to me. I saw the resentment of my parents and my callowness and my immaturity and my—and I sat there for about an hour and cried this stuff out. And got up a better person. And to this day, I've never had to go back and revisit those things and then I could call up my parents and tell them I love them and I could accept their Catholicism and their conservatism and the differences. It was just like ten years of psychotherapy in an hour. And it was real. So that's worth everything. And that's what I saw LSD as. It wasn't to me about the far-flung reaches of metaphysics or—it was about getting straightened out.

NG: We all have these intensely personal reactions to things, because I always argue with anybody who says LSD does this and mushrooms do that, because my first experience on LSD was that I totally went out of the body and into another realm and all I remember is trying to get back down to this earth, which was just so far away, I knew I had to put my foot down on it somehow but I didn't know how to reach it, and later I knew that I had a body hanging around somewhere and I didn't know where or what it was. So that was LSD for me. I never went on any personal trips with it.

TM: I remember my first LSD trip very clearly and I've never had a trip like that before or since. I mean it was so bizarre—

RF: Was that the one that you talked about?

TM: No, no. The first LSD trip I had, the world, after about—it didn't come on for a long, long time, and I was with somebody who was basically trying to lead me through it, and then the world divided into two concepts. One concept was God-like, profound, dark, huge, awesome, impressive, and it was called the Iosteck—it came to me, yes, the name was what the trip was all about—the Iostecks. And the other thing was small, brightly colored and funny and reassuring and warm and silly and absurd, and it was called the Pinkastairs. And I for about four hours went from—I would just say one or the other of these words. I would say, "the Iostecks" and it would just like rise up, this thing, until I couldn't stand it anymore, and then I would say, "the Pinkastairs" and just dissolve into hysterical laughter. Finally my friend put me out on the front porch and said "Call me when it's over."

RF: Thanks, Terence. That sums it up perfectly.

TM: You guys want to do a bath now?

From Harvard to Zihuatanejo

RALPH METZNER

I first met Timothy Leary in the fall of 1959 when I was in my second year of graduate study in psychology at Harvard University. The story we heard was that he had become profoundly disillusioned with the results of his research on the efficacy of psychotherapy (it showed that therapy did no better than the simple passage of time); that his wife had committed suicide; and that these events precipitated him into a personal crisis and caused him to quit his job as research director of the Kaiser Foundation Hospital in Oakland where he had developed a widely used diagnostic test of interpersonal behavior. He then moved with his two children to Florence, Italy, where he met Professor David McClelland, the director of the Center for Personality Research at Harvard, who persuaded him to come to Harvard and teach there.

Ralph Metzner, Ph.D., is a psychotherapist and a professor of psychology at the California Institute of Integral Studies. One of the pioneers in the study of nonordinary states of consciousness, he coauthored The Psychedelic Experience, *with Timothy Leary and Richard Alpert. His other books include* Maps of Consciousness, The Well of Remembrance, The Unfolding Self, *and a forthcoming volume on ayahuasca. His* Green Psychology *will be published by Inner Traditions in 1999.*

Tim Leary was the classic professor type with graying hair, heavy glasses, a hearing aid, and a kind of detached, quizzical air. His personal style was genial and affable and he was very popular with the students. Then, in the summer of 1960, while spending his vacation in Mexico, Tim was introduced to the "sacred mushroom" by an anthropologist friend named Lothar Knauth and had an experience that completely turned his life around. In his autobiographical book *High Priest** he has described how he was taken back through the evolutionary process right down to single-celled life and then back up through the layers and strata of oceanic, amphibian, and terrestrial evolution. Since experiences with psychoactive plants have traditionally been described in mystical or mythical language, Leary may have been the first person to recognize and identify them as evolutionary visions or genetic memories. He resolved at that time to devote the rest of his life to the exploration of the awesome potential of these plants to alter consciousness.

When he returned to Harvard he could speak of nothing else. He soon discovered that the sacred mushroom was known as *teonanácatl*, "flesh of the gods," to the Aztecs and denounced as diabolical by the Spanish clergy at the time of the conquest of Mexico. For several hundred years they had been generally considered to be nonexistent, mythical or symbolic entities, until they were rediscovered in the 1950s by R. Gordon Wasson. Wasson was a wealthy banker whose interest in mycology was stimulated by his mushroom-loving Russian wife, Valentina. After several years of searching in Mexico, they contacted Maria Sabina, a famous Mazatec *curandera*, and she initiated them in a nighttime ceremony in a remote, impoverished mountain village in the Oaxaca mountains. The Wassons were deeply moved and transformed by the experience.[†]

---

* Timothy Leary, *High Priest* (New York: New American Library, 1968; Berkeley, CA: Ronin Publishing, 1995).

[†] R. Gordon Wasson, *The Wondrous Mushroom: Mycolatry in Mesoamerica* (New York: McGraw-Hill, 1980). In this book, Wasson points out that the accepted translation "flesh of the gods" is incorrect and served the clergy's accusations of blasphemy against the mushroom cult. "Teonanácatl means divine or wondrous or awesome mushroom, nothing more and nothing less" (p. 44).

R. Gordon Wasson then began a collaboration and friendship with Albert Hofmann, a brilliant and outstanding research chemist. About ten years earlier, in 1943, Hofmann had discovered the astounding effects of lysergic acid diethylamide (LSD), a chemical he had synthesized in 1938 as part of his research for the Sandoz Pharmaceutical Company in Basel, Switzerland. Hofmann had since developed a deep personal and professional interest in substances of this type. Upon obtaining samples of the Mexican mushroom from Wasson, Hofmann was able to identify and then synthesize the psychoactive ingredient, which he named *psilocybin*, after the psilocybe mushroom.

Thus it came about that psilocybin, the active ingredient of the Mexican hallucinogenic mushroom, was manufactured in tablet form by the Sandoz Company, which had a branch in New Jersey. They offered to supply Dr. Timothy Leary of Harvard University with as much of the drug as he wanted, free of charge, for research purposes.

The Harvard Psilocybin Project was formed to investigate from a psychological point of view the astonishing properties of this plant-chemical. Right from the start Tim Leary adopted what he called an "existential-transactional" approach to this research. He rejected the impersonal clinical atmosphere of the traditional psychiatric experiment. Having taken the substance himself in a sacramental atmosphere, he knew how important it was to have a warm supportive setting to experience the ego-shattering revelations of the mushrooms.

Aldous Huxley was at M.I.T. that year, and he immediately became an advisor to the Harvard Psilocybin Project. In 1953 and 1955, Huxley had published two widely read books on his mystical experiences with mescaline, *The Doors of Perception* and *Heaven and Hell*. Huxley described the experience at its best as a "gratuitous grace," providing access to what he called "Mind-at-Large," beyond the "reducing valve" of the ordinary egoic mind. He and Tim developed a strong rapport and had psilocybin sessions together during that period, working out a nonclinical, supportive, yet objective and safe framework for this kind of experimentation.

The sessions were mostly held at Tim Leary's house. Initially,

Dr. Frank Barron, a noted researcher in the psychology of creativity, was the only other Harvard faculty member involved in the research. After some time, Frank Barron returned to his original position at UC Berkeley and ended direct involvement in the project. Subsequently, another psychology professor, Dr. Richard Alpert, became involved in the psilocybin research project. He went on to become Leary's closest associate during the entire time of the psychedelic research, at Harvard and then later at Millbrook. The close friendship and partnership of the two men led Leary later to compare themselves to those archetypal American rule-breaking, authority-defying adventurers Tom Sawyer and Huck Finn.

Some of my fellow graduate students at the Center for Personality Research had became involved in the psilocybin project and would talk about their sessions at Tim's house. Overhearing their conversation, I noticed there was something different in their tone of voice—a new quality of intensity and feeling. They were talking of ecstasy, love, and sharing in a way that was vivid and personal to them. This was unusual in the austere and cynical mental atmosphere of the Center for Personality Research.

I became fascinated, and yet I was scared of drugs and addiction. I examined what I could of the literature and found, to my surprise, that for this class of drugs there was no evidence of physiological damage, and they were absolutely not addicting. I wanted to try them. An opportunity presented itself when Tim decided it was time to apply these drugs to the problem of behavior change. He wanted to give them to prisoners, for a kind of rehabilitative therapy, based on self-insight. If there was a decrease in the amount of criminal behavior after they left the prison, one would have an objective behavioral criterion of personality change. "Let's see if we can turn the criminals into Buddhas," he said privately. Those participating in the research had to experience the medicine themselves, which is what I wanted.

Thus, on March 13, 1961, I had my first psychedelic experience. It was a chilly Sunday afternoon when I arrived at Tim's house. Two other graduate students, Gunther Weil and Lyn K., were involved in the session, as well as Gunther's wife Karin, the prison psychiatrist, Madison Presnell, and his wife. After we had made ourselves comfortable in the living room, Tim gave everyone six little pink tablets, each containing 2 mg of psilocybin. He took probably a smaller dose. It had already become the preferred policy to not stress the role of guide or teacher, but rather to work on the assumption that we were fellow explorers. Nevertheless, in sessions in which he participated, Tim generally set the tone of the experience.

My first reaction was lassitude. . . . I lay down on the floor and stretched out, feeling very relaxed and yet very alert. Tim had said there would be a period like a decompression or slight disorientation. My body seemed for a while to be in a strange sort of limbo. . . . All of a sudden I found myself in a completely new and magical world. The little green strands of the shag rug were writhing and undulating, like a mass of worms, yet in a most delightful way. The lights reflecting off the glass coffee table top sparkled with a kind of moist luminescence. The furniture, the walls, the floor, were all pulsing and undulating in slow waves, as if the whole room was breathing. I felt like I was inside a living structure, like a vast cell. The rate of the waving motion seemed to be coordinated with my breathing.

This extraordinary sensory fluidity was not at all disturbing; in fact, it was extremely pleasurable. There was clear rational awareness that this was a room with solid walls and a floor, etc. The ordinary world was not erased, it was expanded, enlivened and made infinitely more interesting. For example, I became totally engrossed in contemplating the fascinating edges of things, the curiously beautiful patterns of light and energy weaving around edges and radiating out from them. The telephone was a veritable marvel of diamond-studded, gem-encrusted, crystalline sculpture— yet itself also moving, breathing, changing as if it were alive.

Simultaneously with this unbelievable sensory feasting, Gunther and I were engaged in a kind of verbal interplay, a mock-serious philosophic exchange that had us both convulsed with laughter. Words and concepts exploded in the brain with multilevel ripples of meanings that set off cascades of feeling and physical sensations. Deep philosophic questions arose and dissipated in a stream of paradoxes and absurd riddles punctuated by convulsive giggles. . . .

When I closed my eyes, fantastically beautiful and intricate geometric depth patterns were interweaving behind my eyelids, washing, colliding, streaming by at great speed. Occasionally, there would be images of precious stones or different parts of bodies, but nothing stood still long enough to congeal into anything definite. It felt as if my eyes were giving off a white-hot radiance; my mouth and the sense organs in my face and the rest of the body were glowing, flashing, oozing with liquid light, my nerve fibers crackling with white lightning; my bloodstream felt like a seething stream of lava. My skin was embracing me, enwrapping me, in a kind of alternately wet and dry, hot and cool, almost unendurably pleasurable embrace. . . .

A moment of panic occurred that illustrated the fantastic amplifying power of the psychedelic. When I looked at the faces of the others, they were bright and strong and clear. I thought, "This is how archangels look." They were somehow naked, shed of a fog of dissimulations, anxieties, and hypocrisies. Everyone was true to their own self and not ashamed. I looked at them without shyness and with frank admiration. At one time all the faces were suffused with a soft greenish light. I looked at Karin across the room and told her she was beautiful, and I loved her. She just looked back without saying anything. Then she got up and started to leave the room (probably to go to the bathroom). I began to panic. I implored her not to leave, that dreadful things would happen if she did. Lyn, who was sitting next to me, said it would be all right, but I got more and more upset and terrified, pleading with her not to leave. Karin said she would be back, but I said, "No, no, don't leave." She asked, "What will happen if I leave?" I replied, in a tone of desperation, "Something terrible will happen . . . the music will stop." At that point she got up and walked through the door, and somehow that action became identified with all feelings of abandonment and loss I had ever experienced—there was a moment of acute anguish. And then she was gone, and I felt fine, amazed and relieved. I said to Lyn, "She left, and it was all right." And Lyn said, "Yes, it was all right."

Then, holding Lyn close, I suddenly felt myself shrinking in size. . . . I was very rapidly regressing back into childhood consciousness. I actually felt for brief moments what I had felt as an infant, even to the feel of a baby bottle in my mouth. And then, just as rapidly, I was shuttled back to my adult awareness.

At a certain point I noticed that the intensity of the experiences began to diminish, like a slow gliding down. The body felt very warm and re-laxed. I understood how my normal perception of the world was constricted by many prohibitions I had somehow accepted. For example, I went outside and on the porch was a box. I looked inside and saw that it was garbage *and immediately turned away. Then I realized I didn't have to turn away, that it was okay to look at it, that I had a choice and was not bound by a set of rules regarding what could or could not be experienced and perceived.*

*   This was to me perhaps the most significant revelation of this experience: that I was basically in charge of what I could perceive and think about, that I was not bound by external forces but rather made choices that determined the extent and quality of my awareness. To exercise my newfound freedom, I made some snowballs and threw them at the screened window of the room in which the group was sitting. I felt greatly exhilarated. Somehow, Tim must have sensed my expansive mood and thought, because with a grin on his face he picked up some small orange pillows and tossed them gently at the window from the inside toward me. The brief interchange had an edge of freshness and spontaneous clarity that made me feel superbly happy.*

That first experience with psilocybin had an immeasurable effect on my life. It was radically and totally different, yet during the course of the experience I felt closer to my true self than I had ever been and more aware of my innermost feelings and thoughts. I had also been fully and intensely aware of people and things around me and did not lose the reality perceptions that govern our ordinary world. Rather, ordinary perception was enriched and enlivened beyond comparison. It was clearly false that these drugs were "hallucinogenic" in the sense of hallucinating something that isn't there.

    I could see how much of the sensory phenomena could be attributed to a temporary suspension of the perceptual constancies—those neural mechanisms that keep the visible shapes and sizes of things constant, even though the optical image is obviously changing. An illustration of that happened during the session when I was lying on my side on the ground and Gunther rolled a ball toward me. As the ball approached it grew enormously in size, as the retinal image would. Also the undulating and apparent "breathing" of objects I could trace to the movement of eyes, the constant slight rhythmic oscillations, which become, under the drug, magnified in their action. All the processes that filter, screen, and regulate perception seemed to have been suspended. As Huxley put it, the mind's "reducing valve" had been inactivated.

The week after that initial session we began the prison project. My second exposure to the drug took place behind prison walls. We wanted to avoid giving the convicts the feeling that they were to be guinea pigs in the drug experiments of a mad professor, so we decided that some members of the project would always take the drug with them. My first trip in the prison environment, among convicts, was a visit to hell. Anxiety was magnified to terror, loneliness to profound abandonment, discomfort to agonizing despair, accompanied by horror visions of devouring machine-monsters. Then, while feeling trapped in the depths of isolation . . .

From a very long way off I heard a tiny voice saying quietly: "I get this feeling of being alone in the universe, just the self." A human voice. There were others! Cautiously, incredulously, I opened my eyes. A scene of incredible peace and serenity presented itself. Gunther and two of the men were sitting quietly, talking, bathed in a stream of afternoon sunlight coming through the window. One of the convicts was lying on the bed peaceful and relaxed, smoking and reading a paper. Two others were sitting silently, playing chess. A wave of relief washed over me. The prison walls were down; the whole world was wide open. Objects again had that extraordinary depth-dimension, as if there were soft crystalline formations in the space between them and me. People had mellow greenish faces and shining eyes. Someone said: "There is one of everything," and in some strange way this oneness of everything was the essence, the essence of feelings—one joy, one sadness, one terror, one pleasure.

Suddenly, there was chaos. The psychiatrist burst in: "Everybody back to prison routine, change of guards, out of this room." There was a mad scramble as everyone put together their belongings, straightened their clothes, tried to force peacefully dissolved identities back into the mold required in prison life. As we walked out through the prison yard, I could feel the guards watching us. "Control, easy now," I said to myself. As the heavy doors clanged shut behind us with loud rattling of keys, the grim strangeness of it all was somber in our thoughts.

The revelations of this experience were perhaps even more far reaching than those of the first session. I began to see how the suggestibility factor operated: feelings of fear or guilt or blame could be triggered by chance remarks, and these negative emotions could drastically alter the course of the experience. Conversely, a warm word or a reassuring touch of the hand could provide instant comfort to someone racked by inner pain.

We entered into a contract with each of the convicts who volunteered for the study. We told them what little we knew about the drug, about our own experiences, and stated the goal: to facilitate insight that would enable them to make a noncriminal adjustment to life outside once they were paroled. The agreement also called for psychiatric interviews and psychological tests, before and after the sessions, and written reports on each experience.

The results of this work with about thirty convicts were published.* Although there was no reduction in the rate of recidivism, there were significant personality changes. Subjectively, the men themselves almost always regarded the sessions as beneficial, even those that were painful. Contrary to the dire warnings of many professionals, there was never a moment of violence. Actually, in our research we found that the most violence-prone subjects were psychiatrists and theologians, who had massive repression systems going that could be exposed by the drug experience.

(A year or so later, the power of the suggestibility factor was demonstrated for me again, in an ironic manner. A psychiatrist friend called me from New York, asking for help and reassurance in the middle of his first LSD trip. Recently, the first article had appeared in a medical journal, warning of "untoward reactions" to LSD, and citing nine cases. My friend, under the influence of the drug, already visualized the next issue of the journal with a follow-up report citing case #10—himself. The psychiatric profession, with its training and orientation toward pathological psychic states, was

---

* Timothy Leary, Ralph Metzner, Madison Presnell, Gunther Weil, Ralph Schwitzgebel, and Sara Kinne, "A New Behavior Change Program Using Psilocybin," *Psychotherapy: Theory, Research and Practice* 2(2), 1965, 61–72. For Leary's account, see *High Priest*, 191–211. See also: Rick Doblin, "Dr. Leary's Concord "Prison Experiment: A 34-year Follow-Up Study," and Ralph Metzner, "Reflections on the Concord Prison Project and the Follow-Up Study," both in a forthcoming special issue of *Hallucinogen: The Journal of Psychoactive Drugs*.

particularly vulnerable to the "national negative programming" of psychedelics, as John Lilly called it.)

As a result of my work in the prison, I grew to like and respect some of the men very much. Al was a man of somber mien and the enormous heavy muscles of a weight lifter. In one session, all in the group were touched as we saw him enter totally, incongruously, into the consciousness of a little boy, expressing wide-eyed, innocent wonder and delight at the photographs in a *Family of Man* book, or the feel of water running over his hands—and the look of intense inner searching that came over his face when he saw his arm turn into an eagle's talon.

Donald was in his fifties, serving a twenty-year sentence for armed robbery. In one of his sessions, he had visions of lines and patterns that he traced with careful, probing eyes as he saw in them the patterns of his life. "Does it have any meaning?" he asked, and after a long silence, answered his own question, slowly and haltingly, but deliberately: "Is ego our god? Do we do things so as to have a good image of ourselves in our own eyes?" We talked for a long time. Those of the group that were on longer sentences and were not released organized a study group after the project was terminated. They continued to meet on a regular basis for years after we had been there, working on self-help, self-understanding, becoming guides and helpers for younger convicts. Such was the power of those few initial revelations.

Besides the prison work, we were also experimenting among ourselves. Tim let the graduate students who were involved in the Harvard Psilocybin Project have access to the drug, with the proviso that the sessions be supportively structured and that written reports and other data be obtained from all subjects. We faithfully filled out lengthy questionnaires after each session, wrote accounts, and conducted tests. I was especially interested in the tremendous changes in time perception that occurred with the drug, and ran several ex-

---

* Timothy Leary, George Litwin, and Ralph Metzner, "Reactions to Psilocybin Administered in a Supportive Environment," *Journal of Nervous and Mental Disease* 137(6), 1963, 561–73.

perimental tests, which during the sessions always seemed extremely ludicrous. Nevertheless, the questionnaire results were collated and analyzed and the results written up in psychological journals.*

At the same time, it was becoming increasingly obvious that this conventional approach to the study of these experiences was grossly missing the point. The truly significant aspects of the sessions were entirely nonverbal and nonconceptual, and slipped through our category nets like water through a fishnet.

These experiences made us aware that the content of the drug experience was only partly, even minimally, a function of the drug. Rather the internal attitudes, expectations, and feelings, as well as the external atmosphere and mood prevailing at the time, were the crucial factors. Tim Leary called this the *set and setting* hypothesis, and over the years it has become widely accepted in the professional circles of those who have studied the psychedelic drugs. Contrary to this is the popular idea, promulgated by law-enforcement types committed to a "war on drugs," that it is the drug per se that is responsible for all the visions and trips.

It was interesting to note the different interpretive models and frameworks that different groups in our society had imposed on the experience provided by these drugs. The first was the *psychotomimetic*, the psychiatric-pharmacological model, that regarded the drug experience as a simulated psychosis, and treated it accordingly. Concurrent with this model was the CIA-Army interest in the drug as a weapon for brainwashing and mind control. In the sixties many researchers suspected that such work was going on, but only in the late seventies was it made public.* The military's interest in LSD waned when the unpredictable nature of the drug reaction became clear: you couldn't tell whether unknowingly drugged soldiers would become meditative pacifists, agitated madmen, or atavistic animal figures.

Then there was the *hallucinogenic* model and label, which treated the drugs as tools for studying the brain mechanisms of visual perception and the associated mental states. This type of inquiry is

* Martin Lee and Bruce Shlain, *Acid Dreams: The CIA, LSD and the Sixties Rebellion* (New York: Grove Press, 1985).

exemplified by the work of the German researcher Heinrich Klüver in the 1920s and the American psychopharmacologist Ronald Siegel in the 1980s.*

Then, paradoxically, it was discovered that the very same drugs used to make some people psychotic were being used to make disturbed or addicted people well. Two models for psychotherapy with these drugs developed. In the European literature, the drugs were referred to as *psycholytic* ("mind-dissolving" or "mind-loosening"); this approach involved repeated administrations of gradually increasing doses, adjunctive to psychoanalysis. A second model developed in North America, particularly through the work of Abram Hoffer and Humphry Osmond, who successfully used high-dose single sessions to treat alcoholism and other addictions. Osmond, who had introduced Aldous Huxley to mescaline, coined the term *psychedelic* ("mind-manifesting").†

This model was close to that espoused by the Harvard project, except we were less concerned with individual psychotherapy using psychedelics. We used the term "consciousness-expanding" for the drug and the experience; which is reminiscent of the "consciousness-raising" language of women's liberation groups in the 1970s. This model said: provide a safe, supportive set and setting, with a small group of peers, and the experience will probably be enlightening and productive. Meanwhile, another group of researchers in Menlo Park, California, including Willis Harman, Myron Stolaroff, Robert Mogar, James Fadiman, and others, were developing a *creativity* context for the drug experience: allowing for architects, artists, designers, scientists, and others to work on new problem-solving strategies during their session.‡

The *religious mystical* approach to psychedelic drug experiences was expressed strongly in Leary's writings from the beginning,

* Heinrich Klüver, *Mescal and Mechanisms of Hallucinations* (Chicago: University of Chicago Press, 1966); Ronald K. Siegel, *Intoxication: Life in Pursuit of Artificial Paradise.* (New York: E. P. Dutton, 1989).
† Lester Grinspoon and James Bakalar, *Psychedelic Drugs Reconsidered* (New York: Basic Books, 1979).
‡ Jay Stevens, *Storming Heaven: LSD and the American Dream* (New York: Atlantic Monthly Press, 1987).

stimulated no doubt by his conversations and collaboration with people like Aldous Huxley, Alan Watts, and Huston Smith, all of whom collaborated and consulted with the project. During the Harvard period this approach was exemplified in Walter Pahnke's epoch-making Good Friday Experiment, a carefully controlled scientific study of drug-induced religious experience (described below). This study led to spiritually oriented LSD-therapy with terminal cancer patients at Spring Grove Hospital in Baltimore, which was conducted and described by the Czechoslovakian psychiatrist Stanislav Grof.* The religious-mystical paradigm is of course also evident in Leary's adaptations of the *Tibetan Book of the Dead* and the *Tao Te Ching* as guidebooks for psychedelic experiences. Here we find ancient texts in which specially amplified experiences were regarded as *initiations*—pre-visions of states and levels of consciousness, to be later known and perceived by yogic, magical, or spiritual practices. In a further fascinating line of inquiry, Wasson, Hofmann and the classicist Carl Ruck in 1978 presented evidence suggesting that the Eleusinian Mysteries may have involved the ingestion of the ergot fungus, known to contain LSD-like alkaloids.[†]

The sessions we were having were forcing us into rapid and in-depth confrontation with our own issues as well. Those of us that had experienced traditional psychotherapy found that the relationship interactions there remained almost entirely on the mental level. They did not even remotely approach the spiritual intensity and emotional power of the experiences we were having with psilocybin. In the heightened state of consciousness induced by the drug,

---

* Stanislav Grof and Joan Halifax, *The Human Encounter with Death* (New York: E. P. Dutton, 1977).
[†] Timothy Leary, Ralph Metzner, and Richard Alpert, *The Psychedelic Experience: A Manual Based on the Tibetan Book of the Dead* (New Hyde Park, NY: University Books, 1964); Timothy Leary, *Psychedelic Prayers: Adapted from the Tao Te Ching* (New Hyde Park, NY: University Books, 1966; Rev. ed. Berkeley, CA: Ronin Publishing, 1997); R. Gordon Wasson, Carl Ruck, and Albert Hofmann, *The Road to Eleusis* (Los Angeles: Hermes Press, 1998). See also the recent collection of essays edited by Robert Forte, *Entheogens and the Future of Religion* (San Francisco, CA: Council on Spiritual Practices, 1997).

for example, one could observe one's own psychological projections externalized (i.e., manifested): your feeling states and thoughts would appear on the wall in front of you, or on a friend's face, displayed in living color like a movie. If there was fear or paranoia in a group, one could feel it physically, like sticky tentacles, palpably spreading from one person to another, pulling them into swamplike miasmas of suspicion or despondency.

A high-dose experimental session with psilocybin that we ran in 1963 exemplified some of these complex dynamics (and risks), as well as illustrating Tim Leary's laid-back, humorous and yet caring style of supporting our explorations. Tim gave us a lot of leeway in setting up the sessions. Several of us, with already two years of experience, had decided to explore the effects of a higher dosage of psilocybin, to see if they would compare to LSD, which we had also started to use by that time. Some took 40 mg, I took 60 mg, and George Litwin, with his pioneering spirit, had decided to take 80 mg. These dosages, though higher than any we usually took, were still well below toxic levels. It was in this session, however, that I came the closest to suicide that I ever did in the years of working with psychedelics.

When the drug began to work, George was shaking violently. As I looked at him, his face looked strangely distorted and seemed to be coming apart in layers, like one of M. C. Escher's weird paintings. When he spoke, his voice sounded nonhuman, as if his mouth were filled with metallic mud. He was talking about finding the button that made his heart stop or go.

As I looked around the room I saw great bands of moving streams of energy particles traversing the space, passing through and between myself and the other people. We all seemed to be part of these moving, ever changing bands of energy. They were familiar to me from other mushroom sessions, when I had seen them as luminous vibrating filigree networks. But this time, the intensity frightened me. As my fear level increased, the energy bands congealed and stopped moving; they took on a grayish hue, like prison bars. All at once I felt immobilized and trapped, like a fly in a gigantic metallic spider's web. I couldn't even talk and explain what was happening to me; my voice felt paralyzed. Everyone, including George (who was no longer shaking), seemed to be frozen into immobility by these metallic web-cages.

I felt my mind was paralyzed too. I couldn't think or understand what was happening. I couldn't tell whether what I was experiencing was real or a drug-induced hallucination (an experience psychiatry refers to as "de-realization"). I did however decide I should try to call Tim on the telephone for help. Gunther Weil, who seemed to sense my dilemma, accompanied me to help with the dialing. The telephone set was wiggling and jiggling like a demented jellyfish. Somehow, we managed to reach Tim on the line. I wanted his help to establish some kind of "reality." I said, "Tell me something real, Tim. What's happening over there?"

Tim immediately got the message and said, "Well, Jack's sitting at the table eating a hamburger, Susie's watching television with her hair in curlers, Michael's drinking a beer . . ." I started to feel a little better. These were messages from "reality." Nevertheless, I told him we needed help, and asked if he would come over.

While waiting for Tim to arrive, I was holding on to my sanity with the thought that when he got here, he would free us all from this monstrous spider's web we were caught in, which also had the effect of making us speechless. It felt like I couldn't hear, say, or understand anything. I felt completely dehumanized, not even like a biological organism, more like a mechanical puppet or device.

I was so relieved when Tim came through the door—I could see him moving freely through the sticky web of gray steel bands. But then, as I watched in horror, his movements slowed down, became mechanical, robotlike, his voice thickened and slurred, and I plunged into despair as I realized he too was helplessly caught.

This was in the days before we had learned how to take someone through a really deep psychotic experience, how to reach them in consciousness, set up communication, and bring them back. Tim and the others simply laid me out on a bed and hoped for the best. Corky Litwin patted and stroked me reassuringly.

After some hours of objective time, and a hellish eternity in subjective time, the intensity of the experience began to diminish somewhat. I remembered I had taken a drug, and the effect was beginning to wear off. I felt like a living human being again, though thoroughly shaken by what I had gone through. We needed to learn how to bring someone back from psychotic hell-states, as well as preparing for ecstatic heaven-states.

As we proceeded with our explorations, still under the aegis of the Harvard University Psilocybin Research Project, we were increasingly moving into the consideration of religious and mystical concepts and images. Such ideas were foreign to our humanist psychological orientation, but were thrust upon us by the nature of the experiences. Sometimes when Tim was talking to groups about these kinds of experiences, he seemed inspired by an almost messianic fervor that made a powerful impact on his listeners. At the same time the issue of leadership, with its associated complex of idealization and disappointment, was beginning to rear its ugly head.

One strange and moving session on a cold November night in 1961 was particularly memorable for its focus on these issues. Six of us assembled in Dick Alpert's apartment: Dick, Tim, Michael Kahn, George Litwin and his wife Corky, and myself. Gunther Weil had said he would join us later, as would Maynard Ferguson, the musician, and his wife Flo. Everyone was in excellent spirits. We had never all taken psychedelics together and were looking forward to it.

Our thoughts became serious, almost grave. On the way to the session Mike and I had been talking about the idea of the sin against the Holy Ghost—what used to be considered the one unpardonable sin. We had discussed it as a kind of universal projective test in the Middle Ages— revealing whatever it was you considered your greatest failing. Theologically, it was the attribution to the devil of what really came from the Holy Ghost, thus cutting oneself off from the source of all grace and redemption.

During the session, Mike returned to this topic and related our earlier thoughts. George, who had a marvelous sense for practical detail, was wondering about borderline sins. He asked Tim, as the only Catholic present, "What did the Church do with those rare cases which the existing rules didn't cover? How did it handle totally new events or occurrences? For example, take a peasant who comes to the priest and says: 'I took these pills last night, and I met Christ, and we shook hands and spent a wonderful evening together, but somehow everybody goes around telling me I'm bad.' How would the Church handle that? What would the priest say?"

When we had all finished convulsing with laughter, I looked over and saw that George had stopped smiling and was looking at Tim and saying, "I'm serious."

I felt a wave of sympathy for George and looked at Tim. Tim said nothing. I looked at him very intently and repeated, "What would the priest say to George's question, Tim?"

Tim became very confused. He did not seem to hear and was fiddling with his hearing aid. We repeated the question. Then he looked at me in silence for a very long time. I became aware of how important the question had become to me. It was the question about this night, about our work, about our whole life, which had come to revolve so much around these drugs—was it good or bad?

It had become a very basic question about existence, and personal worth, the question to which each one must find his own answer. This was what I felt Tim to be saying by not answering the question—that everyone must come to terms with their own condition. When I realized that this was what he meant, I felt tears streaming down my face—not tears of sadness.

After a while Tim began to tell a story about a Catholic man he used to know who always referred to a boy with certain sexual habits as "the monster." I felt this was the priest's answer to George's original question about how to define sin; at the base of the Catholic concept of sin lies a strong disgust toward sexuality.

As I was trying to tell Mike how I felt about these two "answers"—the human one, and the Catholic one—I realized that Tim had "said" all these things unintentionally. He protested that he did not even hear half of what was going on, and that he felt "like a figment of George Litwin's imagination."

Outside in the street with Mike and myself on this cold, snowy November night, Tim said he was in a terrible bind and didn't know how to get out of it. He said he had always regarded us as equals and felt betrayed that he was suddenly being called upon to answer religious questions. "What have you guys been doing all these months?"

Mike was saying intense things about Zen masters and Buddha and Jesus very fast, the main gist of which seemed to be that Tim had to suffer so that we could learn. All leaders have to go through the same process of awakening to the fact that they are being regarded as leaders, not as equals, as they would like to be.

We went back inside and Gunther was saying the time might come when he would decide to leave Tim because he disagreed with him and didn't want this pure thing corrupted. He saw Tim being sucked into an evil game because he was so naive.

Tim said, "You like your work at the prison and want to continue with that, don't you?" His voice sounded almost plaintive and apologetic.

The room had become almost totally dark. We were all sitting quietly for a long time. Then Gunther said, "You know, Tim, only a Jew and a Catholic could have this sort of discussion."

Tim asked, "What is there of me to leave?" He said how he had always regarded us as equal work-partners, as a group working together for common goals.

"Yes, I see that now, I recognize the different roles we play. But there was a time when I exalted you, looked up to you, worshiped you—now you have come down to a human level."

There was a terrible groan of protest from George Litwin. "Wait a minute, wait . . . I am neither Jew nor Catholic so I can speak here with some impartiality. There was a time before when the Jews exalted a man and made him divine, and then nailed him up when they discovered he was human after all. Whether it's a fact or not is irrelevant; it is a tradition, and one that we should cease to live by. It's the Jewish tradition that some people are closer to God than others. But there is another one, the one of the Declaration of Independence, where men gather together to draw up a petition in equality."

George was magnificent. He was fighting for a new start, away from the ancient modes of exalting people and then tearing them down, toward a vision of true equality between men and common goals and shared responsibility. Most of us heaved a profound sign of relief. Maynard and Flo cheered.

The bubble had been broken. When George finished talking, Tim got up abruptly and without a word went to the kitchen and left the door open. A bright shaft of light streamed into the room. The depressing fog of incipient religious bigotry was dispersed. The tendency to overidealize a potential leader had been clearly revealed and uprooted, at least for that group and that time.

In our discussions at the Harvard Psilocybin Project in those days, we would sometimes semihumorously regard Tim as being the most "far-out" of our group—one who was so extreme in his attitudes on the psychedelics that he defined one end of the scale that we didn't want to go to. As if we would say, "Well, we won't go to that extreme, that's just Tim in his craziness." But, more often than not, due to the power and inner logic of our own experiences, we'd find ourselves following in his footsteps and eventually coming to share his vision. At least for a while.

Our work continued through the winter and spring of 1961/1962. After the initial experimentation to develop methods for producing positive, valuable experiences that, as in the prison project, could help bring about therapeutic change, Tim was intensifying exploration of the creativity aspects of the drug. For this reason he moved into New York literary and artistic circles to find subjects who were creative professionals. As soon as people heard about psilocybin they wanted to take it. Numerous requests had to be turned down. Our files began to swell with reports from writers, jazz musicians, poets, painters, and philosophers.

Allen Ginsberg and Peter Orlovsky came and sampled the drug, as did Jack Kerouac and Charles Olsen. Allen became so enthusiastic during the session that he wanted to call Khrushchev and Kennedy to talk them into taking it. William Burroughs stayed with Tim's family in Cambridge for a while. Initially positive, he participated with Tim at a psychological convention in New York that drew overflow crowds where he presented a scholarly paper based on his personal experiences with about a dozen different drugs he had tried. Later, he soured on the project and denounced it in tones of virulent paranoia in one of his books: "stay out of their Garden of Delights, it is a terminal sewer . . . they give you love, love, love in slop buckets . . . their immortality cosmic consciousness and love is second-run grade B shit . . ." and so forth.

Gerald Heard, the distinguished English philosopher, friend of Aldous Huxley and author of many books on the history of religion and mythology, visited the project early on and was very positive about the drug. He gave fascinating discourses on the role of psychedelic drugs in mystery cults in ancient times. He advised us not to publicize our findings, to stay underground, following the example of historical esoteric groups and secret societies. Needless to say, his advice was ignored; nothing could have been further from Tim's whole nature.

During the years to come I often wondered what would have happened had we followed Gerald Heard's advice—letting psychedelic drugs become the exclusive province of a small group of visionary researchers and explorers. It did not seem to be the script we were called upon to follow. The experiences were too positive to not want to share them with everybody. It would appear that the time had come when this kind of experience should be made available to large numbers of searchers, so that "the doors of perception" could be opened, so that expanded consciousness was no longer something attainable only by rare individuals. The experience was genuine; a view of what was possible. Those who felt the call to search could do so with a vivid knowledge of the goal.

Meanwhile, the world of academic psychology was becoming increasingly strange. I concentrated on finishing my Ph.D. in the spring of that year, because I knew that it was my last dance with the stimulus and response variables of that world. The time of running rat maze-learning experiments in a Harvard basement, as I had done the previous year, seemed already eons distant. Teaching introductory psychology courses to move up the ladder of university success was equally remote. One of my professors, Dr. Brendan Maher, said he couldn't understand why I was throwing away the opportunity for a really good career in academic psychology. I couldn't explain it to him.

The Psilocybin Project was generating more and more resistance from the university community. One of the things resented most by Leary and Alpert's faculty colleagues was that several of their graduate research assistants were deserting them for the more glamorous and exciting work with the drug project.

Professor McClelland, chairman of the department, issued ominous warnings about the social effects of drugs. He pointed to India as an example of a society that had allegedly become degenerate as a result of excessive use of consciousness-expanding drugs—a theory open to serious question, even apart from the equating of cannabis with psilocybin.

We were criticized that our research was loose and our approach uncontrolled and irresponsible. To the contrary, as far as research is concerned, the project carried out and published several extensive statistical and questionnaire studies on the drug experience. Everyone who participated as a subject was required to undergo psychiatric screening at the University Health Services. No one was ever given a drug without their knowledge, or against their wishes, or without full and complete preparation before, and support during, the experience. Tranquilizer antidotes were always available but no one ever requested their use.

Among the rules established by the university was one forbidding us to use undergraduates as subjects. We had not been doing this anyway: our subjects were graduate students, or older people outside of the university. Nonetheless, our activities stimulated a lot of interest in psychedelics and thus led indirectly to a good deal of drug experimentation among Harvard students. Supplies of mescaline, peyote, and other substances were at that time easily obtained by anyone with a little ingenuity.

The supervisory committee also attempted to lay down rules governing the use of the drugs privately, outside of the university context. At this time, there were no state or federal laws governing their use. Dick Alpert, being an Aries, objected to this attempted restriction of his freedom and private life. Tim Leary, being a Libra, agreed to the rules in order to keep the peace, and continued doing what he was before.

It must also be said that although Leary and Alpert flooded the academic community with research papers, memoranda, and descriptions, some of their written and verbal pronouncements had a quality of messianic overenthusiasm that turned a lot of people off. Tim was constantly inventing slogans such as "You have to go out of your mind to use your head" that antagonized many intellectuals. Typical of that period is this passage from an article Tim wrote for the *Harvard Review:*

> Must we continue to jail, execute, exile our ecstatic visionaries, and then enshrine them as tomorrow's heroes? . . . Society needs educated priest-scholars to provide structure—the intellectual muscle, bone and skin to keep things together. . . . The nervous system can be changed, integrated, recircuited, expanded in its function. These possibilities naturally threaten

every branch of the Establishment. . . . Our favorite concepts are standing in the way of a flood-tide, two billion years building up. The verbal dam is collapsing. Head for the hills, or prepare your intellectual craft to flow with the current.*

With pressures mounting, we began to think of ways to carry on the work completely out of the university context. Tim said it was "as unfair to expect a university to sponsor research on visionary experience as it would be to expect the Vatican to support research on effective aphrodisiacs." And so, in the summer of 1962 about twenty members of the psilocybin project rented a hotel in the small Mexican fishing village of Zihuatanejo (which has since become a major resort town) in order to pursue in-depth experimentation with the drugs, away from the social and political pressures of Cambridge, Massachusetts.

The Mexican sessions were strikingly different from the Harvard psychodramas. Here the setting was the exuberant lushness of jungle flora and fauna, the ceaseless rhythmic pounding of the surf, extravagantly beautiful sunsets, silent lightning storms over the Pacific Ocean, tropical heat and balmy air currents, mysterious sounds of night insects, and the sweet aromas of exotic flowers. In the sessions, a boy playing a flute would become Krishna enchanting the Gopis. The women often transformed into sea nymphs or mermaids; the men, Aztec warriors or jungle shamans.

At the suggestion of Aldous Huxley and Gerald Heard we began using the Bardo Thödol *(Tibetan Book of the Dead)* as a guide to psychedelic sessions. The Tibetan Buddhists talked about the three phases of experience on the "intermediate planes" *(bardos)* between death and rebirth. We translated this to refer to the death and the rebirth of the ego, or ordinary personality. Stripped of the elaborate Tibetan symbolism and transposed into Western concepts, the text provided a remarkable parallel to our findings.

---

* Timothy Leary and Richard Alpert, "The Politics of Consciousness Expansion," *Harvard Review* 1(4), 1963, 33–37.

The Bardo Thödol describes the first phase, the first bardo, as a state of complete transcendence, of pure radiant light, that occurs immediately after death; it tells us it can be maintained only by those with high yogic training, who are able to remain undistracted. This first phase usually quickly dissipates into the second bardo, the longest phase of hallucinations and visions of peaceful and wrathful deities, heavenly or hellish experiences. The third bardo was the phase of rebirth, or reentry as we called it, in which you returned to your ordinary personality.

The basic advice of the Tibetan yogis was always the same: remain detached and centered within yourself, don't become attracted to the pleasant visions or repelled by the painful ones. Remember they are all in your mind. Accept them and float downstream. During rebirth, or reentry, don't rush, stay balanced, maintain the light for as long as possible. Actually one could move into the complete transcendent consciousness even after having already entered into the second or third phase, if one was able to follow the light from within.

This ancient text—which before our experience with psychedelics would have been so much gibberish—contained in uncanny detail descriptions of many aspects of the voyages we had been taking. Of course, we knew perfectly well that the method the Buddhists were using to explore inner space was not psychedelic drugs, but meditation. However, the vivid descriptions of inner states in their texts made it clear that these were realms that were recognizable and real. Suddenly we were no longer a crazed bunch of psychologists, recklessly plunging into completely uncharted terrain. There had been previous explorations. There was a history, a tradition. There were maps and guidebooks. Though trained in the Western methods of scientific research, Leary (and the rest of us) felt affirmed in our spiritual approach to psychedelic experiences by the discovery of these ancient writings. Our initial work on this text was later developed and published as *The Psychedelic Experience*.

We also "discovered," to our delighted surprise, Western authors who had traversed some of these strange inner worlds, without drugs. Hermann Hesse, in his novel *Steppenwolf*, gives a marvelous description of the psychedelic "magic theater" of the mind; and in *Journey to the East* tells of the pilgrimage of a group of explorers toward the elusive "home" within, of the secret league of dedicated travelers who shared a vision of fulfillment. The French Gurdjieff disciple René Daumal in *Mount Analogue*, a mysterious unfinished allegory, portrays an inner mountaineering expedition, describing the pitfalls and challenges of such a mystical journey.

We decided to run an individual session to "test" the Tibetan Buddhist model we were working on, using a moderate dose of LSD. I would be the journeyer, Tim would be the guide. We used our "session room," with a balcony facing the jungle; the ocean surf roared below. We agreed that if I felt fear I would say so, rather than struggling with it myself.

We started off in silence. Tim read some passages from our new "manual." For about an hour nothing happened. I was restless and annoyed at myself for not being able to let go. I was thinking too much and too hard. Tim said he'd found focusing on sensory awareness had helped him get out of obsessive thinking. So he lit a candle, opened a cool bottle of beer (which I simply touched) and encouraged me just to focus on pure sense perception. This seemed to cut through the excessive mentation like a knife through butter. I suddenly felt released from a heavy fog of restless and pointless thinking.

I looked at Tim's face, and to my amazement it became the face of godlike Being, radiating light. Then, as I continued gazing at it, it changed and half of his face looked ugly and demonic. Simultaneously with this visual outer perception, I felt subjectively like a piece of protoplasmic jelly stuck to a rock. The part of me that was floating free in the ocean saw Tim's face as radiant and divine; the part of me that was still stuck to the rock saw it as ugly and cold. My mind felt like it was cradled in a beautiful, clear, empty space, but then I would slip back into fear and distress.

"I keep on losing it."

"How do you lose it? With your mind?"

Silence.

"How do you get it?"

"It just comes. I see divinity in half of your face, but the other half changes to horrible."

"Remember, both come from within you, and pretty soon you'll be able to see divinity in the whole face, or in the candle, or the cigarette, or the whole following day, if you're good at it."

Tim got up and sat by the door. I lay down on the floor, closed my eyes, and again tried to reach that state of ecstatic weightlessness by emptying my mind. I couldn't do it and got discouraged; I thought I could only reach it with his or somebody's help. I started to hallucinate—the peaceful and wrathful visions of the second bardo phase. When I saw fearful images, I remembered the admonition of the Bardo Thödol that they were in my mind only, so I told them to go away. To my immense surprise, they did.

Then, with an electrifying shock of insight, I realized that I could do this not only with these relatively trivial demons, but with all my fears. I thought about a friend of mine, whose behavior sometimes scared me. Then I thought how absurd it was that I should let fear feelings that were in me interfere with the relationship I had with someone outside of me. My whole head opened up spherically in every direction simultaneously, and I felt both serene and exhilarated as never before in my life.

I sat up and looked at Tim. He took one look at my face and said, "You made it." I told him about the fear insight and he added: "Not only the fear of that person, but the love for them is within you too. The point is you have to know your own mental machinery, otherwise it scares the shit out of you."

We talked for a while about possible ways to maintain this state, where everything you looked at was pulsing and glowing with divine radiance, and the difficulties of living permanently at that level of consciousness. We finally agreed that "in order to live at that level . . . you have to live at that level."

During this time, for about two or three hours in clock time, though it was subjectively timeless, I had no problem maintaining that state of spherical openness.

It was effortless. I knew I was in my body, and could quickly tune in to any part of it, but I had no identity in it. My identity and awareness seemed to be spread throughout the room and even beyond into the forest outside. This meant when somebody came into the room, as they did, it was as if they were walking into "me." They were accepted like thoughts entering my head. I could with complete equanimity examine various relationships "Ralph" had with various people, parents, friends, parts of himself, etc.

I felt freer than I had ever felt before. Gradually and gently, over a long period of time, "I" returned back into my usual personality and body-self. The memory of the state of consciousness experienced remained with extreme lucidity.

Many things happened after that first summer in Zihuatanejo. We were more enthusiastic than ever about the potentials of the drug experience for revealing new levels of consciousness and bringing about changes in personality and behavior faster and more effectively than any other method known to us. We also became more serious about communicating what we had already learned to our colleagues in the academic world and the public at large.

Some people tried to fit us into the categories of missionaries, proselytizers, or drug pushers, but this was not the image we had of ourselves at all. We felt like people who had stumbled, almost by accident, onto a possible cure for a virulent plague that was scourging the country. No doubt this was the "emotional plague" that Wilhelm Reich, another misunderstood pioneer, had diagnosed. Yet the majority of the inhabitants, sufferers from the plague, were denying that there even was this condition. Hence anyone proposing a cure for it must inevitably be seen either as a religious nut or a depraved fiend, or both. Nevertheless, we decided to do the best we could in communicating our findings.

Leary and Alpert went back to their Harvard teaching positions. I had applied for and received a NIMH postdoctoral fellowship in psychopharmacology. I signed up for the second-year Harvard Medical School course in pharmacology and read everything I could find about these strange drugs, anything that would help explain their extraordinary action on the human brain. I read thousands of studies, yet nothing really shed any light on this mystery. No one had the faintest idea how the drugs worked. To my surprise I found out that this was also true of most of the drugs used in psychiatry, and even, to a very large extent, of regular medical drugs such as aspirin. They were used because they "worked," and that was that.

We started a journal, the *Psychedelic Review*, to publish scholarly, scientific, and literary articles in this field. Alan Watts, who was at Harvard at the time, and who had taken psilocybin with Tim and written about it in *The Joyous Cosmology*, helped us put the first issue together. Paul Lee, Rolf von Eckartsberg, and I were the joint editors. Paul was a graduate student in philosophy of religion, a close associate of Paul Tillich; Rolf was a psychology graduate student interested in existentialism and phenomenology. After the first year, they left. I continued editing the review, as a more or less quarterly, for about six years.

We also decided to try communal living. This came about in a rather simple way. We were spending almost all of our spare time talking about the research project and doing a lot of driving back and forth from each other's houses and apartments. It seemed the obvious thing to do to live in the same house. The first house we lived in, in Newton Center, was shared by Tim, his children Susan and Jack, Dick Alpert, Foster Dunlap and his wife Barbara and their baby, and my wife Susan and myself. Susan and I had met several months before and I had proposed to her during a mescaline session in Zihuatanejo.

After we'd lived in the house for a few months, the city of Newton Center brought suit to evict us, on neighbors' instigation, for living in a single family dwelling. Dick persuaded his father, George Alpert, a prominent Boston attorney, to defend our case in court. We won because the law defined "family" by reference to sharing of the household, not by blood lines.

One room in the house was set up as a meditation and session room. It was a converted closet, remodeled in such a way that it could only be reached from the basement—you had to go downstairs and then up a ladder. Inside, the walls and ceiling were hung with India print cloth, and luxuriantly colored pillows covered the floor.

The Newton commune, while unsatisfactory in many respects, was the scene of many new and different kinds of psychedelic research. We carried out experiments in which we deliberately invoked problem situations for an individual, who in the expanded state of consciousness would attempt to see through his blind spots. We also performed experiments in language learning, where a person under the psychedelic would listen to recordings of a foreign language being spoken, for several hours, in order to imprint her brain with the sounds and inflections of that language.

Tim, ever the inventive research psychologist (at least at this time of his life), started a collaborative project with Ogden Lindsley, a behavioral scientist who was an associate of B. F. Skinner. Lindsley had pioneered the objective continuous recording of the physical behavior of psychotics in a mental hospital. He designed, at Tim's request, a device that looked like a typewriter, with a dozen keys that activated strip-chart recordings, each key representing an experiential category. Tim called it the "experiential typewriter." The idea was that during a session the person, who might be unable to talk quickly enough to describe his ever changing experiences could code them with the push of a button in a few basic categories, such as "body sensations," "cellular memories," "thought patterns."*

We used this device in experiments with dimethyltryptamine (DMT), a powerful new psychedelic that had been discovered by the Hungarian scientist Stephen Szara. It was not orally active, so had to be taken by injection (though later amateur researchers developed a smokable form). It produced a thirty-minute experience of profound transcendence. In one experiment, described in *High Priest*, Tim was the subject and every two minutes I would ask him to indicate which of the twelve keys on the typewriter best represented his current state of consciousness. I felt the device was a remarkably effective aid in the attempt to objectify internal states.

Generally, during this year and subsequently, we used LSD more, psilocybin decreasingly. LSD was very different. Psilocybin had been the "love-pill." LSD was never a love-pill; it was a death–rebirth trip. I remember when Tim told me about his first session with LSD that he had taken the night before. He was a changed man. He was stammering about the "plastic doll world," the total death of the self. I was somewhat frightened and dismayed.

LSD was introduced to us by Michael Hollingshead, an eccentric Englishman, who had held a mysterious, vague job relating to American-English "cultural exchange" in New York, and who arrived one day at the offices of the Harvard Project. He was broke, depressed, and suicidal. But he also had an extraordinary sense of

* Timothy Leary, *High Priest*, 264–79.

humor, was a consummate storyteller, and a genial, good-natured fellow. Questions about his prior activities always brought evasive answers and wildly improbable, hilariously funny stories. Inquiries we made indicated that certain criminal elements in New York City considered him a con man to be shunned at all costs. He himself expressed fear of being beaten or killed by gangsters.

He had, with the aid of a physician friend in New York, Dr. John Beresford, obtained LSD from Sandoz for the purpose of studying its effect on bacterial molds. The two decided first to try it on themselves, and from their account it must have been an enormous overdose. They were incapacitated for weeks, trapped in inner space networks they could not unravel. He arrived seeking help, and Tim began a lengthy, strange association with him, referring to him as a "divine rascal."*

I always found Michael's descriptions of his psychedelic experiences completely baffling. I could not relate to what he was describing. He completely shattered all our assumptions and premises. Instead of following our code of openness, trust, sharing, and sincerity, Michael made use of the awesome suggestibility of the LSD state to confuse, bewilder, astound, and manipulate awareness and perception. Yet, when confronted with this, he would deny it stoutly, and protest his innocence in such a guileless, humorous, and friendly manner that it was impossible not to like the man.

Michael used to take a large dose of LSD every day, while he still had the supply. He had it made up into a kind of paste, like peanut butter, and would spoon it out of a jar. He thought of it as a kind of daily consciousness vitamin. Often he would, while on the trip, mix himself a stiff drink and then watch TV. He had been invited to stay in Tim's house and help take care of the children, which he did quite well, considering what he was pouring into his system all the time.

Michael's approach to psychedelics was much more like that of the hippy "acid freaks," the trips of Ken Kesey and his Merry Pranksters, as described in Tom Wolfe's *The Electric Kool-Aid Acid Test*—

* See *High Priest*, 233–61; also the autobiographical *The Man Who Turned On the World* by Michael Hollingshead (New York: Abelard-Schuman, 1973).

not growth, not spiritual experience, not insight or learning, just freak out, go as far as possible to the outermost edge of the hitherto experienced and beyond, blow the mind and yet stay cool and in control, keep up the game.

Taking LSD made the religious dimensions of psychedelic experience inescapable. You were plunged into realms where all hitherto accepted belief systems and identity structures were suspended, as everything you called "you" dissolved in pearly streams of liquid color, in pulsing waves of ecstatic sensations, or shattered silently into perfect, symmetrical, crystalline lattices, or shimmering nets of electronic wave-trains. As you returned from these experiences of pure contentless energy, the world of images and categories in which we live our normal lives did indeed seem like a "plastic doll world."

People came out of these sessions reeling with awe, overwhelmed by experiences of oneness with God and all other beings, shaken to the depths of their nature by the grandeur and power of the divine life-energy processes going on within their own consciousness.

We turned to religious professionals for help. Huston Smith, Professor of Philosophy at M.I.T., friend of Aldous Huxley and author of the bestselling book *The Religions of Man*, was one of the first to join our project. He remarked that his experiences confirmed and validated what he had been writing about for years. Some of his students came and joined our project. Walter Houston Clark, Dean of the Theological Seminary at Andover-Newton, a kindly, distinguished old gentleman, became, much to our surprise, an enthusiastic advocate of the potentials of psychedelics.

We ran a series of sessions for ministers, priests, rabbis, and theology students. Some of these were more dramatic and violent than any we'd ever experienced at the prison with hardened criminals. Some got caught up in hell-fire and judgment visions; others wanted to immediately force everyone around to convert, confess, and turn to Jesus; some forgot about God and turned to their wives for solace; some left the ministry; some were deeply confirmed in their calling.

One theology graduate student I worked with in a session, a huge, red-haired bear of a man, wrestled with some nameless monsters in his unconscious for hours, sweating and groaning and finally finding release and peace. However, the next day he announced that he didn't see any value to it, that it wouldn't help him write his thesis, or help America beat the Russians, and therefore he didn't want any more of it—an attitude I found frankly bizarre.

Walter Pahnke arrived and began his famous "Good Friday" study, the first and to this date the only controlled, double-blind, bona fide experimental study of mystical experience. Walter was an M.D. from the Midwest, an ordained minister, and getting his Ph.D. in the history of religion at Harvard. His idea was to give a group of divinity students psilocybin, during a Good Friday service, in a chapel. He understood the set and setting hypothesis, and wanted to maximize every factor to produce religious experiences. A control group would be given placebo, at the same time and same place, and neither subject nor experimenter would know who had the drug and who had the active placebo.

It seemed like an insanely outrageous idea, even to us, and we didn't think it could work. But Walter was a determined, gee-whiz, clean-cut, Boy Scout type, with totally impeccable credentials and impressive backing. Dean Howard Thurman of Boston University Divinity School agreed to the use of his chapel for the service. Andover-Newton Seminary, through Walter Clark, provided volunteer subjects, highly motivated, pretested, and screened. Harvard University, through our psilocybin project, provided the trained guides, who would work with the twenty subjects in small groups. Huston Smith, of M.I.T., was on his doctoral committee.

Walter had the good sense to turn down our strong recommendation that he should experience the drugs himself first. He knew that if he didn't maintain his psychedelic innocence that he would be accused of bias and his study would be criticized for lack of objectivity.

The experiment was a complete success. Walter had culled nine criteria from the literature on religious experience, particularly the writings of W. T. Stace. In terms of these criteria the psilocybin subjects experienced states and levels of consciousness indistinguishable from classic mystical experience, whereas the control group did not.

The study became famous through psychological and religious circles and was widely written up in the press. Walter got his Ph.D.*

Despite successes such as Walter Pahnke's experiment, the political pressures at Harvard University continued to mount. Professor McClelland announced that students who participated in the drug work would be dropped from the Ph.D. program. Newspapers played up the sensational angles with abandon: "Weird Drug Studies Bared at Harvard," "Harvard Eats the Holy Mushroom," "Drug Craze Grows on Campus," and so forth.

We decided to reduce the embarrassment to Harvard by separating the drug research completely from the university. A nonprofit corporation was established, entitled International Federation for Internal Freedom, or IFIF for short, with offices in Cambridge. The Board of Directors was Leary, Alpert, myself, Walter Clark, Huston Smith, Alan Watts, Paul Lee, Rolf von Eckartsberg, Gunther Weil, and George Litwin. The purposes were to sponsor and support research in consciousness expansion.

The plan was to supply information and the drugs (all still perfectly legal at this point), at cost, to small research groups all over the country, formed for the purpose of expanding consciousness. Most of these would be psychologists, ministers, educators, and other professionals. We would act as research center, collating and distributing information and findings. Requests were already coming in by the hundreds.

But because of the escalating sensationalist publicity, IFIF ran into difficulties from the start. At first we had attempted to set up offices in a prestigious medical building across the Charles River in Boston. We had barely moved our furniture and boxes in—and not yet arranged them—when pressure was put on the owners of the building by the medical people who held offices there, and we were evicted. Offices were then set up in Cambridge.

---

* Walter Pahnke and William Richards, "Implications of LSD and Experimental Mysticism," *Journal of Religion and Health*, 5(3) 1966. Also, Rick Doblin, "Pahnke's Good Friday Experiment: A Long-Term Follow-Up and Methodological Critique," *Journal of Transpersonal Psychology*, 23(1), 1991, 1–28.

The drug supply was the next big problem. We could no longer use the free psilocybin that had been supplied by Sandoz for years. This had been turned over to university health authorities. We decided to approach Sandoz in Switzerland and Dr. Albert Hofmann directly.

We knew that time was running out. The drugs were still legal, but it was obvious they would not remain so for much longer. We decided to risk all and sent an order for a million doses of LSD to Sandoz, Basel, which had quoted us a price of one cent per dose. The order was typed on Harvard stationery and accompanied by a check for $10,000.

But it was already too late. Sandoz checked with the Harvard administration and found they were not at all in favor of this purchase. Furthermore, the funds we had counted on to back up the check did not materialize.

Thus our attempt to set up a legitimate distribution system for open-ended, nonpsychiatric research in psychedelics failed. The supply lines of psychedelic drugs then went in two directions. One, into the psychiatric research hospitals, which became more and more tightly controlled, regulated, and supervised. The other direction was underground: black-market chemists made LSD and other drugs in basements, in increasingly vast quantities, varying in quality from very fine to very poor and dangerous.

For our group, the pressure of events was increasing to crisis proportions. Tim had arranged his schedules so that he could be absent in the spring semester and he left for Mexico. Dick Alpert was publicly accused by the *Harvard Crimson*, the student newspaper, of having given LSD to an undergraduate, despite his agreement not to. The fact that the student stated the experience was the most meaningful and helpful event of his life made no difference. The incident provided the university with the needed excuse, and Alpert was fired. Leary's dismissal was ostensibly for failing to show up for classes. It was the first time in over one hundred years that Harvard had fired any faculty member, and it put the story all over the nation's newspapers. It put LSD in the public eye and made it a symbol of fear and danger. For ten years, until the early seventies, psychedelics remained an almost constant headline news item.

McClelland had said that the drug experiences made the users less sensitive to others. Those of us in the Harvard psychedelic project did not feel that this was so. We were quite acutely aware of the emotional reactions of others to the work we were doing—it would be hard not to notice it. But we felt that the work was too important to stop or slow down because of the fear of those not only unwilling to try it themselves, but who also wanted to prevent others from using it.

My own feeling is that it was our group's task, our assignment so to speak, to explore the uses and values of these consciousness tools that had suddenly been rediscovered, and to disseminate the findings to the scientific and academic community and to the public at large. The fact remains that by and large the helping professionals (doctors, psychologists, ministers) were unable to accept these methods and develop a growth-enhancing structure to use them for human welfare. Our technological society was (and is) evidently still too fixed in and identified with old nineteenth-century materialistic-rational paradigms to be able to view these excursions into other realities with anything but fear and nervous withdrawal.

From a sociological point of view, it is instructive to compare this process with the response of the Native American cultures to the introduction of peyote in the late nineteenth century. Large numbers of the tribes throughout the North American continent adopted the psychedelic cactus and developed a socially and legally circumscribed religious structure for its use.*

In our culture, by contrast, the failure of the mind professionals opened the doors wide to the uncontrolled activities of black-market exploiters and profiteers, whose products were chemically impure and whose services were spiritually empty. To be sure, there were exceptions—humane, sensitive therapists and explorers here and there—but the last formal psychedelic therapy program in the

---

* Ralph Metzner, "Molecular Mysticism: The Role of Psychoactive Substances in Shamanic Transformations of Consciousness," *Shaman's Drum* 12, spring 1988. Also in: C. Rätsch, ed., *The Gateway to Inner Space* (Avery Publishing, 1989).

United States, at Spring Grove Hospital in Baltimore, closed in the midseventies.

Because of the Harvard firings and the increasingly vehement opposition and condemnation by both academic and medical authorities our group decided to move our entire operation again to Zihuatanejo, Mexico. By this time we had learned quite a lot about how to prepare the set and setting of a psychedelic session in such a way as to maximize the chance for a beneficial, educational, and growth-enhancing experience. We decided to open a psychedelic training center in Zihuatanejo, where people could come to be trained in the use of these substances, learn what we had learned, and then return to their own communities and apply it in their professional, therapeutic, and creative activities. Our version of the *Tibetan Book of the Dead* as a session manual was available as a conceptual guide. One couldn't imagine a more perfect environment for such explorations.

We rented the Hotel Catalina again and sent out brochures to our IFIF mailing list. The response was overwhelming, since the opportunity was unique. For $200 people could spend a month in one of the world's most idyllic tropical places, learning to expand their awareness with powerful new aids, in a protective and supportive environment. Applications poured in by the hundreds and were screened and processed by Dick Alpert and assistants, who remained behind at first in the Cambridge office. They also published the first issue of the *Psychedelic Review*, which served to establish our scientific and scholarly authenticity.

In Zihuatanejo, we converted one of the cabin units into a session room, decorated with India print drapes and equipped with pillows, candles, and incense. Often, however, a good part of the session would be spent on the beach or in the water. We found that the surf, in the protected bay, proved to be an excellent way to bring someone through a difficult phase of a trip. Simply to lie at the water's edge, letting the waves wash over you, rolling the body across the sand, merging into the eternal currents of air, ocean, sun, and earth, seemed to clear away much fear, suspicion, frustration, and other emotional baggage.

There were usually three or four persons in a session, which might consist of a psychologist, a television actress, a businessman, and one experienced guide. Much of the guiding was done by my wife Susan and myself. We were on a very busy schedule; sessions were started every morning and every evening. A minimum of three to four days had to elapse between sessions for all participants, to let the tolerance effect wear off. Thus, there were always groups either starting or ending a session, or in the middle of one. Sometimes Susan and I went several days and nights without interruption. We learned to sleep "on the wing," as it were.

The atmosphere was extraordinary. Dr. Joseph ("Jack") Downing, a prominent psychiatrist from the San Francisco Bay Area, experienced with psychedelics, had come down as an observer. In a chapter he contributed to the book *Utopiates*, describing our project, he noted a highly unusual occurrence: a young woman in a psychotic state who simply arrived one day in Zihuatanejo and was supportively accepted into the community in such a way that her wild bouts of terror and paranoia were attenuated to a significant degree without the use of psychiatric medication.*

Tim guided some of the sessions, but much of the time he was away in Mexico City, handling the political and diplomatic work necessary to allow the operation to continue. He delivered a paper on our work to a meeting of Mexican psychiatrists. The reaction was frostily hostile, and a campaign was initiated to have our work stopped. Journalistic distortions and fabrications contributed to the problem. For example, an axe murder that had occurred in the area shortly before our arrival was promptly laid at the feet of the *gringos* and their *hongos alucinantes* by a local chief of police overzealous for promotion. Other accusations were made, some by applicants to the center who had been turned down—but anonymous accusations in a newspaper, once made, are difficult to refute. Our project also inadvertently attracted a sizeable number of uninvited Ameri-

---

* Joseph J. Downing, "Zihuatanejo: An Experiment in Transpersonative Living," in Richard Blum and Associates, eds. *Utopiates: The Use and Users of LSD-25* (New York: Atherton Press, 1964).

can marijuana smokers who camped out nearby, adding yet another layer of suspicion and notoriety.

Considering the history of the use of mind-altering plants and mushrooms in Mexico, we had assumed that that country would be more liberal than the United States. This belief was undoubtedly naive. Furthermore, we made the mistake of not securing Mexican medical supervision and cooperation. (We did not regard the psychedelic experience as a medical procedure requiring supervision.) We activated fears of exploitation by foreigners, even though our operation was ridiculously cheap and clearly unprofitable. However, for about six weeks the scheme ran according to plan with about thirty to forty participants—the first wave of several hundred who had been accepted. Almost all were overwhelmingly positive in their evaluation of their experience. The results exceeded our highest expectations.

One of Tim's creative inspirations was to build a ten-foot high tower-platform on the beach, open to the sea. Here, one person would be on a trip at all times. We thought of him or her as a sort of inner-space lighthouse, a beacon representing the highest state of consciousness; one could tune in to this "high witness" in order to recover one's bearings when overinvolved in the mundane, or when lost in the hellish bardos. Each morning and evening, someone else took over, and we would have a little ceremony, a changing of the celestial guard, the cosmic watcher of the day or night.

I spent an unforgettable night on the tower, watching the moon rise and travel over the bay, its silvery radiance reflecting from the murmuring surf. I watched it set behind the mountains as the pink-orange light of dawn suffused the sky. Swimming at night, one could move one's hands through the water and watch strings of pearly phosphorescent particles cascading from each fingertip. Hour-long electrical storms soundlessly shattered the sky into shards of yellow, turquoise, and violet.

During the day one could sit on the beach, and by field telephone order drinks from the bar, which would come down the hill on a tray moving by a pulley on a rope. Digging fingers and toes into the warm sand and opening the pores to the sun, you could discard the false masks of civilization and tumble into the strong, cool, and brilliant surf, awakening billions of sleeping cells to the eternal cycles of sun and sea and earth. The experiences of those days and nights were etched into memory with exquisite clarity and precision.

I believe that in Mexico we violated territorial instincts. Perhaps the Mexicans felt that we were there to do something that would be considered too crazy to do at home—and in a sense they were right. Medical and government authorities in the United States were condemning what we were doing and passing laws to make it illegal as fast as they could. It's as if your neighbor were to come to your yard and stand on his head. Even if he did no harm to your yard, you would wonder why he didn't do it in his own, and be naturally suspicious.

Two journalists arrived from Mexico City to do a story. They were curious about our project and very friendly. They drank with us, told stories, and exchanged jokes. One of them even took an LSD trip. After being with us for several days they announced that they were actually federal agents and gave us notice to leave the country within five days. The technical reason given was that we were running a business while only on tourist visas. Tim tried pulling all the strings he knew, with many phone calls to Mexico City, all to no avail. While we had been absorbed in paradise, our goose had been cooked.

The serene, almost otherworldly atmosphere of our little paradise was shattered. People started dispersing; there was sympathy, but also disappointment. Some guests had just arrived and had not yet had any sessions. They pleaded with us to have just one. Unwisely, to minimize their disappointment, we permitted it. Since the whole ambiance had been poisoned, most of these sessions were bad; some of them very bad.

One man developed a religious mania and shouted the Lord's Prayer at the top of his voice across the Zihuatanejo bay. Later he fell off some stone steps and fractured his jaw. He punched Tim out and bruised his ribs. It took four men to hold him down while Jack Downing gave him antipsychotic medication (which we normally never used).

Another man, for whom I was the reluctant guide, on the day after his session decided to walk home to Boston, taking off on foot and in underwear, heading toward the village. While everyone else was packing, we kept having to send someone out to bring him back from his long walk home. He was impervious to any rational persuasion. Once we got to the Mexico City airport, in the late evening hours, our restless traveler continued to pace up and down, tailed by tired staff members. He would go to the ticket counter and demand a ticket to infinity. The clerks politely asked him to return in the morning. Finally, by trickery and luck, we managed to get him into a taxi and to our hotel. But our troubles were not over. Running on manic energy, while everyone else was dead tired, he paced the streets, demanding a taxi to take him to Boston. We finally took him to the American hospital, where, to my surprise, after one last maniacal lunge, he meekly followed the nurse's orders to undress and get into bed.

This was the first time I understood something I was to experience personally and observe several times: under certain conditions, when all the internal structures maintaining our view of reality have been undermined, a person might well accept any available external structure as better than none at all. We learned later that this man stayed in the hospital for two weeks. He wrote us, stating that the experience, though painful at the time, had taught him some valuable lessons. Part of the reason for his excessive paranoia, we found out, was that he had come to Zihuatanejo against his employer's wishes. He was involved in national security work and feared that the drug might make him reveal classified information. This fear was enormously heightened when the *federales* arrived to evict us.

We regrouped our scattered and battered forces at the house of a friend in Mexico City. Tim arrived, bandaged and limping from his encounter with the religious fanatic. Dick Alpert and Peggy Hitchcock flew in from Boston. We had a long discussion about what had happened and debated what to do next. Several hundred people had signed up for the training and sent in deposits. We wanted to salvage the operation somehow, in view of the positive results we had obtained with the few we did take through the program before the final fiasco. So we decided to try to relocate somewhere else immediately.

Most of us returned to Massachusetts, to our house in Newton Center. A reconnaissance group consisting of Gunther Weil, David Levin, and Frank Ferguson was sent to the Caribbean. We had received an invitation from an American living on the island of Dominica, in the British West Indies. The initial reports of the scouting group sounded positive, so Tim took off. Pretty soon the reports coming back to the rest of us sounded very positive, fairly bubbling with enthusiasm. This was the place, Tim wired. We prepared to leave. A few days later, another wire: something had happened, the group was leaving Dominica. But they were going to the neighboring island of Antigua, which was much better anyway. So we should come down. And bring the morning-glory seeds (this was to be our LSD substitute).

I was the last of the group to arrive in Antigua, where a motley crew of fifteen had assembled. They included Gary Fisher, a psychologist from Los Angeles who had done pioneering work using LSD in the treatment of autistic children, and also his wife and children. Several other couples with children were there, as well as Tim's children. There was a familylike atmosphere, with excited speculations about pirate adventures. However, there was also a considerable amount of tension, some of it between Leary, Alpert, and myself, some generated by our repeated expulsions and what was emerging as a pattern of persecution.

We rented an empty hotel compound by the beach, ominously named "The Bucket of Blood." This was evidently someone's idea of a joke, associating it with pirate marauders, but the place had peculiar vibrations. Most of the sessions we had there were "bummers"; some were horrendous. Nevertheless, we strategized how to get the psychedelic training project going again. We rewrote the Tibetan Buddhist manual. We talked to all of the island's six medical doctors, trying to enlist their support for our venture, getting lukewarm responses at best. Moreover, when we talked to the British Governor of Antigua, he waved *Time* magazine, which carried a story on our Mexican fiasco, in our faces. He did not want a British protectorate to be associated with anything like that—

no, Sir! Judging by the *Time* article, we could hardly blame him.

Meanwhile, at the "Bucket of Blood," events had taken a sinister turn. Charles, one of the most gifted and competent members of our group, a veteran of many trips, who had never before had a negative experience of any consequence, went on such a freaky session that it became the last psychedelic he ever took. It shook everyone deeply to see Charles of all people get caught in such a nightmare. For several days we could not determine what was happening to him. He would sit morosely silent for hours, saying very little, apparently trusting no one except his girlfriend.

Finally, we pieced together that he had decided, in his madness, that the main opponent of our operation in Antigua was a certain black psychiatrist who was a lobotomy specialist, and very conservative. Charles wanted to sacrifice himself by offering to be lobotomized in exchange for our getting permission to stay and work there. One day, he actually started toward the capital in order to carry out this demented martyrdom. His girlfriend stayed with him constantly, gradually nursing him back to health, over the next several weeks. He did not, however, communicate with any of the rest of us for years. I found out that he reconverted to the Catholic Church—exemplifying again the pattern of grasping at any available strong structure from an experience of maximum disintegration. As far as I know, he never came anywhere near psychedelics again.

These events dealt the coup de grâce to our stay in the ill-fated "Bucket of Blood," in Antigua, and indeed in the Caribbean. Gary Fisher and I briefly explored the option of moving to the French-controlled island of Guadeloupe, but our money ran out after a week. Everyone returned to the States. Indeed, it seemed that Fate had sealed our attempted psychedelic training center forever. Escalating political sanctions and legal prohibitions by now had made open experimentation with psychedelics virtually impossible.

Leary, Alpert, and myself, together with a few others, moved to a huge estate in Millbrook, New York, owned by the Hitchcock brothers, where we established a research and training center for consciousness expansion without drugs. The Millbrook center, named the Castalia Foundation, became a sort of unofficial national headquarters for information and advocacy concerning psychedelics. It was also the center of an ever changing scene of magic and creativity, with extraordinary stories so far only partially told.* Other members of our little band of adventurers dispersed to different parts of the country to build careers and normal family lives. Raising children and having a mortgage does wonders for making pragmatists of us all.

Many erstwhile psychedelic voyagers, myself included, went on to study and practice meditative, yogic, and psychotherapeutic modalities of consciousness expansion during the 1970s and 1980s, becoming initiated in Hindu, Buddhist, Taoist, Christian, or shamanic traditions. Some have stopped using the botanical and chemical amplifiers, grateful for the opening vision they provided. Others continue their explorations into the many dimensions of consciousness and reality, absorbing the lessons learned from plant teachers, animal guides, ancestor spirits, human elders and gurus, wise artists, tricksters, and nature deities. I went on to a ten-year period of intense involvement in a Western esoteric school of light-fire yoga (Actualism) and subsequently immersed myself in the study and practice of shamanism. As for Tim Leary, "to hundreds of thousands of his friends and admirers, he remains one of the outstanding visionary geniuses of the twentieth century. To me he was the perfect exemplar of one of those who in the last of the *Psychedelic Prayers* are listed as likely to be closer to the Tao—"smiling men with bad reputations."†

* In part, the Millbrook story has been told in some of Leary's later books: *What Does Woman Want?* (Los Angeles: 88 Press, 1977); *Neuropolitics* (Los Angeles: Peace Press, 1977); and *Flashbacks* (Los Angeles: J. P. Tarcher, 1983). See also the whimsical memoir *Millbrook*, by Art Kleps (San Francisco: Bench Press, 1977).
† Ralph Metzner, Introduction to *Psychedelic Prayers*, 20.

The Esalen Institute, Sacred Mushrooms, and the Game of Golf

AN INTERVIEW WITH MICHAEL MURPHY BY ROBERT FORTE

RF: I'll start by saying what motivated me to compile a Festschrift for Tim. At a meeting in Switzerland commemorating LSD sponsored by the Swiss Academy of Medicine and Sandoz, whenever Tim's name, or the spirit of the sixties, or humanistic psychology, or transpersonal psychology came up, generally it was dismissed as nonscientific, radical Californian esotericism.

MM: Well, that's a Swiss perspective.

RF: That kind of sets the context for the book.

MM: It puts you in a warlike mode.

RF: A little bit, I suppose, yeah.

MM: I guess that haunts Tim Leary, the iconoclast, the rebel. It doesn't have to be in that mode.

Michael Murphy founded the Esalen Institute (with Richard Price) in 1962. He is the author of Golf in the Kingdom, The Kingdom of Shivas Irons, *and* The Future of the Body, *and coauthor (with George Leonard) of* The Life We Are Given.

RF: Tell me what you mean.

MM: Well, you know, you can be visionary without being revolutionary, although they often go together. But anyway, you're setting the dials.

RF: Right, I guess I am. Though I felt *they* set it up that way.

MM: But to do a Festschrift you don't *have* to do it that way. In other words, you're choosing to do this.

RF: Yes.

MM: OK. All right. I mean I'm not objecting, I'm just pointing it out.

RF: Right. That was my inclination: Tim busted loose and he's blamed for having set the field of drug research back twenty years. Lots of folks think he set the field *forward* twenty years.

MM: What about the Beatles? What about our great other musicians of the era? What about the Grateful Dead? What about—you know, Allen Ginsberg and company? What about Stan Grof? In other words, Tim's not alone.

RF: No, Tim's not alone.

MM: But there were mighty forces opening up consciousness. Much of it went far too far. But the culture assimilates, you know, digests this stuff, and we go up the spiral hopefully. So anyway, go ahead.

RF: What is it about that Irish spirit—his and yours—that caused such a ruckus thirty-five years ago?

MM: We both set out pursuing a vision of greater life, of greater human possibilities, and like all such visions of going beyond, of renewing, you run into the constraints of the given culture, the homeostasis of the social order, and there's resulting *Sturm und Drang*. It's a law of life. When you bear witness to greater possibilities and when you bring an energy forward that's going to change people's practices and ultimately, therefore, their ways of perceiving, and their feelings and their bodies, there's going to be the tendency to try to hold fast, to keep things as they are. It's normal. The Irish have been doing that now for about 1500 years. It seems to be genetic. I believe that it is. The English have still not figured out that when the Irish are deadpan, they're joking, and when they're smiling, they're deadly earnest. They still haven't figured that out.

RF: Somewhere I heard that one of the original visions of Esalen was for it to be a psychedelic initiation center.

MM: No, that's not right. I took an early stand. You know, temperamentally, Robert, I did not find drugs to be my allies. I had eight trips between '62 and '66 and I had the best folks with me on them. My first trip was alone with peyote. It was marvelous. Then Aldous Huxley gave me some Sandoz LSD and Laura, his wife, was my sitter down in Mexico. Those first two trips in '62 were just as we were starting Esalen's programs. Then Dick Alpert and Tim came to Esalen, and they gave me a trip—that was '64. It was mainly Dick—although Tim was there that night—with me and Dick Price. That was great. Then I had a wonderful trip over there at Myron Stoloroff and Willis Harman's place, the Institute for Advanced Studies. And that was wonderful. So I had wonderful sitters, but each trip got worse, more painful. The whole message was, "this is not good for you." So my last trip was in '66, and I just had those eight trips in there from '62 to '66.

RF: So you followed Alan Watts's advice: "When you get the message, hang up the phone." This raises the question of using psychedelics as a path in and of themselves, or whether they work best in the context of initiation. Even Jerry Garcia said his most intense and magical time with psychedelics lasted only about a year.

Could you say something about the effect of psychedelics on Esalen? Do you think they have been more, or less, consequential there than the hot springs, the mountains, or the ocean?

MM: Well, I think much of the influence of psychedelics at Esalen has been unfortunate. The place exploded in '62. I mean we had to keep scheduling extra programs. But psychedelics were not there in '62, '63, '64. There was talk about them, and there were these occasional trips like the one I had with Laura Huxley, but I felt constrained to go to Mexico to have that one. You know what I mean? It started going public I would say, on the grounds, big time, '65 maybe, but certainly '66, and by '67, the Summer of Love, our canyons were full—I mean it *exploded*, and to some extent we lost control of the place. I would say—'66 through '70—that was the most tumultuous, out-of-control time. It's a miracle that Esalen survived that period.

RF: There was an energy that was out of control and really dangerous, not the sort of positive disintegration of Dionysian madness.

MM: Out of control in terms of . . . I mean Charles Manson was developing his cult down at Lime Kiln Canyon. He would recruit his folks down there. That's a symptom of the age. The Hell's Angels would come through. We had a big confrontation with them. They came down in a very threatening way and we didn't have any police support. About 30 of them, one of their squadrons, black jackets, all stoned. They threatened to take the place over. These would be symptoms. We had at least three suicides I know of in the larger Esalen orbit when people were stoned and it just fed their depression. Those happened in and around Esalen in those years. The reason the institution survived was we had enough going for us to hold it all together. We were all in our thirties, unmarried, no kids, full of energy. It was a wild time. The seminars were always full, people were having great experiences. It was very exciting. But at the same time, as you know, many of those experiments in that period fell apart. In fact, most of the communes were falling apart by the late '70s. That's what led me to see that you needed life-long transformative practices.

Along the way, we were under surveillance by a number of agencies, the Food and Drug Administration and others. I met twice with the head of the Northern California FDA. to clarify what was going on, what our obligations were. Under the Bill of Rights, you cannot go in and search people's rooms if you're an innkeeper. So we were clear with everybody, our lawyers, everyone, that we were not obliged to go Gestapo-like into the seminarian rooms. But the great reason that our institute never went under—because there was a huge amount of drug use on the grounds—was, we prohibited any sale of drugs there or the use of any in workshops. We said that if we caught anybody in the act of taking drugs, they would be kicked off the property. And in fact we were kicking people out of there. You know, we had some criminals—I mean we had real drug dealing. We told them they couldn't come back. So we took that public stand, and it was in resonance with my own strong negative take toward psychedelics as a way forward into greater consciousness. I'd been meditating since 1950 and been to India, so that was, and that remains, my path; the non-drug route.

We never conceived of the place as a psychedelic research center. But we had seminars about psychedelics. And people were taking drugs down there, there's no doubt about it. But we kept announcing you cannot sell. You can look someone in the eye and know perfectly well that person's stoned, but you can't go and force him to have a blood test and then kick him out because of that.

At the same time Dick Price used psychedelics some in his own personal voyaging, but was with me in wanting to preserve the public viability of Esalen. In other words, we had to be law-abiding. He was completely with me on that. Psychedelic drugs were more of an ally for him, but they weren't for me.

RF: I was surprised that you were happy to contribute to this tribute to Leary, knowing that your attitude toward psychedelics was conservative. When I mentioned the idea back in July, I noticed a genuine enthusiasm in you.

MM: I just was expressing my love and admiration for Tim, that's what I thought. It's not psychedelics, it's Tim. I don't see any contradiction whatsoever. I'm saying that what we learned at Esalen is that psychedelics don't provide by themselves a path to these permanent graduations of human nature which I really want to work for—which I see as my life's work.

I have to say also that through psychedelics many people have had real openings into these great things. I mean all through history. I'm just telling about what happened in Big Sur and I'm telling about my own past, but I'm not talking about the intrinsic worth of psychedelics—if they're done right, in a ceremonial fashion with conscious, creative, and experienced folks.

Tim is a real pioneer and hero. That's all.

In principle I am for the idea of free exploration, and I always was attracted to Tim. I love his visionary spirit and that great Irish charm, and what he basically stood for. The same you could say about Fritz Perls. I mean I hated a lot of the things Fritz Perls did, but I so appreciated what I still believe is his true genius, as both a clinician and a theoretician, although he could be a mean son-of-a-bitch a lot of the time.

RF: Do you think psychedelics were the prime cause for the importation of Eastern meditational systems and philosophies in the early 1960s?

MM: No, I disagree. I became interested in all this at Stanford in 1950 studying with Frederic Spiegelberg. I watched this underground fire at Stanford during the '50s and it was not drugs at all. It was a readiness in the culture to go beyond the very tight upbringings all of us had had in our churches and synagogues. We were ready. I mean hundreds of thousands of Americans were ready to break out. I remember Spiegelberg's lectures, I mean, my God, he would fill every auditorium, speaking about the *Vedas*, the *Upanishads*, the great Buddhist scriptures, Ramana Maharishi, and Sri Aurobindo. You cannot credit it first and foremost to psychedelics. Psychedelics certainly fed into it. But I would say it was *one* of the prime causes.

RF: More synchronistic than causal?

MM: Well, it was one of the prime causes. I think you would have to name five or six primary reasons why the whole thing opened up the way it did in the '60s and psychedelics would be one of those five or six.

RF: OK, you've named two: the constrained upbringings in the '50s and psychedelics. What are some of the others?

MM: The exposure to Eastern thought and practice, to shamanism, to esoteric Judaism, Christianity, and Islam. All those started to pour in, Neoplatonism and the rest of it. Then the tremendous impact of—it was a package that would consist of—existential therapies, humanistic and transpersonal psychologies ... Maslow, Rogers ... It was going to erupt. Put yourself back in the fifties with psychoanalysis and behaviorism in the saddle. There was bound to be an eruption, and it became a very popular movement. Then you had all these dozens of major somatic disciplines appearing—you know, from Rolfing to Feldenkrais, to Charlotte Selver; they just exploded on the scene. All of these events happening at once. You had the real disillusionment about government that came from the Vietnam war. Then this explosion of music. There was so much. The Beatles invented so much new music. The biggest explosion of new invention in music since the invention of jazz. You could go on. There were maybe eight or nine major events. But it certainly did not depend upon psychedelics. That fed into it. The time was right for the culture to open up. All of those things contributed.

RF: Wasson was the first to suggest that religion may have originated out of early humans eating psychedelic mushrooms. Terence McKenna has recently jazzed up Wasson's theory on the origin of religion, suggesting that mushrooms are the missing link in evolution that accounts for this exponential rise in brain size and culture and religion and so on. So do you think we saw a recapitulation of this in the '60s?

MM: First of all, I don't even believe those theories. It gives much too short shrift to all our other activities. I mean, look, Robert, for twenty-five years I have been getting reports of mystical experiences on *golf courses* because of *Golf in the Kingdom*. I call golf "a mystery school for Republicans." If you can have such experiences playing golf, think of all the other activities ... Take the initiations in the great caves of Lascaux and elsewhere, you know, to come into rapport with the hunt, and all the shamanic rituals, I mean, God, swimming in the cold sea, and going on those long runs, going to the mountain tops, and all of the others. No, I simply don't buy those theories.

RF: Confrontation with birth and death and sex and other forces.

MM: All of that, in our day, produces these incredible openings to the astonishment of being and all of these powers. There's is a reductionist theory. There are higher reductionisms, and I would say Wasson's and McKenna's is a higher reductionism. I just don't believe it. Psychedelics certainly had a role, no doubt. And sometimes a ritualized role. But as the *only?* Give me a break.

I would say it's in the nature of this universe to keep graduating. We're in the graduation business. We graduate to new levels of complexity and awareness. It's been going on for fifteen billion years or more in this universe. Since the first life appeared it's been going for 3–4 billion years on Earth. In the human race it's been going on from the beginning. To say it's all one mechanism—I say in *The Future of the Body* to watch for the fallacy of single mediation. It's the fact of our forward march, this opening up, of this stupendous event of the universe opening to higher and higher levels of functioning, more complex orders, ecstasies—reclaiming the world's latent divinity. To say it all depends on drugs is just ridiculous on the face of it. Forgive me for getting so heated up here.

RF: Your book *The Future of the Body* is the most complete assemblage of scientifically confirmed mystical or metanormal experience there is. Charlie Tart calls it "the most important work on the relationship between mind and body ever written." I've not read all 785 pages, but so far there's not one mention of psychedelic experience. That's incredible.

MM: No, I've never dealt with it. Probably in a new edition I would. After seven and a half years it was time, finally, to put the book to bed. So in that respect it does show my predilections, there's no doubt about it. I had it vetted by various critics; I did that with each chapter and then the book as a whole. We had two conferences on the book before it was published to get criticism of it, to make it as solid as I could.

RF: And in these conferences this omission of psychedelics didn't come up? Did you deliberately leave that out?

MM: Well, it was just finally, you know, at the end of the day I'm not that interested. I didn't have any big sections on tantric sex either, and *that* I could have expanded. The psychedelics I certainly could have put in. It was partly just my bias; I have to admit it. But it was not a kind of policy decision or anything like that. I had worked on that thing seven and a half years and it was time to get it published. Also its size. We had cut it in half. So, all of that contributed, but it was not a policy decision to leave psychedelics out. I would say it's just a shortcoming of the book.

RF: I'll say. *The Future of the Body* with no sex and no drugs either? Will there be a second volume?

MM: I doubt it. I'm writing a sequel to *Golf in the Kingdom*, in which I mention mushrooms at Muirfield.

RF: You do?

MM: Yes.

RF: I should send you my chapter on it.

MM: Well send it to me. I mention it once in a manuscript by one Mortimer Crail, who was a professor of Classics at Edinburgh in a book written in 1893 entitled *Golf: Its Roots in God and Nature*, telling about a case of apparent demonic possession during a tournament for pairs at Muirfield. It was attributed variously to demonic possession, a hemorrhage of the psyche that produces a phantom, or the mushrooms served at lunch at the Muirfield Clubhouse. I have you to thank for that reference.

RF: I have a whole section on the origin of golf, that golf was originally a cover for mushroom hunting.

MM: Where? In Scotland?

RF: In Scotland, yes.

MM: This is an incredible revelation.

RF: A man at Muirfield told me "golf" is really an acronym. It means to GO Look For—mushrooms of course, which were prohibited by the orthodoxy. The game was invented to disguise their searches in the meadows and links land. He showed me an old manuscript he kept carefully hidden.

MM: I could refer to your text, whether it's published or not.

Listen, I would love it. I would just mention it in passing. GO Look For.

RF: Yes, to GO Look For. You see, I found the mushrooms at Muirfield. They grow there naturally. Psychedelic mushrooms I mean.

MM: Well you told me this.

RF: And played two under par from that point on.

MM: This is what inspired that reference.

RF: It finally got to be too much. Fortunately the fellow who gave me the mushrooms found me near the 17th green, on the ground, in ecstasy. He took me back to his home where I would be safe and warm. He cared for me till I came down and told me the story of the origin of golf.

MM: Oh God, Robert, you've got to publish this. Listen, can I . . . What's the title of your book?

RF: *Whole in One.*

MM: I might refer to this.

RF: Tim should have known. If he wanted to transform society, he shouldn't have insulted and antagonized the war mongers the way he did. He could have simply and quietly proved that higher consciousness makes life more meaningful in terms Republicans could relate to and aren't threatened by. I suppose he tried that in the famed "She Comes in Colors" *Playboy* interview, but golf is more important than sex to Republicans. If word got out that small doses of LSD or psilocybin improved concentration, visual acuity, reaction time, and therefore improved golf scores, there could be another epidemic.

Your current madness, Michael, as you put it, is bodily transformation.

MM: But not cryogenics or something like that, no. I mean the graduation of the flesh into more luminous forms of embodiment. I like to talk of it as the human flesh mutating in accompaniment with mutation or the graduation of consciousness. Now I was oriented to that, Robert, as you know, by Sri Aurobindo, but the more I look into it, the more fertile it seems. That's what my current book is about, by the way.

RF: Your sequel to *Golf in the Kingdom*?

MM: Yes. *The Kingdom of Shivas Irons*, meaning this metanormal embodiment, where Shivas seems to have transcended both life and death as we know them now. In other words, death will become a new deal and life too if we could live in this new flesh or if you want to call it "new spirit bodies." I actually believe that.

RF: What happens to the physical body?

MM: I think just as consciousness by slow degress and sometimes large degrees can develop, you know, can expand, can graduate, however you want to describe it, can be suffused more completely in the light of God—so can the body. But the body then begins to change. Oh God, don't get me started on this. That's what *The Future of the Body* is pointed to. I'm going to write a follow-up volume to that. Not Volume II in encyclopedic form, but a more speculative book. For the rest of my life I'll be working on that.

Euphorion Returned

Claudio Naranjo

I am pleased to participate in Timothy Leary's Festschrift, though it puts me in the position of having to disagree with Tim's view in the IFIF days. Indeed, though a Festschrift is often taken as a stimulus for a premortem epitaph, I think that it would not be honoring Tim Leary, the seeker of truth and liberation, to flatter him through beautification of his public image. I, at least, feel that I owe him a less conventional response and hope that in the following I can convey both my appreciation and some criticism. I owe him true communication for the simple reason that he is still among the living, and I feel that I will be writing to him and not only about him.*

I anticipate being both warm and polemical, since I, too, communed in the spirit of the sixties, yet it has been a long time—I no longer believe in the deregulation of drugs. I always admired Tim's talent and empathized with his dream of "a better world through

---

Claudio Naranjo, M.D., is an internationally renowned psychiastrist and teacher of transformational disciplines. He is the author of The One Quest, The Psychology of Meditation *(with Robert Ornstein),* The Healing Journey, Techniques of Gestalt Therapy, Ennea-Type Structures, The End of Patriarchy, *and other books and articles.*

* This piece was first written in 1995—ed.

chemistry," yet I think that in his desire to be a youth hero he was a bit too impetuous in his defiance of the authorities and the medical profession, and I am inclined to think that his all-too-impetuous plea for freedom has proven to be a mistake.

Yes: conservatism has set in, and the psychedelic revolution, by becoming too "revolutionary," was aborted. And we cannot put all the blame on the establishment and on the forces of darkness. Different attitudes would have yielded different results, and already in the sixties I thought that it would be better not to make such a fuss about psychedelics, but keep the secret for those ready to partake of it—channeling the new resource through the appropriate therapeutic, spiritual, and perhaps even educational networks. I even sent word to Tim about my thoughts when in the midsixties Frank Barron inquired about my views of recent developments.

Yet I cannot blame Tim very much, because we all get a bit fanatical at the time of our initial liberation. I have been saying for a long time that it is unavoidable that when spirit first shines upon us this makes our ego take most of the credit and talk excitedly about it. We know that sometimes the excitement of one serves to kindle that of many others in such a way that it speeds them into a path of transformation; yet we also know that at other times the "post-illuminative inflation" of the sorcerer's apprentice is quite destructive. I cannot presume to be wise enough to know how relative the weights of + and - will compare on Tim's day of reckoning—yet was not Tim's disdain a major determinant in the alienation of the profession that would have constituted the normal channel in our society for this new resource? Granted, the world of psychiatry has been rather dull and dogmatic, but could the profession not have been educated instead of being shocked into the defensive?

I certainly must give credit to the anarchic impulse of one who sees through the straitjacket of the patriarchal world and has glimpses of true democracy. Yet for many years now I have not thought it functional to push for the democratization of drugs. In spite of having launched the slogan of "democratization of psychotherapy," I think we would have gone much farther in that direction if we had been willing to take a step at a time. (I was present at a meeting where a plea for the legalization of MDMA was the issue—and while everyone pushed for "freedom" I insisted that it should be a prescription drug in the same category as the amphetamines. Of course, it was soon forbidden—to the loss of those in the greatest need.)

I am well aware that I sound like a sexagenarian and no longer like a teenager. I have learned to compromise in certain things. Yet I appreciate the beauty of the noncompromising attitude of Tim, and the beauty of his near-suicidal courage as he preached his dream, exposing the forces of resistance for what they are. Perhaps Jung would have said that he was possessed by the Christ archetype. By letting himself be crucified he has certainly drawn attention to the extent of the psychedelic taboo and the prohibitionist society.

As I think of Tim's willingness to step into the role of a scapegoat some two decades ago, I think of Goethe's "Euphorion"—that beautiful creature born of the visionary romance between Faust and the mythical Helen of Troy. Though Euphorion in the Faust drama stands for a stage in the inner path, we know that Goethe associated him with Byron, whom he admired more than any other contemporary poet.

"Let me be leaping! / Let me be springing! / To the wide ether / Would I were winging," exclaims Euphorion as he indeed leaps in such a way that Faust fears disaster may overtake him. "Hold ye my hand not! / Loose ye my garments! / Are they not mine?" he responds, and goes on frolicking and bounding so high that his concerned parents (those who had crossed all boundaries!) fear his daring and madness will be his undoing. Like Byron and the Byronesque Tim, Euphorion's way of being in the world is—to use the character's words—"fight and fall," and he warns Faust and Helen that he will not hang back. As he casts himself into the air for the last time, his head radiates and a luminous trail glides after him—while the chorus calls him Icarus as if to remind us of still another embodiment of suicidal enthusiasm through the memory of the one whose waxen wings melted as he soared too close to the sun. How can anybody deeply disapprove of a euphoric excess that seems inseparable from spiritual youth? It impresses us as no less archetypal than the Faustian seeking spirit, a sort of divine madness put into human life by providential design.

As you see, I agree with the contention that in the appropriate set and setting psychedelic drugs have enormous transformation potential, and yet, in spite of great appreciation for Tim's talents and for his intuition of what psychedelics could do for social transformation, I am inclined to think that we are not to blame the dominant ideology of the day that he has been cast as a fool. Maybe it is a matter of perspective and unbiased understanding. I think that a fool he was, back then—though one, like Don Quixote, more interesting than average humanity.

Let us hope that his heroism of the sixties, however contaminated by hubris it may have been, is in the end not lost. Let us hope that the day comes when looking back on these decades we see Hegel's dialectics validated and understand that an excess opposite to that of the repressive establishment was necessary before a cultural synthesis could arise.

A Few
Memorable Moments

Mimi Raleigh

I've only known Dr. Timothy Leary for six years, but I feel as if I've known him my whole life. My mother (a 1957 Radcliffe grad wearing purple sunglasses and love beads) idolized Dr. Tim, while my father (the consummate businessman) frowned on his and her "misbehavior."

Years later, after I graduated from Harvard and Cornell and my mother passed away, I began dating a wonderful guy—Tom Davis. On what will always be remembered as a very special evening, Tom invited me to join him and his friend Tim for dinner. We were having a delightful time when I excused myself and went to the ladies room. Tim then turned to Tom and said, "Marry that girl." Fortunately Tom, as usual, took his advice—thank goodness. I never say "thank God" anymore because an innocent "oh my God" in front of Tim once led us into a six-hour door-slamming discussion on Catholicism, as only two Scotch-motivated Irish Catholics could.

A year after Tom and I were married, we kidnapped Tim after *Saturday Night Live* and his cryogenics lecture, to bring him to our

---

Mimi Raleigh is a graduate of Harvard and Cornell University. She works as a replacement veterinarian in upstate New York where she lives with her husband, Tom, four cats and two dogs.

house in upstate New York. As we passed Millbrook, a flock of wild turkeys passed in front of us on the Taconic. We were all thrilled— a magical moment. All of a sudden I felt my mother's presence next to me in the back seat as Tom and Tim were deep in a combative conversation in the front. Silently I said, "I know Mom, I wish you were here with us, I'm so happy." At that point, Tim's left hand reached into the back and grabbed mine. He said, "Say hello to your mother for me." My hair stood on end. It was a powerful moment. The wonder of the evening continued as Tim stood proudly and read a passage of *Ulysses* to me as the sun rose.

Once wishing I could bottle his happiness and enthusiasm, I asked him if he believed people were born happy or worked to achieve it. He, I found out, was born with that contagious lust for life and knowledge.

No one has ever challenged me or stimulated me more intellectually, spiritually, musically, generationally, or emotionally than Timothy has. I can only wish some day to be as young and energetic as Tim. He is more than my friend—he's family.

Farewell/Greetings to Timothy Leary

Thomas Riedlinger

Dear Timothy:

Yesterday I heard again that song which says you're not dead but only "outside looking in." In truth you've been dead now for over a year. Since I know that you didn't believe that your personal consciousness was going to survive your body's death, it would seem that the Timothy Leary game has finally come to an end without entering overtime. Yet here I am, writing this letter to you on a lovely clear morning in early December 1997. I'm sitting alone on a beach near Olympia, Washington, my back against a driftwood log with Puget Sound glittering blue straight ahead and an evergreen forest behind me. It is warmer than normal for this time of year, with a gentle breeze rising and falling like breath all around. There is a pleasant smell of moss and leafy loam and mushrooms

Thomas J. Riedlinger, M.T.S., F.L.S., is a writer and lecturer, a fellow of the Linnean Society of London, and a graduate of Harvard Divinity School. His published works include The Sacred Mushroom Seeker: Essays for R. Gordon Wasson *and articles appearing in the* Journal of Humanistic Psychology, Journal of Psychoactive Drugs, Journal of Transpersonal Psychology, Medical Hypotheses, Gnosis, *and* Shaman's Drum.

mingled with the salt sea tang. In this cradle of peace and contentment I let my mind wander, remembering you.

"Let's have some fun," you used to say at the start of new projects.
I distinctly remember the fun that we had in July 1993 at the annual
conference of the Association for Humanistic Psychology in San
Diego, when you and I and two of the students who worked with
you at Harvard, George Litwin and Gunther Weil, presented a panel
discussion on your early work in psychology. Afterward, back at your
home in Beverly Hills, I asked if it really were true, as you'd written
in *Changing My Mind, Among Others*, that your life had been "a
faithful, dutiful follow-up" to the work of Gustav Theodor Fechner.
You answered yes, for the reason that Fechner, a nineteenth-
century physics professor in Germany, had pioneered the scientific
field of psychophysics, which inspired your own work in
neurophysics. Furthermore, Fechner, like you, had a midlife mystical experience that altered his view of the world forever. But while
yours was induced by ingesting sacred mushrooms, his resulted from
infirmity. Almost blinded by an optical experiment in 1840, Fechner
languished for over a year with his eyes bandaged in a darkened room.
One afternoon in October 1842 he impulsively tore off the bandages,
rose from his bed, and went outside into his garden. What he saw
there seemed, he later wrote in *Nanna, or the Soul-Life of Plants*,

> like a glimpse beyond the boundary of human experience. Every
> flower beamed upon me with a peculiar clarity, as though into
> the outer light it was casting a light of its own. To me the
> whole garden seemed transfigured, as though it were not I but
> nature that had just arisen. . . . I thought I saw an inward light
> as the source of the outward clarity of the flowers, and within
> that the spiritual production of colors which in the flowers
> were merely outwardly translucent. I had no doubt then that I
> saw the shining of the plant souls, and I thought: So it must
> seem in the garden which lies behind the walls of this world;
> and all the earth as well as each body in the earth, is a fence
> which separates outsiders from this garden.

I asked your opinion of Fechner's most popular book, *On Life*

After Death. To my surprise you said you'd never read it. On returning home to Boston I sent you a copy. What you thought of it
I never heard. But when I and my future wife, Beverly, stopped by
to see you in November 1995, about six months before your death,
I noticed it shelved with a few other books within reach of your
work station. The letter I sent you along with that book included
the following passage from William James's introduction to an English edition of *On Life After Death* in which he describes Fechner's
afterlife theory:

> Movements can be superimposed and compounded, the smaller
> on the greater, as wavelets upon waves. This is true in the
> mental as well as the physical sphere. Speaking physiologi-
> cally, we may say that a general wave of consciousness rises out
> of a subconscious background, and that certain portions of it
> catch the emphasis, as wavelets catch the light. The whole pro-
> cess is conscious, but the emphatic wavetips of the conscious-
> ness are of such contracted span that they are momentarily
> insulated from the rest. They realize themselves apart, as a
> twig might realize itself, and forget the parent tree. Such an
> insulated bit of experience leaves, however, when it passes away,
> a memory of itself. The residual and subsequent conscious-
> ness becomes different for its having occurred. On the physi-
> cal side we say that the brain process that corresponded to it
> altered permanently the future mode of action of the brain.
>
> Now, according to Fechner, our bodies are just wavelets
> on the surface of the earth. We grow upon the earth as leaves
> grow upon a tree, and our consciousness arises out of the whole
> earth-consciousness, just as within our consciousness an em-
> phatic experience arises, and makes us forget the whole back-
> ground of experience without which it could not have come.
> But as it sinks again into that background it is not forgotten.
> On the contrary, it is remembered and, as remembered, leads
> a freer life, for it now combines, itself a conscious idea, with
> the innumerable, equally conscious ideas of other remembered
> things. Even so is it when we die, with the whole system of our
> outlived experiences. During the life of our body, although

they were always elements in the more general enveloping earth-consciousness, yet they were themselves unmindful of the fact. Now, impressed on the whole earth-mind as memories, they lead the life of ideas there, and realize themselves no longer in isolation, but along with all the similar vestiges left by other human lives, entering with these into new combinations, affected anew by experiences of the living, and affecting the lives of the living in their turn.

Fechner's afterlife theory evolved from his concept of souls. By his definition, a soul is "a unified being which, in our case as in every other, is evident only to itself, luminous to itself, to every other eye obscure, including in itself at least sense perceptions, above which, in proportion as it rises in the scale of consciousness, higher and higher relations develop." (This and all following Fechner quotes are from *On Life After Death*.) The soul of a human being is "the conscious principle and bond of a circle of bodily activities which . . . [in] sleep sink below the threshold above which consciousness shines," and on waking "rise above it." It is not strictly identical with consciousness but rather appears to experience consciousness differently above and below the threshold. Below the threshold it participates with all other terrestrial souls, including those of plants and animals as well as human beings, in comprising the soul of the earth. In Fechner's opinion, the souls of human beings when their bodies die disperse into the earth soul. Echoing through nature as a kind of spiritual waveform, they induce new relationships with other souls living and dead by intersecting them and causing what today we know as interference patterns, a component of holography. In this state, according to Fechner, we achieve immortality. For in life a man (or woman) experiences nature "through the windows of his senses, and draws fragmentary knowledge of it as in little buckets." But after death,

> when his bodily frame sinks into decay, the spirit, fettered and encumbered no longer, will roam throughout nature in unbound liberty. Then he will feel the waves of light and sound not only as they strike his eyes and ears, but as they glide along

Beverly Jean Jenden-Riedlinger, Timothy Leary,
and Thomas Riedlinger, 1995

in the oceans of air and of ether; he will feel not only the breathing of the wind and the heaving of the sea against his body
bathing in them, but float along through the air and sea himself; he will no longer walk among verdant trees and fragrant
meadows, but consciously pervade the fields, and forests, and
men as they walk about them.

James's own thoughts on the subject appear in his book-length
essay *Human Immortality*. In it he acknowledges Fechner's great influence on him, as you did in *Changing My Mind, Among Others*.
Others haven't been so generous. Many Fechnerian concepts have
been surfacing in recent years without being credited to him, in
areas such as consciousness theory, morphogenetic field theory and
especially the Gaia theory of planetary consciousness. Sooner or
later these oversights are bound to be corrected. I'll leave that for
others to do, as it remains for future scholars to investigate and

deconstruct the basic correspondence between Fechner's psycho-physical ideas and your neural circuit theory.

In the meantime, Fechner's writings are sufficient in themselves to help alleviate my sadness at your death. That is why I came here, to this beautiful place on a beautiful day, my heart open to nature, to experience your presence in the earth soul as it penetrates my own. As Emerson put it so well in his infamous Harvard Divinity School Address of 1838: "We mark with light in the memory the few interviews we have had . . . with souls that made our souls wiser; that spoke what we thought; that told us what we knew; that gave us leave to be what we inly were."

So farewell, Timothy—and greetings! Our paths will intersect again, I'm sure.

Godfather

WINONA RYDER

Winona Ryder and brother Uri with Timothy, March 1996

Three months after I was born my dad, who was Tim's archivist, went to see him in Switzerland where Tim was living in exile after escaping prison and being called "the most dangerous man in the world" by Nixon, who was furiously trying to hunt him down.

My dad and Tim took acid and went skiing and my dad pulled out a picture of me—the first one ever taken (I was a day old)—and showed it to Tim and asked if he would be my godfather. Tim said, "Sure."

We didn't meet until seven years later, after Tim was

Winona Ryder, Timothy Leary's goddaughter, is an award-winning film actress who has performed in twenty films, including The Age of Innocence, Little Women, *and* The Crucible.

released from prison and came to visit us on our commune up in Mendocino. We were walking on a dusty road on a remote mountain ridge. It was sunset and we were holding hands. I looked up at him and said, "They say you're a mad scientist."

Tim just smiled and said, "I know." I think he liked the sound of that.

Around the time I became a teenager I wanted to be a writer. This of course thrilled Tim and we constantly talked about books. My favorite literary character was Holden Caulfield, his was Huck Finn. We talked about the similarities between the two characters—especially their feelings of alienation from polite society. I wanted to catch all the kids falling off the cliff and Tim wanted to light out for the territory. It was a time when I was in my first throes of adolescence and experiencing that kind of alienation. And talking to Tim was the light at the end of the tunnel.

He really understood my generation. He called us "free agents in the Age of Information."

What I learned from Tim didn't have anything to do with drugs but it had everything to do with getting high. His die-hard fascination with the human brain was not all about altering it, but about using it to its fullest. And he showed us that that process—that journey—was our most important one. However we did it, as long as we did it. "You are the owner and operator of your brain," he reminded us.

Tim was a huge influence on me—not just with his revolutionary ideas about human potential, but as someone who read me stories, encouraged me, took me to baseball games—you know, godfather stuff. He was the first person outside my family—who you never tend to believe while growing up—to make me believe I could do anything. He had an incredible way of making you feel special and completely supported.

F. Scott Fitzgerald wrote a letter to his daughter in which he said that he hoped his life had achieved some sort of "epic grandeur." Tim's life wasn't "some sort of" epic grandeur. It was *flat-out* epic grandeur.

It's easy sometimes to get lost in all the drug stuff that Tim's famous for—all the "turn on, tune in, drop out" stuff, especially in a society that loves a sound bite. But that wasn't Tim's only legacy. It was his vitality, enthusiasm, curiosity, humor and humanity that made Tim great—and those are the *real* ingredients of a mad scientist.

Climbing Jacob's Ladder

ZALMAN SCHACHTER-SHALOMI

Tim,

You may not get the credit or for that matter get blamed for what you did. But you did deep and far-reaching subversion of the old architectural cosmology and the accompanying rule of the rationalistic academic-intellectual hierarchy.

Because of LSD and other substances and—and this is essential—the way in which you showed us how to sacramentalize our relation to them and to their openings we learned that one can make mind moves and look at the shifting panorama from any perspective one wants. I can still hear your mantra, "You can be anything you want" from that record you made at Gerd's.

Did you know that the very day on which LSD was invented was also the day of the Ghetto Uprising in Warsaw? I feel that there is some profound connection here, the words for which elude me.

Zalman Schachter-Shalomi is a rabbi who received ordination from Lubavitch. He is the author of From Age-ing to Sage-ing *and is considered by many to be the founder of what is now known as Jewish Renewal. Reb Zalman is open, fluid, and energetic and steeped in Yiddishkeit and Torah Judaism. He now teaches at Naropa Institute in the Chair of World Wisdom.*

The trickster gods used you well in prison and in flight. Here, too, you taught us to see past the facades of law and order. You do care about life and health, harmony between all creatures of this planet and who knows what other forms of life. I remember that during the night you initiated me you were concerned about how people will use this most powerful "transporter," how kids would not know if they were not gently shown how.

Those kids are now getting ready to get ready to retire. What are they going to do with their awareness? Maslow at his end had the right idea. Check out what's ahead and spend some time in that consciousness. Oh if Castalia would be a retirement home! What a high ecstasy count in that place. Strobes and music, color organs, fine incense, a lot of loving touch, Terry McKenna as dietician, and the intimacy of shared is-ness. We might surf the Intranet.

Your fantastic introspection made you surf the information highway of our nervous system and talk about it—even as a stand-up philosopher—tripping through chakras, ancient texts, symbols, and myths—raising kundalini.

And you understood that we are getting the global spinal column together and beginning to raise the kundalini in it. The againsters have reason to fear, but not the pornography on the net. That is only the global kundalini at the second chakra. Wait! We are climbing Jacob's Ladder. What a vista when we get up to chakra four and more.

And you wanted more. You found that in the infinitesimal there was the nexus of the infinite and the cosmic. I suppose you can't wait until you get to do your head with a being from the implicate dimensions.

Thank you, Tim, for modeling the guy at the sky light, the bodhisattva. You helped us get ready for the third millennium while you moved on to the fifth or more.

Who are you, really, masked Anthropos? May you live long and prosper!

A hug to you from Zalman.

LSD: Let's Save Democracy?

AN INTERVIEW WITH PHILIP SLATER
BY ROBERT FORTE

RF: This conversation might be something of a prologue to a book on Timothy Leary. Although you never knew him, there are some interesting parallels between your life and his. First of all, you worked on an LSD research project at Harvard seven years before Tim arrived there. Then, after you attained some prominence in the academic world, you dropped out of an academic career at a prestigious university. You've written about contemporary culture in a book that helped to define the humanistic movement of the sixties and seventies and that became a bestseller, *Pursuit of Loneliness*. You've also written *The Wayward Gate*, which discusses humans' failure to perceive what does not fall within their worldview; you've written about *Wealth Addiction;* and you've written about the state of American democracy in *A Dream Deferred*. You are a living example of the best that the social movement of the sixties offered. First let's talk about your early work at Harvard with LSD that was sponsored by the CIA.

Philip Slater is the author of the 1970 bestseller The Pursuit of Loneliness. *From 1950 to 1952, while a Harvard graduate student, he unwittingly assisted in CIA-sponsored LSD studies. He is now a novelist and a playwright who lives in northern California.*

PS: OK. I had done a little research at the hospital, which is now called Mass Mental Health Center. It was then the Boston Psycho-pathic Hospital. I heard that they were getting funds from a foundation to study a drug that nobody had heard of at that time. The drug was something that would make you psychotic for a brief period of a day; you would learn what kind of psychotic you would be if you became psychotic. This wasn't necessarily the official view of the drug, but it was what everybody talked about—everybody who was involved in the project and who later took the drug. It was the scuttle-butt around the hospital. There was a group that met every day up in the occupational therapy department which consisted of the OT director, the recreational director, a nurse, a psychiatrist, an x-ray technician, a social worker, and various other people from time to time. We hung out together and occasionally went out for drinks and so forth. So a lot of those people were interested, as well as a couple of Harvard graduate student researchers like myself. When I heard about this drug it sounded fascinating so I wanted to be on the project. Those who were on the project were going to be the first subjects so we would know what the hell we were dealing with. I was number four in the series. It was a very clinical orientation: two people following you around with clipboards taking down everything you said, making observations about you. We started at eight o'clock in the morning. At eleven you had an intake interview with the admit-ting psychiatrist of the hospital, who then wrote a diagnosis; later on you had a therapeutic interview. We did various studies as time went on. I did a study, for example, on the differences between people who took it alone and people who took it in groups of three or four, and found, as you might expect, that the people who took it in groups had a lot better time. They were diagnosed either manic or schizo-affective, whereas people who took it alone tended to be diagnosed as depressive or schizoid or something else.

RF: How did you recruit your subjects?

PS: They volunteered. They were all volunteers.

RF: Were they told that they were going to be given something that would induce a temporary psychosis?

PS: Well, my memory is a little bit hazy on that. But they knew it was going to affect them mentally in some way.

RF: One of the popular misconceptions is that Leary was fired from Harvard for giving LSD to undergraduate students and of course that's not true. Not only did he never do LSD research at Harvard—he worked with psilocybin—but he never involved undergraduates in the study. However, undergraduates were involved in your studies.

PS: Out of 150 subjects that we had, I would say 90 of them were undergraduates. I did a study of people in groups of four as part of my ongoing quantitative research at that time, and I think there were six or eight groups. I'm sure there were at least 32, probably 40. They were all undergraduates.

RF: Did this research instigate any kind of community from having shared this extraordinary experience together?

PS: It varied with everybody. A lot of these people we never saw again. They came, they got their twenty-five bucks or whatever, and went home. I think the people in the hospital who were closer to the project developed a little psychedelic group as it were. And then there were individual people who were very taken with it. One of our subjects was Ralph Blum. I don't know if you know of him.

RF: Ralph Blum who wrote *The Book of Runes*?

PS: *The Book of Runes*, yeah, that's Ralph. He was one of our more verbal subjects. And I know there was another one who became a psychiatrist later on, but I don't think he had a good experience. I'm sure there were other people who became interested and were affected by the experience; certainly we were. We did things like take it out on our own, sneak little bits out.

RF: This is 1952—

PS: '52, '53.

RF: This was before Huxley wrote *The Doors of Perception*, before Wasson had discovered the sacred mushroom in Mexico.

PS: You know, it's interesting, because *The Doors of Perception* was published in '54 but people knew about it then. Hyde knew about it, because I know he quoted it. Robert Hyde was the head of the project. Hyde, as you know, was the first person to take LSD in the United States, and he was my teacher. I initially became involved through taking a graduate course at the hospital with him. It was a fascinating course in psychopathology. He was a great teacher and had a brilliant, really free-ranging mind that could go all over from psychology to cultural-historical things. I learned more from him than from anybody else at Harvard. He just could make connections.

RF: Is he still alive?

PS: I would be very surprised if he was still alive. He was probably in his fifties then, forty years ago. So he'd be very, very old. He's been retired for—the last time I asked anybody about him, he'd been retired already for five or ten years, so he may even be older than I remember. But he liked to try different things. I remember one time we were celebrating something or other. We had a little party up at this bar around the corner, and we spiked the punch with LSD and people realized afterward that they had had enormous quantities of LSD and an enormous quantity of alcohol. We realized then that there was kind of a negative relationship between the two, that they tended to cancel each other out.

RF: It is remarkable that there you were in the early 1950s giving LSD to Harvard undergraduates and nothing resulted from that in terms of social movement, controversy, or visionary breakthroughs. Tim Leary comes along a few years later and there's an uproar and a movement beginning to take form. You were still there at Harvard. Was there a difference in Harvard between 1952 and 1958 or '59?

PS: I think he created the culture. Not single-handedly, but he was caught up in it in a different way. Our little group went way beyond the psychotomimetic definition of the drug, and we had a lot of different experiences with it, and were bonded by it very much. People who had it felt closer to each other because of it. But I don't think we gave it any real spiritual significance.

RF: Was "spiritual significance" even remotely in the vocabulary in the early 1950s in Cambridge?

PS: No, not really. Because everything was taking place in this completely clinical setting. I spent a couple of hours of my first trip on the disturbed ward, which sounds weird and it was, but I hung out there all the time anyway. I was doing research there and so on. I felt very comfortable, and I knew all the patients and everything. But that's the kind of environment we were in. It was very clinical.

RF: What about sexuality? Did that change in your subjects?

PS: I don't think so. There was always sexual content in people's verbalizations, but . . .

RF: I'm surprised news of this "study" didn't spread throughout the campus.

PS: This one course was the only real connection to Harvard, other than the med school and so forth. There wasn't that big a connection between Harvard and the hospital at that time. So it wasn't that surprising. In Leary's department, a few years later, it was different, he was in a completely different part of the university. But you know how colleges and universities are. People can be working three doors down from each other on the same problem and not know it, because everybody is on their own little ego trip. It's just the nature of the beast.

RF: You were allowed to take the LSD out of the clinic?

PS: Well, we managed—it was a little bit loose. The stuff was locked in a safe. I don't remember how or under what circumstances I got hold of what I did get hold of. I know we did a tolerance test once, so I was taking a little bit every day and then a little bit more and a little bit more and then stopping and then taking a full hit and then waiting and taking another hit to see if you'd develop a tolerance to it. So I had access to some. I don't know whether I got extra or what I did. I think that was the only time that I actually had some to carry around, but I know Hyde did. He was suspected of tripping more than once, but then he was a pretty out-there guy anyway.

RF: Did you know at the time that this work was funded by the CIA?

PS: We didn't know. We did two studies. The first one was sponsored by the Geschickter Foundation—that should have been a tip-off—and the second was funded by the Society for the Study of Human Ecology. I never met any of the Geschickter Foundation people, but I remember meeting some of the Human Ecology people. They were a very strange group.

RF: Was Herbert Kelman involved with you guys?

PS: No, not at that time I don't think. He was around, but I don't think he was involved in LSD at all. Why?

RF: Because he reportedly had something to do with Leary's firing and he was involved with the Human Ecology Fund.

PS: Really. Could be. Huh, that's interesting. That was probably later. You know, I got my Ph.D. in '55, so I wasn't involved in any of that then. I was involved in another project in another hospital.

RF: Did your LSD experiences in any sense affect the perspective you then developed in your career as writer and teacher?

PS: It's hard to say, because there was a lot going on in my life, and that was a fairly circumscribed event. I was married and had three kids, and then shortly thereafter I was divorced and paying alimony and I was working three jobs. I was too busy surviving to have time to really process my life or think about anything. It was really a very hard period for me, for six years after I got my degree. And of course I also was writing my dissertation during part of that too. The LSD experiences were all pushed aside. I think the impact it had was latent. I mean there were always certain kinds of music that evoked the experience, and especially Debussy and Ravel, which I'm still very attached to. And I remember one time there was a group of us, all of whom had had LSD at one time or another, and we were sitting around my living room listening to Ravel's Daphnis and Chloé suite, and we all started having recollections and visions or memories of visions. But I think what happened was that after my life calmed down a little bit in the early sixties, I began to get interested again, and also I think personally, psychologically, I began to explore more.

RF: Using psychedelics?

PS: No, not at that time. It meant going to groups, encounter groups and things like that; exploring inner space a lot more. Then in the later sixties I got into doing a lot of pot and so forth, and became interested in the whole thing again. So it definitely had an influence, but a delayed reaction.

RF: Did you ever interact with Tim at Harvard?

PS: I was aware of him. The irony is that there were several of us who were very interested in his earlier quantitative research on interpersonal dynamics, which of course he was totally uninterested in after psychedelics. But we were doing a lot of quantitative stuff with computers, all this factor analysis and everything. We were very interested and very excited that he was coming. Then of course he came and immediately got into the psychedelic stuff, and no longer cared about it. I knew Dick Alpert better. Our fathers were both involved with the New Haven Railroad. His father was president and my father was chairman of the board. With Leary and I there was a definite wave pattern that wherever one was, the other wasn't. We were completely out of phase. When I was interested he wasn't and when he was interested I wasn't, and when I was interested again he wasn't again.

RF: What was your reaction when you saw this psychedelic movement start to congeal out of Harvard in the early sixties?

PS: Well, I could understand it. It made sense to me. I could see it happening. I also knew that he was headed for trouble. That was clear. Rumors flying around.

RF: What do you mean "trouble"? There's so many ways to look at the trouble Tim got in. Trouble with the administration because he was challenging authoritarian systems? Trouble with some of his colleagues who felt he was profaning a sacred substance? What trouble do you mean?

PS: I meant it in the more mundane sense of trouble with the administration and even more with fellow faculty I think.

RF: There was a lot of jealousy because he was such a popular professor and had this really exciting line of research going and all the graduate students were flocking toward him. . . .

PS: I went through that at Brandeis toward the end. When I was department chair at Brandeis in the Sociology Department, I was always having to protect somebody for doing something like that. Whether they were teaching a course in yoga or Zen or they were doing a course in gender, they were doing things that were radical and were breaking academic traditions in one way or another. It was always clear to me what upset academics the most. One was popularity—being popular. They always said to us either we were seducing the students—not literally but emotionally—or being seduced by them. If we're popular we must be lowering academic standards, because learning isn't supposed to be fun. The other thing is, anything emotional or anything below the brain, anything that might involve touching, anything that involved feeling, anything that involved spiritual things, was very, very frightening to academics. Of course Leary was doing all of it. And that was the fifties. We were doing it in the late sixties and people were still getting all in a tizzy over it. So it wasn't hard to imagine, looking back, how intense the reaction was to Leary in the very early sixties.

RF: Do you think he was careless or irresponsible in the way he conducted himself? Or do you think that was an important and courageous, daring move on his part, the way he pushed the limits?

PS: It's hard to say, because I wasn't intimately involved in it, but at the time I thought, he's not protecting himself at all. I could see he was going to get clobbered. You can get away with rubbing academics' noses in emotion and spirituality and your popularity and everything else, but you don't want to give them an opening. You can get away with it if you can play by their rules at least on the surface and he didn't appear to do that. I'm not saying that that necessarily was a bad thing for him. I'm just saying that I could see that event coming.

RF: So now we have this drug war and other evidences of twenty, thirty years of extreme reactionary repression to what was ignited there. Do you think if Tim were more circumspect, more careful, that we could have avoided this?

PS: I don't think so. Yes, he did bring a lot of that about but I think if he hadn't done it somebody else would have. The fifties were so repressive in every way, and it was such an awful, stupid, dishonest period in history, where everyone was pretending a kind of normality which didn't exist, and there was just a lid on everything, and a tremendous lid on sexuality particularly, and really on any kind of experience that was other than to make money and support your family; and for women, to be domestic and support your husband. And to suddenly open all that up and show we've got a new world opening up here—I don't think there's anything Leary could have done differently that would have made a difference. There was just too much pressure behind the opening.

RF: That pressure wasn't built up enough when you were doing your early experiments?

PS: Well it had, but Leary provided meaning. We were still operating in a kind of academic, scientific, psychological framework. It was a private thing and we didn't translate it into anything else. Of course the sixties came along and there was a general shift in attitude, which was huge. A lot of other things opened up as well. I think, when you consider all the other things that were going on then, you certainly can't either blame or credit Leary for all of the sixties. I just feel a kind of inevitability about what happened, that all of that had to happen. He was the guy that comes along with a pretty big ego, puts himself at the center of it, and noises it about. There's always somebody like that, and if it hadn't been Tim it would have been somebody else.

RF: When I was in fifth grade, in '67, my teacher told me that LSD stood for Let's Save Democracy. Of course that went right over my eleven-year-old head, but in the last few years I finally got it. If we look at the political spectrum from authoritarianism to democracy, authoritarianism preys on an unaware populous and democracy requires a self-aware, self-determined populous. Here's LSD, which can activate the awareness of the divinity within—anathema to authoritarianism. Tim realized this and hit the streets with his findings.

PS: Yeah, I think that's right, and I would add that to what I said, that it was facilitating the democratic process for him to do that, even though it cost him dearly and generated a lot of reaction and backlash. But it always does. You would expect it, no matter who did it or how they did it or what happened. And you can say, "Oh well, he made it worse than it would have been." I don't know. I've always said that authoritarianism works within the personality too, and when the ego is authoritarian, it prevents a lot of stuff from getting to the brain. It's like the ego is a repressive dictator often, and acts just like a despot. First of all there's no distinction between the despot and the nation, there's no distinction between the ego and the personality. What's good for me is good for the country. What's good for the ego is good for the organism. Of course it isn't true, and messages coming from the periphery are ignored, the messenger is shot. All these things are very much equivalent. So LSD was a very strong force in the democratization of the organism, let's say, and that reflects itself outside as well, because you can't really separate them. You've got one, you've got the other.

RF: Do you think the authorities were aware of that, and that was the reason that they immediately repressed it? I've had a hunch, I don't know if it's true or this is my own paranoid conspiracy theory, that the government, through the CIA's research of LSD, became aware of its effects on personality very early on, and maybe I'm attributing too much intelligence to the powers that be—

PS: I think so.

RF: But they could have become aware that a high dose of LSD in the right circumstance brings you into contact not only with your deep self but with other dimensions of reality that are beyond the scope of the ruling paradigm—extraterrestrial intelligences, a collective mind, intelligent unity of life, living God, things like that they don't understand and can't control and don't want free and available. Attempted repression backfired. While Harvard thought they were getting rid of Leary, they actually gave his career the best boost it could have gotten.

PS: Yeah, well that's usually the case. But I don't think they thought that deeply about it. I think they thought only that this is interfering with the channeling of youth into the proper tracks, and they're all going out and doing something different from what they're supposed to be doing. That fear doesn't need an intellectual content. It's the same with academics when somebody's really popular. You know, there's something going on here that's threatening. I don't like it. And I can think up twenty different reasons why it's bad, because I'm an academic and that's what I do is think up reasons. And I think with the government it was the same kind of thing. It was just a fear. It's drugs and it's bad and it's corrupting youth. And I don't think they thought beyond that into anything as sophisticated as what you're saying.

RF: Do you think that the sixties worked? I mean there was a movement, a humanitarian and environmental movement away from consumerism, away from militarism, a reawakening of cosmic and ecological concerns that are necessary for our survival. Do you think it worked to help humanity evolve?

PS: Oh, absolutely. There are tremendous changes that took place in the sixties. In the first place, the sexual revolution; that was a tremendous change. In the fifties, if you weren't in New York City or some equivalent environment, you couldn't even rent an apartment and live with somebody unless you faked it in some way, really, until the sixties. And now the percentage of people living together, I think it's higher than the percentage of people who are married up to a certain age, or in a certain age group. And of course what could be shown in the movies or on TV and what can be said, even in the newspapers. The general idea was communicated in the fifties that women weren't interested in sex, and that's of course the old authoritarian tradition, the repression of female sexuality, because nobody ever represses male sexuality very much. That's pretty much over. So that is, I think, one of the most important changes that happened in the last several thousand years. And along with it go a lot of other things. The attitude toward war changed completely. There's a totally different attitude toward war now. People used to think of war as like a tornado, like an act of God almost, and now people think it shouldn't happen. If somebody's fighting somewhere, we should do something to stop it. That's a totally new idea. It didn't exist before.

RF: At the same time we have bigger defense budgets than ever before.

PS: Yeah, sure, but there's always a huge lag in these things.

RF: Materialism?

PS: It's the sort of thing that I'm writing about in this book. There's really two things happening at once. The old systems, when they decay, become more extreme, always. They become exaggerated. They become more monolithic. And that undoes them eventually, because it's like fascism was the purist form of authoritarianism. The dictator has no obligation to anybody, that is, obligation that everybody understands. It's not like the king who has certain obligations to nobles, certain obligations to the populace, and is bound around with traditions of various kinds. A dictator has none of that. It's pure authoritarianism. And it's the beginning of the end. It's like they're falling like flies, because the only places that they can exist are really backward places. Internationalism has grown enormously. I think it's very hard, if you weren't there, to recall how unbelievably naive, insular, conventional, and accepting of authority the fifties were. If the government said it, it had to be true. Nobody thinks that now.

Even television: if you watch what everybody watches, you'll see a tremendous change. Compare *Seinfeld* with *Father Knows Best*, for example. That's like night and day, what's dealt with, what's talked about, what's understood. It's understood that Elaine wants to get laid, and it's understood that people fart and masturbate, and all this stuff is talked about openly. That's a tremendous change.

RF: But at the same time we've seen growth of the one world, new world order, throughout the world, even well into China. We've lost ground since the sixties in the environmental movement.

PS: No, no, no. We have not lost ground. I mean you have to distinguish in all these things—it's like people who think crime has gotten worse or there's more child molesting than there used to be. You have to distinguish between what's happening and what's being made known. People are incredibly environmentally aware now, and they're aware of what's happening. Corporations are not getting away with nearly what they used to get away with. Of course there are more ways of polluting everything and so on than there used to be, but there's more battles over it. Even with all the control of the media that corporations have, they can't ignore that issue, because they know that a huge majority of the population is environmentally concerned, ecologically concerned, and that's a huge change. The sixties was like a handful of people making a row. But there's another 90 percent of the population that doesn't buy it. I was in Paris in 1968 during the riots, and I remember I had this feeling that everybody's out there in the streets, that it was just this tremendous movement. Then, one Sunday, there was a march by the right and what an eye-opener all of a sudden. There were five times as many people in the streets, all dressed in suits and stuff. It made me realize that the left was not the majority. The sixties was really, if you looked at polls and things like that, a very small number of people.

RF: Nixon's silent majority.

PS: Well, it existed then. Today it's different. It's quite different. I mean there's many, many more people, there's a hundred times as many people who are antiwar, who are ecologically concerned, who are into spiritual pursuits, who are antimaterial. But it's not news anymore. Another major change is organic food. Can you imagine, in the sixties, if they'd made that attempt to redefine the meaning of organic? Nobody would have opposed that. They wouldn't have gotten a flutter. Ten people would have complained and they would have ignored it. And alternative medicine; it's huge now. It's a huge thing. All these things come out of the sixties, and they're permanent.

Nobody's going back. But I will predict that magazines and TV will come out within the next two years with something saying the move is back to traditional medicine. I mean they just do that regularly. It's back to the tradition. Because the media themselves are very conservative, and also, they want this kind of novelty pendulum thing going all the time. So they have to go back and forth, they have to have movement without threat is what the media—that's what advertisers want: movement without threat. Novelty without change. Every two years feminism is dead. Every two years. Its as regular as clockwork. Because they're thinking of feminism as bra burning or some other little superficial thing that symbolized it for them, whereas with the real issues, like battered women's shelters and day-care centers, there are huge gains over ten, twenty years ago. So that's the way things tend to get defined. And the media also is into cynicism, because it makes them look intelligent.

There's an interesting book by a guy named Alfie Kohn called *The Brighter Side of Human Nature*, where he talks about this: about the confusion of cynicism with intelligence and how that works. For example, the idea that psychological differences between men and women are biological, and/or that men are inherently biologically aggressive and violent and so on, all this stuff. There are studies and magazine articles about stuff like this all the time, and scientists are in total disagreement. The only stuff that ever gets in the magazines, as Kohn points out, is the dark stuff, the negative stuff, the "it's all biological, there's nothing you can do about it, it's just a given." You know, "men are natural-born killers," and blah, blah, blah. So it's not optimism. It's just looking at the real data as opposed to the media data, which is so skewed.

RF: I agree the media distracts people from deeper issues; for example today attention is on Monica Lewinsky's dress instead of on the U.S. reaction to international pressure on them to lower fossil fuel consumption.

PS: Yeah. Or the U.S. opposition to the World Court. I love that one. It's so funny. They were the ones that pushed for it in the first place and then all of a sudden they're like, "God, they might use it on us!"

RF: I don't mean to harp on what might seem to be a cynical attitude compared to yours, but we just lived through the decade of the 1980s, twelve years of Reagan and Bush in one of the most corrupt decades of American history. I haven't read Kohn yet but I see that Americans are unwilling or unable to see just how corrupt and dark the American political scene is. I, for one, believe the findings that the military-industrial complex has been involved in the narcotics trade since early in the Vietnam War, as reported by Alfred McCoy in his Yale dissertation that became *The Politics of Heroin in Southeast Asia*. It's been reported in many other places too. I'm convinced that military intelligence was involved in the assassinations of the Kennedy brothers, Martin Luther King, and Malcolm X. Most people suspect a conspiracy in these murders. The CIA's beginning is clearly traced to Nazi intelligence joining with the U.S. military just after World War Two, as Martin Lee describes in his fine exposé, *The Beast Reawakens*. The Iran Contra hearings of the 1980s did little to motivate the American people to clean up the obvious and profound corruption of the democratic process. The United States has been in wars in Nicaragua, El Salvador, Iraq, Iran, Panama, and other places. There is some public outcry, but these senseless wars continue. Saddam Hussein was put in power by the United States military; so was Noriega. And the most recent "monster," Bin Laden, was a U.S. hero when Russia invaded Afghanistan. You told me the United States built those terrorist camps that it just bombed. People are aware of all this stuff but it goes on. Global warming is something everyone is concerned with, but doing anything about it lags far behind the GNP in importance. The drug war rages—half a million people in jail just for pot. It is utterly futile, gives jobs mainly to dope dealers, the police force, and the prison industry, while doing nothing to reduce drug abuse, which is a relatively minor health problem—unless you include alcohol and cigarettes, which are foisted upon the American people in slick ad campaigns—but your career in national politics is over if you challenge the sense of the drug war and appear "soft on drugs." There are so many absurdities in firm place in American politics it's hard to see any progress at all.

PS: I think what you are reacting to is the fact that the world is in a major cultural transition—the kind of paradigm shift that takes place over decades, even centuries. And at those times things seem to be moving in opposite directions at the same time, and at accelerating speed. (I'm working on a book now that deals with this.) So, those who cling to the status quo feel the world is going to hell, and those who want fundamental change also feel the world is going to hell (i.e., backwards). It's chaotic, but chaos is necessary for creation.

RF: Yes, and this brings us back to Tim, who titled his last book *Chaos and Cyberculture*. In it he explains that his efforts in the sixties were to induce chaos in an excessively ordered culture. Here again is a fundamental difference between an authoritarian culture (or personality) and a democratic one. The democratic society tolerates some apparent chaos in the world, having trust in a natural order, while the authoritarian seeks control.

Timothy Leary and the Psychedelic Movement

AN INTERVIEW WITH HUSTON SMITH
BY ROBERT FORTE

RF: Huston, it's a pleasure to be in your beautiful home overlooking San Francisco Bay and hear your reminiscences about Tim. I'm hoping you'll also speak more generally about the advent of psychedelics in modern life. Perhaps you can compare the styles of Aldous Huxley and Timothy Leary. You worked closely with each of them.

HS: That's true. I will do my best to speak to your questions.

RF: It may be a surprise to some readers that you have been intimately involved with this subject—psychedelics and religion—for over thirty-five years since your first experience in 1961. You've written over a dozen scholarly articles on the religious importance of psychedelic drugs, and devoted an appendix to the subject in your book *Forgotten Truth*. These writings are being compiled into

Huston Smith is one of the foremost scholars of religion in the world today. His book The World's Religions *is one of the bestselling books on that subject and was followed by the* Illustrated Guide to the World's Religions. *He recently edited, with Reuben Snake,* One Nation Under God, *which deals with the Native American Church. He was a central early participant, along with Aldous Huxley, in the Psilocybin Project at Harvard.*

a book by the Council on Spiritual Practices. Your most recent book, *One Nation Under God*, is about the victory for religious freedom won by the Native American Church. You are widely known as one of the most authoritative and eloquent voices on the religions of the world. You've worked for over thirty years to express the common vision of the world's religions to revive a sense of the sacred in modern life. Yet in spite of your deserved stature you are still somewhat reticent to discuss this subject. Why is that?

HS: Because the psychedelics are so ambiguous. They are like a two-edged sword. They can cut through *samsara* to get to *nirvana*—which is to say, cut through the daze and doze of mindless existence and wake us up—while at the other extreme they can behead us. Just this week, in reading Peter Coyote's first person account of the psychedelic sixties, *Sleeping Where I Fall*, I came upon his mention of one of the Haight-Ashbury's Diggers who took acid on a bad day and became the three hundredth person to jump off the Golden Gate Bridge. The potential of these substances for both good and ill is so great that it is irresponsible to be glib about them. One should know one's audience before one speaks.

RF: This is a subject that has been trampled in the war on drugs. Official sentiment against psychedelics was largely motivated by the ebullient antiauthoritarian spirit of the sixties and Timothy's zeal certainly catalyzed that; or, perhaps the resistance had already been in place for centuries, and Leary's efforts vaulted over that resistance to spread the word—like the I Ching says: when the wild geese find food, they call their friends. So what I'm hoping we can do today is talk about Timothy and what went on during that period, but also discuss the larger subject, the problems and prospects of integrating psychedelics or entheogens into modern society.

HS: You want me to plunge into that?

RF: I brought some documents with me that I found in the Leary archives to put you in the mood of those days, to help you remember the optimism, the intellectual and spiritual enthusiasm around those early openings of consciousness. Wonderful, passionate, excitement and interest from universities throughout the world, and from governments too. Here are just some of the letters from medical schools, divinity schools, prison wardens, the Parapsychology Laboratory at Duke, the National Institute of Health. Here's a letter from William Wilson, the founder of Alcoholics Anonymous, written to Tim in 1961 praising LSD. Another from the distinguished psychiatrist Abram Hoffer in the Department of Public Health in Saskatchewan where they used LSD to treat patients citing "cures in alcoholics and addicts that are practically miraculous."

HS: This is going to be an interesting book for me to read.

RF: Brilliant minds, some of the world's leading scientists and artists, engaged in discovering these drugs and applying them to a whole range of things. Then the whole movement turned into chaos. Harvard and Sandoz chastise Leary and Alpert for being out of line, for seeking publicity more than science, then they're fired. In just a few years Tim is sentenced to twenty to thirty years in prison, ostensibly for marijuana offenses. He's denounced by Nixon as "the most dangerous man in the world." Considering the source, that may be a compliment. Here's a letter from a federal judge in Texas who sentenced Leary to twenty years saying he'd do it again and that he is unwilling to reduce the sentence, in spite of Leary's having cooperated with authorities.

Did you have any idea of what was to come when you first became acquainted with the subject of sacred drugs?

HS: Before answering your question I want to take exception to your calling them "sacred drugs." They have sacred possibilities, I'm not going to back down on that. But Aldous Huxley was wise in calling them "heaven and hell drugs," and hell connotes what is demonic rather than sacred. We're back with my point about their ambiguous character.

Now to your question: did I have any idea as to what was in store? Not at the start. As you noted, during the first year or two the mood was wildy optimistic, for all signals seemed to read green. You have touched on the important ones. Psychologically, the psychedelics promised easier access to repressed unconscious materials, shortcutting the years and prohibitive expense of psychoanalysis. In

W. G. W.

BOX 459 GRAND CENTRAL STATION

NEW YORK 17, N. Y.

July 11, 1961

Mr. Timothy Leary
Center for Research in Personality
5 Divinity Avenue
Cambridge 38, Mass.

Dear Mr. Leary:

It was most pleasant to have your letter of June 30th, along with the suggestion that we may have a number of mutual interests.

The last time I saw Aldous I believe he referred enthusiastically to your work.

A number of us A.A.'s here in New York have been a part of the development of the LSD possibilities. Our chief contact has been Dr. Humphry Osmond of Saskatchewan, whom we consider to be the greatest authority in this whole area. He is very close to Aldous and if you don't know him, you certainly should.

Though LSD and some kindred alkaloids have had an amazingly bad press, there seems no doubt of their immense and growing value. Indeed it seems to make out a statistical case, as of now.

Perhaps, too, you will find some interest in Alcoholics Anonymous - its principles and mechanisms.

In any case, it will be fine to meet you as soon as that can be arranged. Regrettably I shall be away practically the whole of August, plans already having been made.

However, it still may be possible to meet you close to August 1st, if it would be convenient. Failing that, we may be able to arrange something following Labor Day.

Meanwhile, all the best.

Sincerely yours,

William G. Wilson

WGW/nw

P.S. My office telephone number is MUrray Hill 6-1100 in New York City. Please ask for my assistant, Nell Wing, who will know my whereabouts.

behavior change, they held the promise of reducing the recidivism of paroled prisoners. And in the area of my prime interest, they seemed to hold the promise of rolling back the materialistic worldview that imprisons us by showing people—causing them to see directly— that Nietzsche was wrong in announcing that God is dead.

RF: Was it apparent right from the start that these were religious sacraments when they arrived at Harvard in 1960?

HS: To me it was, though set and setting quickly entered the picture—"set" denoting the subject's psychological makeup, and "setting" the circumstances in which the chemicals are ingested. This again makes me restive when you refer to them categorically as "religious sacraments," for that seems to position them in a linear, one-to-one relationship with religion.

Others picked up on the resources of the drugs. Leary's appointment was in the Center for Personality Research, and his chief interest was in the psychedelics' potentials for behavior change, specifically changing asocial habits. One of the first experiments he designed involved his taking psilocybin with prisoners at the maximum security penitentiary in Concord and following up to see if it reduced their recidivism rate when they were paroled, which it seemed to do dramatically. (I have since learned that he may have fudged the data to make this point.) But for me, at the time, the important thing was the altered view of reality—what (in the title of one of his books) Carlos Castenanda called "A Separate Reality"—that the psychedelics repeatedly (though not invariably) brought to view. This was Aldous Huxley's chief interest too. He arrived at M.I.T. for a semester as Distinguished Visiting Professor of Humanities in the same week that Tim took up his tenure at Harvard, and, having written *The Doors of Perception*, he was an important presence at the start of the Harvard experiment.

RF: Do you continue to feel that psychedelics are a way to see into a spiritual plane of reality?

HS: I do.

RF: Would perceiving that plane have social or political consequences?

HS: This a far-reaching and important question. It relates to the whole issue of whether metaphysical and religious outlooks—worldviews—affect history and shape it, or are simply head-trips that "bake no bread," as the saying goes. Needless to say, I wouldn't have gone into philosophy if I held the latter view. I'm with William James, who said that if a landlady were interviewing a prospective roomer she would do better to inquire into his philosophy than to ask about his bank account. Arnold Toynbee raised the stakes on James by asking who in the past have contributed the most to the present generation. His answer was Confucius and Lao-Tzu, the Buddha, the prophets of Israel and Judah, Jesus, Muhammad, and Socrates.

RF: Were you responsible for bringing Aldous Huxley to Cambridge that fall?

HS: Minimally. The Humanities Department at M.I.T. had a line item in its budget to bring a distinguished humanist to its campus each fall, and its chairman asked me what I thought of inviting Huxley. Needless to say, I was enthusiastic. When he accepted, I immediately volunteered to be his social secretary, managing his schedule, shepherding him to his appointments, and generally spending as much time with him as I could.

RF: Was your enthusiasm for Huxley related to his book, *The Doors of Perception*, that he published in 1953? Were you already curious about sacred drugs?

HS: Far more than curious; I found his book riveting. This needs a bit of explaining.

As you know but your readers may not, I was born of missionary parents in China and lived there until I came to the States for college. China was like the boondocks then, and I spent my college and graduate school years scrambling to catch up with the West and trying to become a full-blooded American. It seemed obvious that science and technology were what made the West dynamic and traditional societies stagnant, so I was an easy convert to the scientific worldview which I now see as scientistic rather than scientific.

RF: Some readers may not be clear as to the difference between science and scientism.

HS: Science consists of the actual discoveries of science and the method—the scientific method—which produces those discoveries. Scientism adds to those, first, the belief that the scientific method is, if not the only reliable way of getting at truth, then at least the most reliable method; and second, the belief that the things that science can get its hands on—physical, material, measurable things— are the most important things, the foundational, generating things from which all else derives. Nothing that science has discovered supports, much less proves, that those tacked-on points are true. They are no more than opinions, which my teachers led me to assume are true—there is truth in A. K. Coomaraswamy's quip that it takes four years to get a college education and forty to get over it. I'm fortunate that it didn't take me that long.

RF: What did the trick? What enabled you to see through scientism?

HS: That brings me back to Aldous Huxley. He had a sidekick, another Englishman named Gerald Heard. His name hasn't lasted, but he was brilliant—H. G. Wells said that he was the only radio commentator (his beat was science) that he ever bothered to listen to. Heard is credited with having moved Huxley from his early *Brave New World* cynicism to the mysticism of *The Perennial Philosophy*. Have you heard of him?

RF: Sure. I have some letters here from Gerald Heard to Tim.

HS: Well I hadn't, but I chanced—chance? Is there such a thing?— upon one of his books, *Pain, Sex, and Time*, and it proved to be the most important reading experience of my life. Let me warn those who might take that as a come-on for the book that it is unlikely that it would have the same impact on them. A book's impact depends almost entirely on who the reader is and where he is on his life's journey. I have never gone back to that book because I know I would find it disappointing now, for I am in a different place, but it spoke powerful to where I was then for being the first mystical book—book written from the mystic's perspective—that I had ever read. It is the only time in my life that I read all night, and when dawn was breaking and I closed the book I closed out my naturalistic philosophy with it. The mystics' worldview struck me as the truer of the two and I have never changed my opinion about that.

After that first book I went on to the others that Heard had written, and when I had read them all—quite a few—I decided that I wanted to meet the man, so I wrote him in care of his publisher. He replied, saying that he would be glad to see me but that it might be tricky to get to him, for he was in retreat, meditating as it turned out, in Trabucco Canyon about thirty-five miles from Los Angeles. I was about to move from the University of Denver to Washington University, and as St. Louis is farther from Los Angeles than Denver is, I hitchhiked from Denver to Trabucco Canyon. I had no car and was in debt from graduate school; it was easier to hitchhike then than it is now. As I was saying good-bye to Heard he asked if I would like to meet Aldous Huxley. "He's interested in our kinds of things," he said, and he gave me Huxley's address in L.A. Huxley and his first wife Maria were at their cabin hideaway in the Mojave desert but their maid put me on the phone to them and they told me how to find their place by bus for what turned out to be a glorious afternoon. For the next fifteen years those two men were virtually my gurus, and Huxley's anthology of mystical texts, *The Perennial Philosophy*, virtually my bible. I brought Huxley to lecture at Washington University and Heard to teach for a semester there.

That in itself was enough to excite me when *The Doors of Perception* appeared, but there was more. Mystical texts had convinced me that there is a separate reality but I wanted to experience it so I became a serious meditator in the hope of doing so. Unfortunately I turned out not to be good at that art—in Indian parlance, I'm a *jnana* rather than a *raja* yogi. I don't regret the twelve or so years during which meditation was my spiritual path, and I have not given up meditating some each day. I find it useful for the focus it gives my life and for the way it helps me direct my attention, but I can't alter the focal length of my consciousness by meditating. Even in the instance when I came closest to that goal, during my koan training in Japan, what happened was a radical reshuffling of components of this-worldly experience, not a visionary experience. I needed help to experience what the mystics experience, and Huxley's mescalin held the possibility of providing it. So when he came to M.I.T. in 1960 I naturally raised the issue and he referred me to Leary who had enlisted him as a consultant for his project.

That's a long answer to what sprung me from my naturalistic worldview.

RF: And it leads you to Tim. Do you recall your first meeting him?

HS: It was a luncheon date at the Harvard faculty club and I found him charismatic. His reputation for being brilliant had landed him a dream contract—full-time research on anything relating to personality theory he wanted to investigate. He was urbane, witty, and a great raconteur. On top of which he had style. The tailor in Harvard Square who specialized in outfitting Harvard professors had replaced his California casual wardrobe with natty, expensive English tweeds, replete with stylish leather elbow patches, but it was typical of Tim that he added a distinctive touch to his designer academic fashion by rounding it off with spanking white sneakers that gleaned as if they had been bought that morning. He was a marvelous performer and (I was to learn later) could read *Finnegan's Wake* with such a flawless Irish brogue that he could have gone on stage.

The point of our meeting was to sign me up as a subject in his psychedelic project, which at that exploratory stage involved collecting firsthand reports of what subjects experienced when they took mescalin, or psilocybin, so as our lunch drew to its close, we pulled out our academic datebooks to schedule my first ingestion. The first several dates we tried wouldn't work for one or the other of us, and finally Tim flipped past Christmas, eyed me with a mischievous grin, and said, "What about New Year's Day?" I accepted and it turned out to be a prophetic way to enter the sixties.

RF: Did Tim come across as a spiritual person, or a brilliant intellectual—not that they are necessarily in conflict.

HS: Add his charm and I would say the latter. Also he had

NOTES ON MESCALIN

Huston C. Smith
39 Sandrick Road
Belmont 78, Massachusetts

New Year's Day, 1961. Eleanor and I reached the home of Dr. Timothy Leary in Newton about 12:30. Present in addition to Timothy were Dr. George Alexander, a psychiatrist, and Frank Baron, research psychologist.

After pleasantries, Tim produced a capsule container, saying one was a very mild dose, two an average dose, three above average. We were to take from one to three as we wished. Eleanor took two at once; I took one and a second about a half hour latter when nothing seemed to be happening.

I would judge about an hour after my first pill I noticed mounting tension in my legs which turned into tremors. Went into the large living room and lay down on the couch. The tremors turned into twitches, though they were seldom actually visible.

It would be impossible for me to fix a time when I passed into the visionary stage—the transition was absolutely imperceptible. From here on time becomes largely irrelevant. With great effort I might be able to recall which of the following thought feelings reconstruct the order in which the following thought-feelings occurred, but there seems to be no point in trying to do so.

The whole world into which I was ushered was strange, wierd, uncanny, significant, and terrifying beyond belief. Two things struck me especially. (1) The mescalin acted as a psychological prism. It was as thought the infinitely complex and layered psychological ingredients which normally are smelted down into a single band was weak, nondescript sensation-impressions were now being refracted, spread out as if by a spectroscope, into about five layers. And the odd thing was that one was aware of them all to some degree simultaneously and could move back and forth among them at will, choosing to attend to, concentrate upon, whichever one wished. Thus I could hear the soft conversation of Tim and George Alexander in the study adjoining

2

distinctly, and follow their discussion coherently, even contribute to it in
imagination (and could have in reality had I wished, I am sure). But this
leads to the second marked feature feature. Though the five bands of consciousness—I x say five roughly, they weren't absolutely distinct and I
made no attempt to count them—were all real, they were not of equal importance. I was experiencing directly the metaphysical theory known as emanationism
in which, beginning with the clear, unbroken, and infinite light of God,
the light then breaks into forms and lessens in intensity as it passes through
descending degrees of reality.   The persons talking in the adjoining room
were functioning in an intelligible wave band, but one which was far
more restricted, cramped, and wooden than the bands I was now privileged to
experience. Bergson's concept of the brain as a reducing valve I now saw to
be precisely true.

"Empirical metaphysics" was another phrase, along with "psychological
prism" which kept running through my mind. The emanation theory, and especially
the elaborately worked out layers of Hindu and Buddhism cosmology and psychology
had heretofore been concepts and inferences. Now they were objects of the most
direct and immediate perception. I could see exactly how these theories might
would have come into being if their progenitors had had this experience. But
beyond accounting for their origin, my experience testified to their absolute
truth.

But how could these layers upon layers, these worlds within worlds
be put into words. I realized how utterly impossible it would be for me to
described them on the morrow when I lost this world of perception as I knew I
would. I knew this because I knew how imposs`` it would be right then to
describe what I saw to Tim or F'   ... With all this came the clearest realization
I have had as to what literary genius would consist of. It would consist of
the ingenious use of words to bridge as far as possible the gulf between
the normal state of existence and the world I was now in.

.3

It should not be assumed from what I have written that the experience
was for me pleasurable. The two accurate words are significance and terror.
The experience was positive --awesomely so--in that it was rolling back
range after range of reality I hadn't known existed. Whence, then, the
terror? I suppose from the utter freedom of the psyche and its lordship
over the body. I was aware of my body, laid out as if half-dead on a slab,
cool and slightly moist.   But I also had the sense that that body could
function only if my spirit chose to return to it, infuse it, and animate it.
Whould it so choose??? There seemed to be no particular reason why it should
do so. Moreover, could it do so if it chose. There was in A number of
religious traditions have the idea that no man can see God and its live--
the vision would be too much for the body to stand; like plugging an electric
toaster into in a major power like without a condenser, the body would simply
shatter. This too now seemed to me to be an empirically experienced fact.
I thought of trying to get up and walk across the floor. I suspected that
I could saccced in the attempt. But I didn't want to chance it. To force
this intensity of experience into the physical organism would be to chance
its
shattering the neuro-physiological organism apparatus.

Later, after the peak had passed and I had walked a few stepps and
was sitting down again I said to Tim, "I realize I'm still under the influence,
and xxx thinkgs probably look different in your perspective, but it looks
to me like you are taking an awful chance in these experiments. I xI Objective
tests might reval my heart and body in general to have been functioning normally
through the afternoon, but there is such a thing, as people being
freightened to death. I feel like ''- an operating room, coming out of
dangerousxxoperation having arely squeaked through an operation orderd in
which for two hours my bodyxhungxinxthe life hung in the balance."

I haven't said anything about the visual. Most accounts of the
experience dwell on it. I found myself xxx for the most part uninterested

4

in this aspect. The visual seemed an intrusion, a distraction from
significance, which for me was all important. What did this all meaningx
meanin mean about ike reality and mind and the human condition? Shapes
and colors, however breath-taking, could contribute little to this question.
Only iwexdid twice did physical sight come into prominence: Once xkex
was when George induced me to look at the pattern a lantern-like lamp shade
was throwing on a tope rug. This was extraordinary, the shapes standing out
like blocks in an exaggerated 3-D effect, but more—they would twist and
turn and undulate like a serpent. The other time was xkexxthe involuntary,
when the Christmas tree, its lights turned off, jumpped out at me. Thix
The tree had been in my visual field most of the afternoon, but this was
transfiguration. Had I not been in the room all the time I would have said
someone had re-trimmed the tree, loading it ten times the tinsel it had
previously borne. Wherexx before there had was tree with decorations, now
there were decorations with a bit of tree behind them.

I had a sore throat when I arrived. As the day progressed it
became increasingly accute. I felt dehydrated, with membranes dry and
almost parched. We returned home at 10:30. It must have been close to
5 a.m. before either of us fell asleep. Then slept fitfxily in snatches
until 9. Today myxxisdxhex I feel physically lousy with the cold which
has passed into the runny stage. Mind normal.

enormous self-confidence, which made him his own man. When he considered something to be important he went after it, regardless of what others thought. But I don't recall ever having looked to him as a spiritual model, and I don't think he saw himself in that role.

What I can say is that for the first three years of the Harvard project, my involvement in it was the most exciting thing in my life. Tim may have had other satellites in his orbit—he probably did, for his energy and exuberance were uncontainable—but the twenty or so people I was involved with constituted for those years my most important community. The important kind of experience that we shared, and others were ignorant of, bonded us far more solidly than I was bonded to my academic colleagues or members of my church. Some of the names of those in my group are still remembered in psychedelic circles: Dick Alpert who became Ram Dass; Walter Pahnke, an M.D. who mounted the Good Friday Experiment to earn a second doctorate in the psychology of religion; Walter Houston Clark, Professor of Psychology of Religion at Andover-Newton Theological Seminary; Ralph Metzner, who was to become Dean of the California Institute of Integral Studies; Paul Tillich's teaching assistant Paul Lee, who I hired to teach at M.I.T. and who went on to teach at the University of California, Santa Cruz; Rolf von Eckartsberg, who became Professor of Psychology at Duquesne University; and Lisa Bieberman, who managed a journal that sprang up, *The Psychedelic Review.* Those are the ones I remember best. We would meet about every other week, sometimes for an all-night session with one of the substances, sometimes simply to discuss the religious implications of the psychedelics. During one of the all-night vigils a burning candle overturned and set fire to a lace window curtain. Soon thereafter (it was around 2:00 A.M.) Eleanor, my wife [she later answered to the name Kendra], who was not with us that evening, phoned to ask if everything was all right. She had been awakened by a vivid dream that Tim's house (where we were meeting) was on fire.

There was glamour in the mix, too. Tim's project had become news, and it attracted the rich and the famous along with other curiosity seekers and would-be guinea pigs. More weekends than not Tim would spend in New York and return with gripping accounts of sessions with people we knew only by name. One that comes to mind is Jack Kerouac. He was known for picking fights when he was drunk, but he was mellow under LSD. Tim's parting words to him were, "We had a good time and you didn't throw a bean ball the entire weekend."

There was a lot of humor in the picture. Michael Hollingshead arrived from England via John Beresford's LSD project in New York City with a whole mayonnaise jar, large size, filled with LSD—as you know, I'm talking about a substance so potent that simply licking a postage stamp with a speck of LSD on it will put you into orbit. Basically he was a con man, but he had great plans to strike it rich in America by selling Hollywood this idea he had for a movie. The story line was about a man who wanted to seduce a young woman who had no use for him. He was determined, though, and resourceful, so he figured that if he could learn to levitate, that would get her attention. Transcendental Meditation claimed that it could cultivate that talent, so he signs on with them and practices diligently. Sure enough, there comes an evening when he realizes that his body is beginning to feel strangely light, and half an hour later it begins rising from his meditation pad. Excited, he phones his would-be lover and heads for her apartment. It isn't easy going for his feet have difficulty maintaining traction with the sidewalk, but he gets there and she is indeed impressed—to the point that she agrees to return to his room with him. Taking her arm to keep himself grounded, they make it and by this time she is impressed enough to agree to acquiesce to his overtures. She goes into the bathroom to prepare herself, but when she emerges his levitating prowess has peaked and she finds him plastered to the ceiling, powerless to disengage himself. The closing scene of the movie was to have her stretched languidly on the bed beneath him, saying sweetly, "Anytime you're ready baby, anytime you're ready." The movie never materialized.

The humor carried right through to the end of Tim and Dick Alpert's Harvard odyssey. On the twentieth anniversary of their firings Tim and Ram Dass continued their flamboyant style by appearing at Harvard University to celebrate the occasion. The hall was jammed, and of course jazzed—and the ambiance resembled

May 1961

Dear Tim

How about contributing to my next
prose masterpiece by sending me (as you sent
Burroughs) a bottle of SM pills, with a bill
if that is feasible. Allen said I could knock
off a daily chapter with 2 SM's and be done
with a whole novel in a month.

Really serious about that, if you
can manage it. I'm curious to know what would
come out. As you know, in NY, there was no
chance to write anything.

Your questionnaire required some
modifications on my part, much like the
questionnaires for taxpayers, so I explain
some at the end.

It may interest you, Coach, to learn
with horror that I now weigh 190! Ugh!
I dont wanta be a Guard! I wanta be a scatback!
Oh! Too late!

Have you got Allen's Europe address
other than Paris Am/Express?

Plus tard

Jack
Kerouac

Or I can send bill
ahead of time...
I mean, I really want some
& dont want to inconvenience in any way

Okay, Coach.. my address is JK
c/o Blake
P.O.Box 700
Orlando, Fla.

Am gone to Mexico villages now. Hope
to see you this winter in New England.
for a ragged furious
round of ice hockey!

Jack K

(Kerouac)

Kerouac
Feb

Nov 1 · 61

Dear Pearl and Tim

        Mushrooms just arrived, took only one, had hangover and benny blues now
feel better.

        In answer to yr question "what suggestions about what to do with psilocybin":

        Why not a college course called I N T U I T I O N A L   R E S E A R C H ...

        Or, as I first thought, "Insight Research"

        Or "Subjective Studies"-—

        Idea being that the student, instead of exploring objective avenues
of educational material, explores subjective reservoirs of perhaps "Jungian" data.

        Something like that. When I was at peak of psilocybin high in January
I seemed to know everything about the Khans of Mongolia. Information certainly didnt
come from outside since I never studied that subject.

        This may be silly, but maybe psilocybin releases genetic memories, or
maybe re-incarnation memories, who knows.

                                 Later

                          Jack

LATER:— Took 2 more, Then one more
next day —— got high but
had funny hangover of
brainwashed emptiness ——
Psilocybin is Siberian Fly Amanita?
— is Airapetianz's brainwash
drug? Substituting one
gamesmanship for another?
Me no take no more

(But brainwash doesnt last beyond the drug)   Jack

nothing so much as a concert by the Grateful Dead. The two principles were introduced by David McClelland, Chairman of the Department of Social Relations, who had fired them twenty years before. Wreathed in smiles, he was overflowing with warmth and goodwill, which made the contrast between the occasions captivating. But the contrast between firings and celebration was no greater than the contrast between the routes Tim and Ram Dass had traveled in the two decades. Ram Dass had found his guru in India while Tim had moved into high tech cyberspace. The finalist films for the Academy Awards that year were *E.T.* and *Gandhi*, and Tim, with his characteristic wit, pointed out that the contest was being enacted before the audience's very eyes. He, into cyberspace, was obviously a stand-in for *E.T.*, "while in that corner" he said, gesturing to Ram Dass, with his bald head, mustache, legs folded beneath him, and his eyes closed in meditation, "we have Gandhi."

Underlying all these highjinks, what held us together was our feeling that we were on the cutting edge of knowledge. We were spearheading the acquisition of new and important truths and their potentials. We likened ourselves to explorers in Africa when that continent was still unknown to the Europeans. But given my temperament and my interests, it was always the spiritual value of the psychedelics that were the most important. They didn't change my worldview, which had already become that of the mystics. What they did was enable me to experience their world—experience it as more solid and real than our everyday world, which it demoted to the shadows on Plato's cave. And they taught me, again experientially, what awe is. For more than a decade I had been teaching my students that awe is the distinctive religious emotion combining two emotions, fear and fascination, which (apart from their religious joining) are in tension with each other. Fascination draws us toward the object in question while fear holds us back.

RF: In *Flashbacks,* Tim tells of a meeting with Lama Govinda, the great Buddhist sage and scholar, who reportedly said to Tim, "You are the predictable result of a strategy that has been unfolding for over fifty years. You have done exactly what the philosophers have wanted done. You were prepared discreetly by several Englishmen who were themselves agents of this process. You have been an un-witting tool of the great transformation of our age." Thirty-five years after Lama Govinda reportedly made that statement, how does it sound to you, Huston?

Nena and Lama Govinda

HS: Lama Govinda's Foundations of Ti-betan Mysticism was so foundational in my understanding of that tradition that it took me to Almora, India, in the early 1960s for two weeks of unfor-gettable tutorials with him that lasted in the glorious setting of his hermitage until the sun set behind the Himalayas. But when I try to understand what he was getting at in that statement, I find myself unsure. What strat-egy was he thinking of, and what was it that he thought the philoso-phers wanted done? More than half my career has been in philoso-phy departments, and I haven't noticed my colleagues being at all keen about what Tim was up to. Most important, what great trans-formation of our age was he thinking of? My guess is he was think-ing of exceptional states of mind, and regions of reality that psychedelics can now make available to the public—people who can't devote their lives (as Govinda did) to accessing them through meditation. I can see that as a great incursion in modernity, but has it transformed history? That's difficult to answer.

RF: There came a time when you parted from Tim and Alpert. Was it an amicable parting?

HS: Very, as their parting with McClelland, their department chair-man, had been. The organization that emerged from Tim's experi-mental program called itself the International Federation for Internal

Freedom—its abbreviation was poetic, for, freighted with ambigu-
ities from the start, IFIF was the iffiest organization Cambridge had
ever seen—and I was a founding member of it. But as the three years
unfolded, differences began to appear with Tim and Dick on one side
and Walter Houston Clark and I on the other. They were antiestablishment rebels, whereas Walter and I thought of ourselves as reformers. They were giving up on the university, where we were sticking with it. And—perhaps most importantly, for their was a lot of sex
on their side—they were bachelors and we were married. So one night
a formal parting of the ways took place. It occurred during a Thanksgiving overnight gathering of the clan at Millbrook, Peggy Hitchcock's
estate. Dinner was preceded by the traditional Thanksgiving touch
football game, which Kendra remembers with delight because she
was regularly assigned to block opponents and (as she put it) getting
in people's way was something she was good at. Her moment of glory
was when she was assigned to block Maynard Ferguson.

Not surprisingly, the brownies were spiked with grass; but the
pertinent part of my report came around midnight when Tim, Dick,
Walter Clark, and I decided, with our friendship at full tilt, to face
up to our differences, and Walter and I officially withdrew from
IFIF and the direction it was headed. As we were the "squares" in
the organization, I suggested that we might organize ourselves into
IFIF squared with the logo $IFIF^2$, though we did not in fact institute a parallel organization.

I remember one more moment that night which relates to Dick
Alpert. As an assistant professor who was just beginning his career,
he was so overshadowed by Tim's glamour and status during those
Harvard years that I confess I hadn't paid much attention to him.
But after our "parting-of-the-ways" discussion was over and I was
heading upstairs to join Kendra for the night, he sought me out for
the first one-on-one conversation we had ever had, as I recall. "I am
sure that we will remain friends and continue to see each other," he
said, "but before we formally go our separate ways, I want to tell
you that I have been impressed with the steadiness with which you
have maneuvered these turbulent years." It is self-serving for me to
report that, but I do so because it was my first glimpse of the generosity of the man who was to become Ram Dass. Also, in a way that

brief exchange was to prove prophetic, for in the years that followed I grew closer to Ram Dass than to Tim. Proximity has played a part in that—for the last fifteen years we have been neighbors on opposite sides of San Francisco Bay—but we also think more alike.

RF: I'm noticing now, Huston, as I'm watching your face when you talk about the football game at Millbrook and your other memories of Tim, that you seem to have a lot of affectionate and loving memories of Tim and those times. When I first asked you about contributing to this volume a couple of years ago, you declined. You said you didn't want to be seen as endorsing Tim's behavior, so you felt you couldn't speak about it.

HS: That's true.

RF: In 1961 he spoke at a conference with Huxley on "How to Change Behavior." Already he was seeming very radical as he anticipated his critics:

> Those of us who talk and write about the games of life are invariably misunderstood. We are seen as frivolous or cynical anarchists tearing down the social structure. This is an unfortunate misapprehension. Actually, only those who see culture as a game, only those who take this evolutionary point of view, can appreciate and treasure the exquisitely complex magnificence of what human beings do and have done. To see it all as "serious, taken-for-granted reality" is to miss the point; is to derogate with bland passivity the greatness of the games we learn.

What do you think of that statement?

HS: I think it polarizes, pitting them against us. Whatever Tim's intentions were, what comes through is: you see us as a threat, whereas it's only we who see life's magnificence. His statement is unnuanced. And it is disingenuous, for in other situations he did talk about tearing down the social structure and—in jest but only half so—spiking the public water supply. And though it would be unfair to charge him with cynicism, he could be frivolous in the sense of being reckless and not as responsible as he should have been.

RF: He had a thoughtful rationalization for his attempted "juvenilization" of society. He cites Arthur Koestler:

> Biological evolution is to a large extent a history of escapes from the blind alleys of overspecialization, the evolution of ideas a series of escapes from the tyranny of mental habits and stagnant routines. In biological evolution the escape is brought about by a retreat from the adult to the juvenile stage as the starting point for the new line; in mental evolution by a temporary regression to more primitive and uninhibited modes of ideation, followed by the creative leap.

And in his own words he writes:

> The emergence of Hedonic Psychology in the 1960s was greeted with official scorn and persecution. Larval politicians correctly saw the cultural perils of hedonism. The neurosomatic perspective frees the human from addiction to hive rewards (which are now seen as robot) and opens up vistas of natural satisfaction and meta-social aesthetic revelation. The revelation is this: "I can learn to control internal, somatic function, to select, dial, tune incoming stimuli, not on the basis of security, power, success, or social responsibility, but in terms of aesthetics and psychosomatic wisdom. To feel good. To escape from terrestrial pulls." (*Info-Psychology*, p. 29–30)

HS: There is some truth in all that, but again the polarization and absence of the qualifications and specifics. Suppose we accept Koestler's statement. How, precisely, would/should we act and organize society if we were to "retreat from the adult to the juvenile stage as the starting point of the new line"? Throw tantrums? Play with matches? Expect others to feed us and clean up after us?

RF: I thought I noticed compatible notions in your writings that critique the modern world mindset. Particularly in the essays assembled into your book *Beyond the Post-Modern Mind*, wherein you describe the modern world mindset as an overly scientific, authoritarian, outer-directed, controlled, measured, "disqualified," worldview that is giving way, thank goodness, to a perspective that values more the individual's inner resources. "The supreme human opportunity is to strike deeper still and become aware of the 'sacred unconscious' that forms the bottom line of our selfhood" (p. 178).

You write:

> Our final adversary is the notion of a lifeless universe as the context in which life and thought are set, one which without our presence in it would have been judged inferior to ourselves. Could we but shake off our anodynes for a moment we would see that nothing could be more terrible than the condition of spirits in a supposedly lifeless and indifferent universe— Newton's great mechanism of time, space, and inanimate forces operating automatically or by chance. Spirits in such a context are like saplings without water; their organs shrivel. . . . So we must pick up anew Blake's Bow of Burning Gold to support "the rise of the soul against the intellect" (Yeats) as intellect has come to be narrowly perceived. (p. 102)

HS: Tim was right in calling for that rise. Looking back, I think I agree with him in most of the things he was against. Reformers, as Walter Houston Clark and I regarded ourselves, are no more in love with the status quo than rebels are. The difference lies in how to change it. My concern is basically philosophical—to show that the diminished worldview that modernity's misreading of modern science has caged us in is inaccurate. It was (and is) the promise psychedelics hold for helping to spring us from that cage that drew me to Tim and his Harvard experiment. I'm worried about social problems, too—overpopulation, environmental pollution, the growing gap between the rich and the poor—but I don't have concrete solutions for them. I am not really a social philosopher.

RF: While Tim has become most visible for a kind of trivial psychedelic Pied Piperdom, there may have been some more historical, philosophical substance to his endeavors. Do you agree?

HS: Yes. But again, what were his specifics?

RF: Some folks hold him accountable for derailing the psychedelic movement by alienating it from mainstream society.

HS: Accountable is too strong. He probably contributed to it. There was a rebel streak in him that almost forced those in authority to react—every action elicits an equal and opposite reaction, as the saying goes. But questions of degree are difficult to answer—was Caesar a great man or a very great man? Tim appealed to the rebellious elements in the Western youths, and that's not all bad. I admire Noam Chomsky greatly and he is very outspoken. But he stayed with the university and hasn't lost his reputation. So the line between rebel and reformer is not a clear one.

RF: Letters such as the following from Gerald Heard seemed to provoke him to a revolutionary stance.

> As you say the trinity of the 3 Ps Police, Priest, Paymaster (banker) is always against the journey of the soul but the current of consciousness is against the 3. For better or worse—better if you and the con[sciousness] chang[ing] druggist do it—worse if the politician is bright enough [in] his dark way to get in on the act. In either case, police, priest, and paymaster have had their day. Did you see that Glen Seaborg head of the A.E.C. asked what would be the big breakthrough in the next thirty years said in the consciousness changing drugs.

How did your group hope to infuse the virtues of the psychedelics into society?

HS: As I mentioned earlier, there never was an IFIF[2], so it's inaccurate to speak of my group. After the original IFIF it was for me a matter of cautious networking and writing as I struggled in the trail of William James, Aldous Huxley, and Gordon Wasson—and later, Albert Hofmann and Reuben Snake—to understand the workings of these substances and their import for religious living.

RF: I've been trying in the last several questions to get you to be critical, but you have been pretty muted. What was Tim's shadow side?

HS: Judge not that ye be not judged: he did what he had to do. But his heritage is a mixed bag. He thrived on followers, and as the decades advanced he went to greater and greater lengths to get them—preparing groups to colonize outer space, touring the circuit as a stand-up comic with Gordon Liddy—until in the end it was hard to know what he stood for other than getting attention. And magical thinking seemed to enter the mix, as in his failure to check for the prostate cancer that killed him. He was not given to long-term commitments and the responsibilities that come with them—how many times was he married? His own family did not turn out well. When I asked him about getting addicted to the hard drugs he got into, he said, "You get addicted then you cure yourself." That's a recklessness answer. He never broke himself of the tobacco habit. When I introduced him for his final book reading at Cody's Books in Berkeley—his early books were riveting, but that last one was a paste-up hodge-podge—he had to take a break at midpoint to go out on the deck for a cigarette. I am left looking back on his life with gratitude, and also with sadness. Gratitude not only for the doors to my psyche that he opened but also for the friendship, fun, and excitement he provided during those Harvard years. Sadness for the way his life went downhill. So much talent but a sad conclusion. His spirit remained unbroken, however.

RF: Are you surprised at what a mess there is now? Did you ever imagine back in 1960 that these drugs would be as forbidden, as illegal, as they are today?

HS: Initially I was utopian like everybody else. Whether it could have been different, I have no idea. Oh, things might be better now in little ways. The hysteria regarding drugs might be somewhat less if Tim and Dick had curbed some of their more flamboyant antics. But it remains an open question for me as to whether these substances can be openly integrated into society. I have used the image—lifted from Gerald Heard—of a beach ball in a lake. A part of it is always underwater. Gerald thought it must always be that way with society. There will never be a society where everything is above board because people have different tolerance levels. In the Victorian age you couldn't talk about sex but the state of your soul was fair game. Now those topics are reversed.

RF: But we're talking more about the soul now. Religious questions such as the existence of angels, life after death, spiritual laws of success, are making the bestseller list.

HS: You are quite right. Recently things have changed again. So perhaps the soul is coming back. And Tim may have helped to bring it back.

RF: There is such fear and ignorance that surrounds the mystical properties of psychedelic drugs, in spite of this interest in religion. Do you think that will ever change?

HS: I don't know, but I find something in me resisting saying that it will. One of the thunderclap realizations of my first experience was that (as I have reported) I had never known what awe was, and the way it fuses fear and fascination. I have to confess that for me fear is a part of the psychedelic experience. Every time I approach the prospect of losing control and being ejected from the driver's seat, I find myself fearful. And if that is endemic to the experience, fear may prevent an open acceptance of the psychedelics. Even in societies that don't have the FDA stalking. So I'm not sure that nonacceptance can be chalked up to the three Ps—paymaster and so on. It may reside in the nature of these substances.

RF: You once told me of coming across Tim in Switzerland in the '70s. Something he said to you seems relevant here.

HS: I know what you are referring to, and yes, it is relevant. Kendra and I were involved in a three-week seminar on Jung and Kazantzakis in Switzerland and I got word somehow that Tim was in the country. The original IFIF network was still sufficiently in place for me to track him and we arranged to meet in the town near my seminar site. This was on the heels of his prison break and escape from the United States—as hair-raising a story as I've ever heard—and he was wearing the dark aura of a wanted man. He roared into town in characteristic style on the back seat of a Harley Davidson driven by a Swiss buddy of his. It was wonderful to see him again, out of prison and free, but what I remember best was his statement, early in our conversation, that you are asking me to repeat, which was, "Nobody ever changes, do they, Huston?" Like so many of Tim's observations, it was deeply discerning. Here we were, in a foreign land, thousands of miles from Cambridge, so much had happened for both of us. But I was still on the spiritual journey that was my priority before I encountered Tim and the psychedelics. And he was still a fugitive from lawful society—kicked out of it as he had been kicked out of West Point, Harvard University, and Zihuatanejo.

RF: We still have this conflict between the materialist's "scientific" worldview and that of the mystic. You can end it, in a way, with psychedelic drugs. You can see, in a scientific way, that is, a systematic way, that the numinous does exist, that there is a sacred, that God consciousness may be more fundamental than the materialist's claim. You can prove the reality of the mystic's experience.

HS: You can prove it to me, but then I didn't need proof—I believed that the mystics were right before I encountered the psychedelics. And I'm afraid that the same holds for the disbelievers. Materialists have to agree that the psychedelic can generate mystical experiences, but there is nothing in those experiences that forces people to accept that they tell us what the world is like. Bertrand Russell is a case in point. Asked if he had ever had a mystical experience, he answered, "Many." "What did you do with them?" "I dismissed them."

RF: I'm trying to follow Huxley's thought here. As he said in an early paper, "Visionary Experience," given with Leary in 1961 in Copenhagen:

> These biochemical methods are, I suppose, the most powerful and the most foolproof, so to say, of all the methods for transporting us to this other world that at present exist. I think, as Professor Leary will point out tonight, that there is a very large field for systematic experimentation by psychologists, because

it is now possible to explore areas of the mind at a minimum expense to the body, areas which were almost impossible to get at before, except either by the use of extremely dangerous drugs or else by looking around for the rather rare people who spontaneously can go into this other world. (Of course it is very difficult for them to go in on demand, "the Spirit bloweth where it listeth," we can never be sure that the people with the spontaneous gift of visionary experience will have it on demand.) With such drugs as psilocybin it is possible for the majority of people to go into this other world with very little trouble and with almost no harm done to themselves.

HS: That wise man; I don't recall having read anything by Huxley that didn't strike me as right on. But note the qualification in the passage you quoted. It says that psychedelics are "the most" foolproof, not that they are foolproof, which is what would be required to turn skeptics into mystics.

RF: I'll concede that distinction but even so, doesn't it seem strange to you that theological seminaries and monastaries ignore this "most powerful and most foolproof" way of accessing the divine? Religious training, or metaphysical inquiry, seems to provide the ideal context for these drugs.

HS: Here I'm completely with you. Of course, legal space would have to be carved out for this to happen, and even with that space they should be offered as an elective, so to speak, and not part of the required curriculum. For I don't see that anything that has happened since the Wassons published their groundbreaking *Russia, Mushrooms and History* that counters the premise of that book, which is that "mushrooms" mean close to everything to half the world while the other half views them phobicly, as toadstools.

RF: In that same conference in Copenhagen Huxley raised the question: "Of course we come now to the philosophical problem: what is the metaphysical status of visions, what is the ontological status? . . . it is worth going into, and I hope someone will go into it sooner or later." I wonder if we'll ever get around to that in this culture?

HS: Huxley got around to it, and William James, Gordon Wasson, and Albert Hofmann all got around to it. You are getting around to it and I got around to it in the key essay I have written on the subject, "Do Drugs have Religious Import?" which has been anthologized more than twenty times, mostly in textbooks. So the thrust of your question is whether our society will get around to giving the question the attention it deserves.

Who knows? As Bob Dylan sang, "the answer is blowing in the wind." I am not entirely discouraged, however. I never thought that I would live long enough to be invited to give a well-publicized lecture on psychedelics and religion at a major university. It was at Northern Illinois University, two years ago. It was as if I were back at Harvard when the topic was respectable. Still I don't know where we're headed. It's like when Dizzy Gillespie was asked about the future of jazz. He said, "Man, if I knew where jazz is going, I'd be there already."

Owsley's Leary

AN INTERVIEW WITH OWSLEY STANLEY
BY ROBERT FORTE

RF: I just noticed that it was April 17 that we began this conversation—right in the middle of the anniversary of the discovery of LSD—about Timothy Leary. He's been enjoying a bit of upswing of late. Though pretty much confined to a wheelchair, he has incredible energy and good humor, acting like an adolescent prankster in a seventy-five-year-old decrepit body. He's beautiful and tormented at the same time. Razor wit. Glad to have this chance to discuss him with you.

Bear: I'm not really sure just what I could say about him that others haven't already said. We have hung out a bit over the years, but I have always felt that he was so intent on bullshitting me about this or that, that I never saw the guy's real self. Sorry, but that's the truth.

Some people are saying that Tim is planning to commit suicide live via his Web site. If this is true, then he has abandoned any pre-

---

Owsley Stanley is best known as an artist, scientist, designer, and creator of technologies that expand consciousness. He has produced audio output systems for the Grateful Dead and enhanced receiving capabilities for many others. "Art and music are the pinnacle of man's endeavors," he writes, "the rest of the activity is just support for art."

tense of dignity in his pursuit of celebrity. In the Australian newspaper weekend edition today I read an article by Philip Adams who makes mention of the notion that sustained celebrity status has, as its inevitable consequence, permanent brain damage. I'm inclined to agree, and Tim is making an excellent case in point.

RF: Well, he *is* a public figure, a celebrity. There are certain liabilities of that position. What's that saying? "The farther the monkey climbs up the tree, the more you can see his ass."

When he first announced his plan to have his body cryonically preserved he added, "I just want to keep my options open and when it comes down to it I may decide to fuck this freezer business and have them stick me in the blender." He's actually becoming more private now, but a few press releases make it seem like an all-day party. It's really more like an eight-hour party.

Bear: I am pleased to learn that the article about dying on the Internet is fiction. It really doesn't suit anyone with any degree of enlightenment. The only thing that a man truly owns in this existence is his honor, and a major part of the nature of honor is dignity. All that is the work and is the personal creation of each one of us. Perhaps the greatest work of art, the highest challenge facing an artist in this life, is the work to create himself, and the honor that may become a part of consciousness. I think that is the unconscious goal everyone starts out with, but some of us sorta lose the plot along the way.

RF: Timothy Leary?

Bear: In fact he has, in my estimation, been one of the most destructive actors to appear on the scene since the discovery of the psychedelic effect of the peyote plant by Havelock Ellis and its introduction to Western culture in the 1890s.

RF: He was so vocal and antagonistic. Seems like the whole psychedelic effort has to first clean up after Leary.

Bear: I agree with that, and a mess it has been. An unnecessary effort. I wish that Tim had been able to open up to me. I always approach everyone with a "tabula rasa" in order to learn about them. I guess I wasn't patient enough.

Maybe I'm a bit strong in my statements about Tim and all the things he has done. I don't hate him. Actually I am rather fond of him, or at least of whom I feel or hope him to be. I was disappointed in my inability to penetrate the mask he held up to me. I don't dislike him as a person, I only have a difficult time coming to grips with his motivations. I think of him mostly as a guy who has just missed the bus, and is running around trying to figure out where it has gone. He seemed to come upon where we had just been and think that was "it." Here's an example:

One day a few years ago I was in L.A. and I called him up and dropped by. He was distracted and didn't want to hang out that day because he was in the middle of working on a computer game. "What sort of game?" I wanted to know.

"State of the art," he said. "It will get people really sucked in and turned on."

I had a look at what he was doing with the computer nerd he had as an assistant. The screen was filled with text. "Tim," said I, "computer games aren't text-based any more, they're graphics-oriented."

"Not at all," said Tim. "Everyone will love this game."

This was early in his contact with computers, and the standards for games had already gone far beyond the text-intensive sort that he was writing. Nothing ever came of that game, but I couldn't convince him at the time that the idea was cool but he needed to make something which really was in sync with the "state of the art." A day late and several dollars short. Sad.

I kept getting the vague feeling that he was being a "hail fellow, well met" sort of person in my presence, and that he really wasn't all that interested in who I was, or particularly interested in what I had to say. I felt that he was not opening himself much in the interaction. I definitely got the impression, on several occasions when I had a limited amount of time that I could spend with him, that there were more interesting things that he was into doing during that time.

I was born in the year of the Dog in the Chinese cycle, and I do indeed have a strong need to be friends with the people I know. I form attachments. I have a need to do that. I felt that wasn't all that important to Tim. I could be wrong, I could have misread him; I am quite willing to admit to that. The urge I feel is always toward forming friendships in my life. Can't help it.

RF: He calls you "God's Secret Agent" in The Politics of Ecstasy. Says you're a good bet for "romantic immortality," a "folk hero of the twenty-first century": "He was spinning us along an epic poem trip through the levels of creation. He can really tell it. I've studied with the wisest sages of our time—Huxley, Heard, Lama Govinda, Sri Krishna Prem, Alan Watts—and I have to say that AOS.3 . . . has the best up-to-date perspective of the divine design I've ever listened to." Says you're "a mad saint" and writes about you with great passion: "AOS.3 is that rare species, a realized, living, breathing, smelling, bawling, laughing, working, scolding man. A ridiculous, conceited fool, God's fool, dreaming of ways to make us all happy, to turn us all on, to love us and be loved."

Bear: That chapter in The Politics of Ecstasy is a fictionalized account produced as a sort of extract of a lot of meetings, a sort of digest in the terms of what he was trying to say in that particular book. It does show his attitude toward me, however. I though it a bit of somewhat self-serving fiction at the time that I read the book.

RF: A healthy society needs people like Leary to incite chaos, break down dysfunctional patterns.

Bear: I don't disagree with you about Tim's compulsive iconoclastic bent, but I differ with you about the reasoning behind it. I don't see any purpose in being in constant conflict with everything, and espousing nothing. The impression that it leaves me with is that he will do anything to attract attention to himself: a full-tilt run at celebrityhood. Not because he actually believes that whatever his object of the moment is, is important.

RF: The people at Sandoz and the Swiss Academy of Medicine, among many others, think Leary ruined the chances of this phenomenally important drug, LSD, to work in society.

Bear: This is the "official" stance of the Swiss establishment. Albert Hofmann is ecstatic about the way that acid has spread throughout the world. He was the original Psychedelic Ranger, and he had to work through the scientific community with which he was associated. He was in no way offended by the "esoterics and hippies" using LSD, his only concern was that people not use it to make a lot of money. Later, when the use started to move out into the community at large, the scientific and M.D. people were upset, and still are, because the stuff was no longer the exclusive privilege of their elite group.

The medical and scientific community have only themselves to blame for the loss of access to experimentation with the psychedelics. They stood on the sideline when Senator Tom Dodd and his weasle friend Art Linkletter forced through the legislation. William O. Douglas, too, was taken in by Linkletter. The M.D.'s thought that it would just clean up the streets, but they forgot the lesson of cannabis, didn't they? Nuts to them! They still would rather whine and act righteous than take any real action to return the class of substances to legality.

The effects that Leary produced were of a minimal value to the psychedelic community as a whole. I don't agree with the old saw that there is only good publicity. I don't think that his in-your-face, fuck you kind of approach has put us in a better position today than we would have been if he had been a bit more circumspect. We are much the worse for his actions.

He never seemed to care about the damage that he was doing, even when we told him, which we did on numerous occasions. He always appeared to favor iconoclasm as an end in itself, rather than a means to an end. He certainly is one of those directly responsible for the rapidity with which the laws progressed to the draconian state that we now find them. Perhaps without all his shouting from the rooftops in the loudest voice he could find, things wouldn't have gotten quite so bad. I am referring to things like the practice of sentencing people on the weight of the filler materials in the doses as if it were all active drug. Such things belong to the realm of emotions, not justice, and the fact that they came to be indicates a very unthinking reaction to the scene. We all knew that the advent of psychedelics was important, but we were also aware of the words of the Kybalion: "The lips of knowledge are closed except to the ears of understanding"—a warning similar to the old saying about pearls and swine.

RF: He cast those pearls everywhere. I saw a cartoon of two pigs looking at some pearls while one of them is saying, "Oh my, what exquisite pearls."

Bear: Was it a string of pearls?

RF: No, there were just a few scattered on the ground.

Bear: Exactly my point. I think Leary might have done a lot of damage to a lot of kids, not because he said "take acid" and they did, but because the ways in which he did it caused the laws to be written which have locked them up for life.

RF: He was busted for a few joints' worth of low-grade pot and twice sentenced to multiyear sentences.

Bear: The fall Tim took was entirely of his own doing. There's an old saying, "If you can't do the time, don't do the crime." I don't expect you to point out to me that his "crime" was his big mouth, because I know that full well.

Psychedelics are a part of religion or knowledge, not the weapons of war and confrontation. It only destroys things to expose them. Everyone who needs to know will be told. The media and the government didn't need to have been involved.

RF: Can you really blame Tim for this? Psychedelics have been forbidden in Western Christian society since the beginning.

Bear: You've got to be kidding! It's obvious where the blame lies.

RF: This history is too complex to lay it all on one man.

Bear: That's like saying the match that burned Chicago wasn't the only reason it burned. No one else was talking Tim's talk.

RF: Listen to you! Legend has it that you are the one who fed the hungry masses.

Bear: I guess you're making an attempt at humor here. In three years I made less than 500 grams of LSD.

RF: A mere five million doses.

Bear: Wrong again, we dosed high, and the fact is there were only a little over a million doses, spread over three years, half of which were given away and the others sold to support the trip. Nowadays those who make it run batches of 10 to 20 kilos at a time. You suffer from an overdose of media. Our thing was small and intermittent, as I was not at that time entirely sure if it was okay for the community in the long view. I wanted to be sure that it was a good thing; it is indeed powerful. Also we made the doses a bit too strong. That was a mistake.

RF: Everybody was just learning.

Bear: We didn't figure out for a long time that the doses weren't conducive to the quiet growth of the scene. It was for those who followed me on the Path to figure that one out. I always was in favor of the cosmic experience. Perhaps that is what a person with a big, strong ego needs, but it's not cool on the street. Most people never take only half of a dose, but they will take several if they feel the need, so our tack wasn't the best one.

RF: How did you get involved with psychedelics? Was it through Kesey and the Dead?

Bear: I heard about the Leary/Alpert scene before I was aware of Kesey. In 1963 I became involved with a scene in Berkeley. I suppose it was an extension of the scholastic movement which must have started with Hofmann, except there were students who were cooking up the acid, rather than professors obtaining it from Sandoz. None of the doses were of a very high grade. I had some of the genuine Sandoz material given to me by an old attorney friend who in turn had gotten it from a fellow in Mexico. The real stuff was quite a revelation. I determined to discover how to make it, since no one else seemed to be able to do it right. And so it went.

RF: I gather you had a circle growing quietly underground.

Bear: We weren't exactly underground, but we weren't out in the streets waving flags either. Like rock and roll, there are the ones who are in-your-face like my pal Paul Kantner, and there are those like Jerry Garcia, who just smiled and sang his songs. Who do you think had the greater influence? Perhaps that isn't really fair since Paul is still around, but I think that the point is there. Life is a form of art. There is beautiful art and there is the ugly kind. Why make something which is ugly, no matter how "artistic" it may be?

RF: Do you see *anything* redeemable about Leary's popularizing, or as Ginsberg called it, "democratizing" the psychedelics?

Bear: Leary had relatively little to do with "democratizing" the use of acid, as we already had it done by the time he was being heard. I think he was more like "surfing" on the waves that we found. Of the two, the path taken by Ram Dass has seemed more significant, at least to me.

I am not critical of the spread of the use and knowledge, only the rude, rough, and wholly unnecessary way Tim went about using the thing publicly for his own ego-gratification. Be assured, there are many of us who were appalled by the things some people, including Tim, were up to. Don't confuse me with the elitists, either.

RF: Though now I feel I'm lauding Leary in defense of your negative view, he may have done society a great service by praising the virtues of psychedelics and thereby turning on millions of people. Ram Dass was just one of them. Maybe he would have picked it up somewhere else down the line, but he was an uptight, dysfunctional man—by his own admission—before he met Leary. Probably lots of people fit that description.

Ram Dass says he was a "rascal in training." Its kind of funny that he is known as the saintly one now. Lots of folks deplore Leary's reckless ways but I didn't expect to hear many of the same critiques from you, of all people. Thanks for keeping this adventure unpredictable.

Bear: Maybe the critiques are valid, but the motivations are different for presenting them. I want to see the psychedelics become a regular way of life for people—they want to preserve the status quo.

The point is: Leary's way was *wrong*. The damage has been done, and I for one am not going to celebrate the destruction of a city just because, perhaps, it may rise from the ashes renewed. There's even further to go now, as you yourself admit, than there was then.

RF: You don't value his role as a teacher at all.

Bear: There is no teacher. All such are frauds, especially those who proclaim that status. Find the truth yourself. It's all around you all the time. Once you have acquired the key, you will find you have all the pieces already. Psychedelics are the key. Find the Kybalion; it's got all the information you need.

Stolaroff on Leary

AN INTERVIEW WITH MYRON STOLAROFF
BY ROBERT FORTE

RF: I'm glad that we are going to have this conversation about Tim. Your perspective on what was going on with him at that time is very important in the process to resuscitate the potential of psychedelic drugs. Leary was so popular that many people associate LSD with his style, his exuberance, and in that process a great deal's been lost.

MS: I think it's a question of being thorough, so as to disclose all aspects of the situation. Most of us who have honestly pursued the

Myron Stolaroff holds a master's degree in electrical engineering from Stanford University. He worked for Ampex Corporation as a design engineer and eventually became the Director of Instrumentation Marketing. He helped pioneer the development of videotape recording. In 1956 he was given LSD and declared it was "the greatest discovery man has ever made." In 1961 he founded the International Foundation for Advanced Study. During that period he was the executive administrator for a research group conducting clinical studies with LSD and mescaline where they treated 350 subjects to psychedelic visions. He has published professional papers in the Journal of Nervous and Mental Disease, Gnosis, *and the* Yearbook for Ethnomedicine and the Study of Consciousness. *He published his memoirs,* Thanatos To Eros: Thirty-Five Years of Psychedelic Exploration, *in 1994,* and authored *The Secret Chief: Conversations with a Pioneer of the Underground Psychedelic Movement,* in 1997.

investigation of psychedelics think that one of the real tragedies of our time is that such an extraordinarily valuable and necessary tool as LSD should be held in such disrepute. And Tim certainly understood that as well.

RF: To what extent do you think that this disrepute is caused by Timothy?

MS: I think as far as the scientific community is concerned, he really scared them, and if you followed the exchange of letters with Ralph Metzner and myself that was published in *Gnosis* [winter 1993, spring 1994, and summer 1994], and also the documentation that I pointed out in *Storming Heaven*, I don't think there's any question of what Tim was trying to do. He made it very clear to me personally he thought psychedelics weren't going to be accepted by our current society, especially by our current mainstream scientists, who haven't even accepted the transpersonal aspects of the human being. Therefore he wanted to publicize psychedelics and set up a national network for them to be supplied. His goal was to turn on the country.

Tim appreciated the potential of human beings very much. I think he was very aware of the investment we have in our conditioning that results in the establishment of a kind of self-interest that interferes with clear perception. And he recognized psychedelics as a powerful tool to cut through such conditioning, to bring a person to direct understanding of their own true nature, and the nature of the universe. This is probably the most valuable tool that one could have. I think he was committed to it being understood and accepted. In that regard he and I are very much in alignment.

He and his associates wanted to spread the word. They wanted to make it possible for everyone to have the LSD experience. In their published announcement of their organization, the International Federation of Internal Freedom, they acknowledged this would have to be approved by the FDA. However, the FDA didn't approve it. The FDA wouldn't allow LSD to be supplied to groups like this. So Tim's private agenda was to find ways to have these groups form around the country and to make sure they had supplies of LSD. A lot of this is beyond my direct knowledge but some of it is not. They worked with people who manufactured black-market LSD and had means of distribution. So people around the country began to have supplies and were able to have the experience. I believe that a huge bulk of this was engineered by Tim and his associates. That was his plan. That's what he announced to me that morning when I visited him in Cambridge to invite him to get off our advisory board. He told me that's what he wanted to do—turn everybody on. He was convinced that all you had to do was to take LSD and move into transpersonal areas. Unfortunately its only true for healthy-minded people. Ones who are not can have difficult times with this. That was the problem of his whole approach to setting up a national network for the purposes of turning on the country.

RF: You can see from some of your correspondence at that time there was a spirit of camaraderie. You offered to supply him with LSD, according to this letter that I have here dated January 8, 1963.

MS: [laughs] That's quite a letter. I'm amazed I don't have a copy in my file.

RF: You're offering to provide them with the material and you're working together.

MS: Yes. And of course, I might say that one of their objectives was to obtain drugs and to distribute them in conformance with existing laws to research groups. So the letter I wrote is consistent with that. We very definitely needed approval of the FDA. But the FDA made it clear that approval was not forthcoming for the kind of thing Tim wanted to do. In fact they were extremely adamant about it. So in a way that offer is kind of hypothetical—although it's true. If he'd gotten approval we could've gone ahead with what I said in the letter.

RF: Let's back up a little bit. Tell us about the International Foundation for Advanced Study. How did that come to be? How did you get interested in the subject of psychedelics and why did you start the International Foundation for Advanced Study?

MS: Well, I won't repeat a lot of material that you can get right out of my book: *Thanatos to Eros: Thirty-Five Years of Psychedelic Explora-tion*. To be brief, I had my first spiritual awakening through partici-pating in the Sequoia Seminar, and that got me in touch with Gerald Heard. We sponsored a couple of lectures of his in Palo Alto. I was extraordinarily taken by him, so I spent a two-week seminar with him once at our Sequoia Seminar Lodge up in the mountains. He was one of the great human beings on the planet—totally, abso-lutely fascinating. I began to visit him whenever I was in L.A. In one of these visits he told me about LSD. I was utterly amazed. First of all, since he was such an outstanding mystic, I didn't know why he needed to take LSD, but he assured me that it had enor-mous potential. It created vast openings of the mind that led to an understanding of spiritual realities and it was very valuable.

RF: What year was this?

MS: Probably early 1955.

RF: That was the first you'd heard of LSD?

MS: Yes. I asked him how he got in touch with it. He told me about Hubbard coming down from Canada and administering it to both him and Aldous Huxley.

RF: Gerald Heard really started a lot of fires. Huston Smith says his first opening came from reading one of Gerald Heard's books.

MS: As a matter of fact, one of my spiritual awakenings came from reading his *Preface to Prayer*. Reading that book led to a spontane-ous experience where I awakened into a brilliant, overwhelmingly glorious light. It was very brief but I'd never experienced anything like it in my life. It had quite an impact.

RF: You were coming at this from a field that's not normally associated with mysticism. Am I correct that you were an electrical engineer?

MS: I was an engineer, but I spent a number of years with this Se-quoia Seminar. At the time we're talking about I had been with them four or five years and I was on the planning committee. I'd already had a spontaneous mystical experience with them, so I was deeply into meditation and the study of mysticism. I was reading everything I could get my hands on. And Gerald's books were quite an opening; but *Preface to Prayer* was the outstanding one for me.

RF: The International Foundation for Advanced Study was one of the first institutes set up to explore the application of psychedelic drugs to creative problem solving, personal growth, and to psychotherapy. What were some of the things you were doing there?

MS: Well, I'm not sure how accurate your statement is. At that particular time I don't know if any real work was going on in creativity. I was totally unfamiliar with the work in Europe until I went to visit Hofmann in 1963, which led me to Leurner in Germany and then to Sandison in England, who Hofmann said were the two best investigators. But prior to that time, there was a lot of work done in Canada by Humphry Osmond in Weyburn, and Abram Hoffer in Saskatoon. And the two of them got most all of the Canadian funds for work in the field of mental health research. Al Hubbard was very close with them in that work. Then Hubbard joined J. Ross MacLean who had a small hospital just outside of Vancouver. It was a mental hospital, and they started using LSD there as a treatment for alcoholism. And it was open to people who wanted to come and have the experience. They worked there for several years together. After Hubbard left, MacLean kept the work going for several years. Then Hubbard decided to be independent of MacLean and set up a separate treatment room in Vancouver with a psychiatrist. I was going up and visiting frequently and we were all learning. We had the great vision of setting up LSD clinics all over the world. The next place to start was Menlo Park, where I set up a nonprofit corporation and a clinic after I resigned from AMPEX. We had two separate session rooms. We got Charles Savage as medical director and Dr. John Sherwood to be the immediate medical supervisor and we started to conduct sessions there, which we did from 1961 to 1965.

We started that with Sherwood. Hubbard talked Savage into being our medical director after we'd been operating a few months. And then Savage wanted to do research, so he put together a team of Robert Mogar, who was a professor of psychology at San Francisco State College, Willis Harman, Professor of Engineering at

Stanford, and James Fadiman, a psychologist. Those were the three main ones. Quite a bit down the line Bob McKim from Stanford joined. He was very interested in creativity research.

RF: You keep using the word "clinic," but your work was not solely clinical. It wasn't only for treatment.

MS: It was open to the public. It was open to anyone who wanted to have the experience. It became more and more treatment-oriented as time went on, because as the adverse publicity grew, people became more and more resistant to coming. The people that did come were the more desperate ones so our client group had more and more pathology as time went on. But Savage was the one that made the decision on whether or not they were acceptable to the program.

RF: This is a different program than what was going on in Palo Alto with the VA hospital, where Ken Kesey and Allen Ginsberg turned on.

MS: Oh that was almost purely a pharmacological experiment. They were giving people different drugs just to see what happened. As a matter of fact, Leo Hollister, who was in charge of the Veterans hospital investigation, was very opposed to our operation. He had no understanding of what these things really do. He deeply resented the mystical aspects, and he disliked Hubbard.

RF: There have been allegations that this was under the auspices of the American CIA.

MS: It could have been. Who knows what their contracts were? Hollister was their kind of man. Then there was another group in Palo Alto. You see, the Palo Alto clinic was an enormously famous clinic because the director was Russell Lee. He's the one that's given credit for single-handedly getting Medicare accomplished.

Theirs was a regular clinic that treated many thousands of patients. As a part of it, they set up a foundation for scientific investigation, I think called the Palo Alto Research Center, that was headed by a physician named Jackson, and they did some work with LSD for a while. They administered to about a dozen psychiatrists and psychologists. Karl Pribram turned on there. Out of the twelve I think he had the best experience. Gregory Bateson was involved with them as well. A lot of them had horrible experiences. That's what contributed a lot to the psychotomimetic label—these psychiatrists taking it and having horrible times. Are you familiar with Abram Hoffer's quote? "The people who have the worst time with psychedelics are (1) ministers, (2) psychiatrists, and (3) psychologists." These are the ones with the greatest investments in their status.

RF: When you had your first LSD experience and decided to start the clinic in Menlo Park, what was your vision? What was your dream of what LSD and the other psychedelics could be for our society?

MS: I pronounced that LSD was the greatest discovery man had ever made. It has such enormous potential because the mind is infinite. LSD opens up the resources of the mind. Since the mind is the most important aspect of the human being, what could possibly be more important than a drug that revealed the awesome, infinite potential that lies within? Soon after my first experience, I had no doubt I was going to spend the rest of my life researching psychedelics: promulgating understanding and the development of the potential of psychedelics. That came as a result of my first experience in April of 1956. I didn't have a really good opening until 1959, and that's when I discovered that I truly was God. The Buddhists particularly don't like looking at it that way, but that's how I experienced it.

RF: That's right around the time that Tim had his first awakening. Tim took it first in 1960, in the summer. When was the first time you met Timothy and what were your impressions?

MS: Well, I'll prologue this by saying that we met Dick Alpert first. He was in Palo Alto. He knew people at Stanford, among them Jim Fadiman, who arranged our meeting. Jim knew the group back there in Cambridge and said a lot of good things about them. So we met with Dick Alpert and were very impressed. Later, Al Hubbard went to visit them at Harvard and he came back and said, "Myron, we've got to have Leary and Hollingshead on our advisory board." I was very reluctant to put anybody on that I hadn't met so I didn't do anything about it. Then Tim came to visit—I think it was in the spring of '62—and I was very taken with him. He was extremely charismatic, very bright, very personable. We had a really good time together. I won't go into details here, but I went up to San Francisco and met him and we spent some time together. After that I had no hesitation about putting him on the board, but I never found out anything to encourage me to put Hollingshead on. Tim and I had a very genial relationship.

RF: So when did your relationship start to go sour?

MS: I wouldn't say it ever went sour.

RF: Well, thank you for clearing that up, because you can tell even in this letter where you chastise him, it's done with such a loving tone.

MS: No, I never was down on Tim. I regretted a lot of things that he did. I thought that he was extremely unwise. Abram Hoffer and I went to a conference in San Francisco in the summer of 1966. Leary was tremendously popular. I remember he got up on the stage wearing a white blazer and pants with vertical white and red alternating stripes. He made an appealing presentation—his usual way of telling half-truths and getting people stimulated without discussing the adverse side of things—and everybody in the audience yelled and cheered. Hoffer and I were standing together and Hoffer said, "You know, we hate to see this kind of promotion because there's so much you need to understand before you embark on using these things, but who are we to judge? It may take forty years before we know whether Tim is an absolute hero or whether he brought everything tumbling down." I thought that was very open-minded of Abram and I never forgot it.

RF: Well, Myron, that's one of the main questions I want this book to address. You know as well as I that psychedelic drugs have been most forcibly repressed in Western Christian civilization for a long, long time, for two thousand years. Whenever the European colonialists found them in Mexico or anywhere else in the New World, they dominated those cultures and forbade the use of them.

They were almost totally eliminated from history until Wasson and a few people started to do their work. Eventually this knowledge began to accrue. There was bound to be resistance by the establishment to these substances, so maybe Tim's style was exactly what was needed to make sure the cat didn't get back in the bag.

MS: Perhaps. Time will tell. There is no question in my mind that Tim is largely responsible for terminating legitimate psychedelic research in America, and through our example and persuasion, throughout the world. On the other hand, hundreds of thousands of individuals have had psychedelic experiences through his leadership. Tim will have succeeded if sufficient numbers of persons who have taken psychedelics achieve enough wisdom and responsibility to restore scientific research and obtain public recognition of the value and potential of psychedelics. Psychedelics are powerful. They are intense. It's now clear how you have to approach them and that was totally misunderstood in our culture. You see, one of the things that becomes clear with time, and a point that I wish to emphasize from now on, is that in order to take these substances for benefit, you have to be *honest*. And if you look at how our culture is going, the level of dishonesty has been growing steadily. Here we are, a nation with a five trillion dollar debt. What does *that* tell you about honesty? What does it tell you about morality? Look at what our politicians are willing to say to get elected. Look at the abysmal, politically driven War on Drugs that is dismembering our profoundly wise constitution. Look at our media and the way they handle news. So here's a substance that requires honesty and you look at the level of honesty in our society. Of course they don't want to embrace it. Everybody thinks that they're making the right choices and doing the right thing. Who wants to be shown differently? Only a very honest person and one who is sincerely interested in being a true scientist or true investigator or is truly invested in his or her own personal growth.

RF: I think that you just gave Tim a fantastic compliment. Is that true?

MS: Well, I think he did understand the bullshit. But he did not come from the position of unconditional love. Because he was excited I think by the confrontation. He did a lot to create confrontation and keep it going. If you realize that people are frightened, you have to put them at ease. If they perceive these things as dangerous and they're very reluctant to face the truth, you have to comfort them. You have to make them comfortable until they're willing to objectively look at the data and then make their own decision. He didn't do any of those things. He flaunted it. That was his great error. That's what produced all the commotion.

RF: So your group and Tim's group had very different ways of dealing with the resistance. Your way was going to be work through science, to systematically demonstrate the positive or negative aspects of the drugs. Tim wanted to offer them to the wind and trust the great evolutionary current.

MS: As a matter of fact, when I visited him and he explained his program to me—and this was a few days before I wrote the letter excerpted in *Storming Heaven*—we made an agreement. He said to me that our institutions are too encrusted, they're too invested, their too solidified to ever accept something like this. I said, "Tim, the only way you can go is to win over our institutions, because society is not going to go against the institutions." He said, "Myron, you go ahead, you do the scientific work, go ahead and do the conventional thing of winning the institutions over and having it come through appropriate developments, and I'll do the things to shake them up." Fifteen years later when we had a reunion with Hubbard, Leary, and many others, at Oscar Janiger's, I said to Tim: "When we made this agreement, you said you'd shake them up, but I didn't know you were going to hit them over the head with a baseball bat!" He said "I don't like your metaphor." But it's true. My metaphor was accurate.

RF: So what about now, Myron? We now have a culture where literally millions of people have tasted the fruits of psychedelic experience and we have the most draconian laws prohibiting them. Do you think that you could have done it differently? Do you think you could've sidestepped the resistance and enabled as many people to benefit from these drugs?

MS: Well, you know, the question is meaningless because we could only do what we have the understanding and awareness to do. Back in the sixties, I was a highly neurotic person. I happened to have some natural instinct for sitting in sessions with people, but my God, it's taken me the last several decades to develop some maturity and wisdom. You can't exercise wisdom before you have it. Now if I took today's wisdom back to the 1960s, I think we would have been much more articulate in dealing with the public, dealing with reporters, the whole approach. Unfortunately you just can't go back and start over. We have to deal with the current situation. We have to take the wisdom we've gathered and the understanding, realize the enormous fear people have of these substances, realize the ignorance that prevails, realize that there are a lot of people who benefit from the current perception of psychedelics being dangerous and toxic.

RF: Who are they?

MS: Number one, the psychiatric profession. If they really understood how effective psychedelics can be in therapy, these agents would be an enormous threat to them, unless they were willing to undergo the experiences themselves, advance their own personal being, and learn how to use them. In this field, any really knowledgeable good-hearted person can be of considerably more help to another person than many psychiatrists. Even perhaps with very sick people. There's so much to be learned to properly use these things. But anyhow, that's where a lot of powerful resistance is—the psychiatric profession, because I think they perceive it as a real threat.

The March 1993 issue of *Psychiatric Annals* was devoted to psychedelics. There wasn't a single article in there by anyone who knew much about the proper use of psychedelics. They kept repeating over and over again all the toxic problems, the abuse problems and so on. And that is, I think, an accurate picture of the psychiatric community's regard for these drugs.

RF: I conducted a survey of the American Psychiatric Association back in 1984 that measured psychiatrist's attitudes toward psychedelic drugs. First I measured how much they knew about them personally and in terms of the literature, and then I asked them to rate the perceived potential of their judicious exploration. The first question was, had you ever taken a psychedelic drug? Respondents self-rated their expertise. And sure enough, just as you're saying, there's no informed opposition. The only people within the psychiatric profession who dismiss the significance of psychedelic drugs were the ones who, by their own admission, didn't know anything about them. All they knew was from sources in the popular media. Psychiatrists who had taken them, or who had bothered to read the research literature, usually predicted immense possibilities in fields as diverse as neurology and religion.

MS: Well, if one were a genuine psychiatrist and heard that something made it possible to open the mind and get into one's own unconscious, enabling examination of one's own shadow material and unconscious values, goals, anger, pain, guilt and so on, my God, wouldn't they be interested? One might be skeptical, but how could you not be interested?

RF: Well, this is what brings us back to Tim now and maybe why he decided to just do an end run around the psychiatric profession.

MS: Well, I get back to Hoffer's quote. It may have been necessary for someone like Tim to really shake the boat. Without him we would not have nearly as many people with an understanding of psychedelics. So in a way he did a great service. Probably a few million people know the experience because of him. The unanswered question is: What will be the outcome of the people who have had the experience because of him? We do know that there are areas where there have been major contributions. I think everybody agrees that the computer field has proliferated because of these people. I am told on pretty good authority that practically every leading scientist today in that particular field is an acid head. There's no way to verify this because of the illegality. No one will admit it, but yet it's logical. Because if you learn how to use these tools, they're so valuable, they open up so much, they make so much more possible, how could you *not* use them, law or no law? There are certainly wise people who have been introduced through Leary's efforts who are making headway. On the other hand, look where we stand. Jeremy Tarcher wished to sponsor a book with interviews of fifty people with name recognition who were willing to say that they owed a lot to psychedelics. Charlie Grob was in charge of the project. He couldn't get anybody willing to say public that they had taken psychedelics. Kary Mullis is one of the few who's been wide open.

RF: I quote him in the introduction to *Entheogens and the Future of Religion.* He said, "I think I may have been stupid in some respects if it weren't for my psychedelic experiences." He won the Nobel Prize. But remember when he was going to testify in the O.J. Simpson trial, the prosecutors were going to knock his testimony because he admitted to using acid, as if that discredited his genius.

MS: But he didn't mind saying anything. I went up to him at the Entheobotany Conference in San Francisco in October 1996 and told him about the book. He gave me his card and told me to get in touch with him, but later he wouldn't respond. Perhaps because he was writing his own book, which is now out. But he hasn't hesitated to declare himself in public. I contacted others as well. I was told that anybody would be an idiot to admit in today's culture that they used psychedelics.

RF: Or they'd be honest and courageous.

MS: Now that's what I tried to say. I said it's time to stand up and be counted. How long are we going to be pushed around by this?

RF: I spoke with Huston Smith about this very point. He is a little reluctant to speak favorably about psychedelics. Huston Smith is one of the most dignified and prestigious scholars in the world, and he's afraid for his reputation. That's how subversive this subject is.

MS: He's already written about it.

RF: Yes, he has. But he writes about it very carefully, and is more cautious now because he feels like he's just hitting his stride.

MS: Well, that's great. Now you see you have to take into account another thing, Bob. I don't have many contacts—we're too isolated here—but I have a little bit of evidence that, as people get older, the experiences get more uncomfortable and they abandon them. At the Vallombrosa Psychoactive Sacraments conference in 1995, several of the old-timers doubted that psychedelics are valuable on an ongoing basis. They all admit they're great openers and great initiators, but they imply that you then have to go on to other means of development. There was a bit of sharing of information that perhaps the experiences do get uncomfortable. I personally know people who stopped using them because the experiences are so uncomfortable. One prominent psychologist thinks that the body doesn't process them as you get older. In my own experience, that's not true. I think if you keep on using them, certain priciples need to be taken into account.

First of all, these sacraments, as I prefer to call them, are fantastic privileges. It is an undescribable grace, an undescribable privilege. And to not fully appreciate the experiences and act accordingly begins to create negative karma. And if you keep on using them, seeking the positive effects and not making the indicated changes in your life or not taking on the responsibility for the awareness that you have gained, I think that our inner awareness perceives a violation, which results in discomfort. I say this based on my own personal investigations, because it's true that for me the experiences have gotten far more uncomfortable as I've gotten older, but that's because I'm trying to do more with them. And almost every one turns out better than the last one. I don't think that you can be fully in heaven without being totally in hell. It's like Gibran's section on love in *The Prophet*. "If you want only love's pleasures and love's peace, then get up from life's threshing floor, go out into the seasonless world and laugh, but not all of your laughter, and cry, but not all of your tears." I'd like to get together with other elders and share this, because I may be underestimating the amount of grace that's available. But I have checked this out with several very serious searchers. And of course we have two outstanding people very outspoken on this, one is Kazantzakis in his *Saviors of God*, the other is Andrew Harvey in *The Way of Passion*.

RF: Carl Jung said, "You can't see light without darkness, hear silence without noise, attain wisdom without foolishness. The experience of holiness may well be the most painful of all.”

MS: That’s a beautiful statement. It’s a beautiful statement and unfortunately, you see, there’s not enough information being disseminated, so the people using these substances today are not aware of it and most of them want to avoid discomfort, which really puts a lid on their growth.

RF: This is one of the valid criticisms of Timothy. He was so positive and ebullient in his message that he overlooked the importance of confronting the shadow.

MS: Yes, and he didn’t confront his own shadow. So that’s part of the problem. I think somebody who really wants to be a charismatic figure and a model for people has an enormous responsibility to be honest. To be tremendously honest and committed to their own growth and development so that their own blind spots don’t get projected out onto others. It’s an enormous responsibility.

RF: Well, I watched Timothy very closely. As you know I was with him a lot in the last four or five months of his life to try to get a sense of the man’s relative contentment, you know, and there were some times when he just appeared the most sparkly kind of Zen master, and other times he was such a twisted and tormented and pained man. And he was, I think right up till the very end of his life, he was wondering himself if he’d done humanity a great service or if he set back the advance of knowledge of these sacred magical drugs. I don’t think he knew.

MS: That’s fascinating. Well, I don’t think any of us do yet. It’s a pretty fair balance. An awful lot of good was done. An awful lot of harm was done. And it remains to be seen. I still stand by my statement to Ralph Metzner in the letter in *Gnosis* that the final word will be to see how many sincerely pick up the torch and contribute. Unfortunately the signs are not good. None of the organizations committed to understanding psychedelics except for MAPS, through Rick Doblin, has yet done a good job. The rest of us have had a hard time raising money.

RF: Timothy was penniless when he died.

MS: Yeah. But the thing is, you know, if there are a couple million people who have benefited from these experiences, suppose they all kicked in . . .

RF: A dollar.

MS: I was going to say ten or twenty. But suppose they did? We'd have funds for research, we'd be able to do a number of educational projects. There's something strange about the niggardliness. Is the vision real?

RF: This is another image from Gerald Heard via Huston: that it's by necessity that the psychedelic drugs remain underground. The image that Gerald gave to Houston was like a ball floating in a lake. Half of it is always underwater. And that as soon as it comes up it's going to fall back down. That by necessity these are esoteric devices and they have to remain underground.

MS: I don't agree with that, and neither does the Dalai Lama. Look what's happened in Tibetan Buddhism. If you go back before 1985, I think it's roughly that time, all the esoteric teachings were kept secret for the adepts. But the Dalai Lama, as I understand it—I don't have direct knowledge here, but as I understand it—feels the world is in such shape that anything that can help should be released. And in the last ten to twelve years a lot of these sacred texts are being translated and released. Okay, it's going to fall on a lot of deaf ears, but it's going to fall on some good ears.

RF: Yes. Again I think of Timothy somehow perceiving that this was a time when this most protected religious secret be spread far and wide.

MS: And you know there's another interesting book, *The Jew and the Lotus*, where a bunch of Jewish people got together with the Dalai Lama. It's really a critique of Judaism. One of the things they discovered after learning more about Buddhism and the esoteric side of it was in taking a look at their own religion where the esoteric side is the Kabbalah. Did you know that the Kabbalah is restricted from the general Jewish population? The average Jew in the average congregation doesn't know anything about the Kabbalah. And they realized what a mistake this was. Sure, it would be great if you could get everyone who was exposed to dedicate themselves to the value of the privilege and earnestly commit themselves to the study. But if you are unwilling to make it available because of possible misuse, there will be a lot of people you miss because they don't even know about it. And these things weed themselves out. The ones who are sincere will advance. If you're not sincere it catches up with you and bites you.

RF: There are at least two different ways of looking at why there has been secrecy. One is that things like the Kabbalah had been kept from the Jewish people because it was the Jewish Orthodoxy that was trying to preserve their own power. On the other hand, these teachings may have been kept secret because if they were exposed outside of just the right context, then they would lose their power. On one hand it's wise to protect secret teachings. On the other, it's political control.

MS: The real problem you face is that you don't want to dissipate valuable things. This is what happened to LSD. It's what happened to MDMA. We have a living example of what happens if you try to spread it out without instruction, without understanding, just indiscriminately. And I think there are people who feel that's the way. Tim obviously felt strongly, let anybody use it. It will be self-adjusting. In due time those who abuse it will lose interest in it, which according to Jerome Beck's studies happens with MDMA. It's a way to go, but if you don't want to pay the price resulting from ignorance, then let's at least be able to publish some guidelines and key factors that are important to know before people experiment with these substances.

RF: When the government took away your permissions and your research supplies, why didn't anybody challenge them? Why didn't you or Hubbard or Janiger or Cohen and everybody else say, "Wait a second, these are valuable scientific instruments. You can't punish us because of some nonscientific social activism over here"?

MS: I don't know. When I go back and feel myself in that situation, I think we all viewed the government as having great power and we viewed ourselves as having very little power. It looked hopeless. Today I would be very outspoken. I would have press conferences. I'd probably do a lot. I mean it's an opportunity to educate. But back in those days we didn't feel that at all. We felt that the whole medical profession in our area was against us. So we didn't feel we had the strength or the power to do anything about it.

RF: But now you feel that you would've had the strength and the power?

MS: Well, I feel I personally do. Of course you know I'm old enough that I don't care what happens to me personally anymore. When you're young, when you have a career ahead of you, you have to be more careful. But also I have a much greater understanding of why society is doing what it's doing, and a much greater understanding, I think and hope, of knowing the right things to say. You see, the very first thing to say is this issue of honesty. Let's face it folks, this is for honest people. Let's hope there's quite a few out there.

The Most Kind Man
I Have Ever Known

DANNY SUGERMAN

Thus far, there has been a lot said and a lot unsaid, and written, all of which I think Timothy would've enjoyed—positive or negative. He liked being a celebrity, and much more will be added since his death—more tributes, and Tim deserves every one, every kind word, remembrance, good-bye, farewell, love. . . . Not only was his spirit indefatigable, his heart was enormous in its boundless love of people, art, artists, LIFE.

He was, of course, the first in his class to die (not to disrespect

Danny Sugerman, perhaps best known for his friendship with Jim Morrison, is the author of Morrison's biography, No One Here Gets Out Alive, *which has sold over two million copies and has been translated into twenty-two foreign languages. Today Sugerman continues his writing career and oversees the operations of the Doors' estate. He is credited with the Doors' staying power and bringing the band's music and Jim's poetry to generation after generation. Sugerman also wrote* Wonderland Avenue: Tales of Glamour & Excess. *The book, released in 1988 to wide critical acclaim, led to his friendship with Timothy Leary who read the book and contributed an enthusiastic quote for the back cover. The two became close, forming a similar mentor-student relationship to the one Sugerman had once had with Morrison.*

Michael McClure, Timothy Leary, Barbara Leary, Jello Biafra, and Danny Sugerman backstage at the Roxy after a reading

Abbie Hoffman) a natural death. But, from what I've heard, Tim was the first at many things. When I first learned of his egalitarian "Every man has a right to meet God!" approach to LSD versus Aldous Huxley's more British, reserved, "Must be very careful with this, only the best and the brightest," it confirmed for me Tim's true enthusiasm, complete abandonment, and unbridled faith in his fellow man and the unity of all living things.

He had a way of making whomever he was with feel as if they were the most important person on the planet. A rare gift. Some people couldn't believe their initial encounter with the man. My wife, Fawn Hall, couldn't accept Tim's instant acceptance of her, while much of Hollywod judged and mislabeled her as a far-right republican. He didn't care what other people thought. He just liked her. He had no agenda. She would come to love him as much as I. Forget the old "I'll give you the shirt off my back" breed of humble generosity many people can summon (especially for people in need), Tim gave you not only his home and food and good company—he gave you him. And on many occasions he gave people, myself included, back their own selves. To my knowledge he did this with every sentient being he encountered.

This energy cannot be faked. Timothy Leary did not simply offer up true Irish charm and wit, although he gave that too. Timothy Leary held back nothing. He gave people, especially those he loved, everything. And of course in acts of true gratitude for such friendship people naturally gave back to Tim.

He was one of the few true friends I've had. I considered it an honor to meet him and even more of an honor to consider him a friend. But he wasn't just a friend. I'm proud to say Timothy was like a father to me after I lost my own, a priest to me when I needed ministering, a kindred soul, a tribal elder, a mentor, an inventor, an artist, anarchist, writer, performer, philosopher, scientist, psychologist, guru.

He was one of the most kind men I've ever known. In a town plagued by ego and riddled with judgment, Timothy loved me with complete, unconditional love. Nothing I said or did, from the time my first book hit No. 1 through the time my last book came out, as a psychotic, paranoid crack addict seriously in need of a miracle . . . on top or in the gutter, Tim was always there for me. We spent hours together researching Ibogaine as a cure for my methadone addiction.

In his final years I tried to pay him back but the debt was too big and he was too much of a gentleman to accept it. Still, I tried to let him know I was now there for him, if he needed me. I had his house cleaned, brought him groceries, drove him to doctors, told him I loved him. "Yes," he said, "now love yourself." He was not a taker. But how do you give, what do you give, to a man who has everything?

Let's Do Lunch

Jeremy Tarcher

It was 1975 at 9110 Sunset Boulevard, Los Angeles, California—a time and place when everything was still possible—so when my secretary said tremulously, "Timothy Leary is here to see you," I wasn't surprised. My lunch date had arrived. I had diligently read the popular press of the prior ten years, and had no trouble identifying the despoiler of American youth when he came calling under his own name. (I have since had it on good report that Timothy has been known to come calling under a variety of names, genders, and disguises.)

Jumping out of my seat and tingling with fear (is he catching?), anticipation (will he catch me?), and righteous loathing, I showed him to a chair. What a nice anecdote this will make, I thought. Timothy Leary, Mephistopheles himself, in my office, asking me to read a manuscript. Not a chance, Leary. I won't be associated with a cultural criminal of mythic proportions, but I'll listen anyway. Maybe that battered folder contained an appropriately contrite confession.

Jeremy Tarcher is a publisher of many important books on psychology, modern society, and the evolution of consciousness, including Flashbacks, *the autobiography of Timothy Leary.*

Those papers weren't a mea culpa, and I was neither under-standing of what they were (I still have that problem with Tim some-times), nor interested in what I didn't understand.

We lunched and as a public service, with the Osso Bucco, I pointed out some of his shortcomings so widely reported in the press. Where his mind could have been I really don't know (and I'm not at all alone in this), but the heavier the axe blows of my accusation, the broader his smile and the more quizzical his expres-sion. I think he had heard it all before.

Good-bye, Mr. Leary, and good luck. Try elsewhere.

Apparently he didn't hear, for it wasn't long before he was back on my luncheon calendar and sitting in my office, still smiling with more unpublishable-by-me ideas. We sat at Le Dome, my warm duck salad disappearing while Tim seemed to have lost his appetite but not his sense of having something important to tell me (and I'm still not entirely clear as to what it is). All I do remember is that I hadn't felt that optimistic, that full of possibilities since I first read Henry Miller.

Dammit, I felt good. Being with Timothy Leary made me feel good.

And so over the next few years when Tim would call from time to time, we would go out to lunch and I would return to my office with a broad smile on my face, but never quite clear on what had transpired.

I had worked with many famous people in the television indus-try and had been out in public with many of them, but I noticed something different when I was out with Tim. No one who recog-nized him failed to smile. Apparently he had devoted strangers posted on every corner. A stroll with Prometheus in ancient Ath-ens would, I imagine, have brought the same words and winks of pleasure, gratitude, conspiracy, and community as a stroll with Timo-thy in Beverly Hills. It was clear I wasn't the only one who liked to be with him. The Leary energy field made these people feel posi-tive about life's potential. (It's his gift—grace, direct from God.) I could tell that there was a little bit of what Tim symbolized in ev-ery one of these at-least-once-ignited souls, and they were happy and proud to know about that part of themselves. I wasn't conscious of it at the time but I wanted to be part of that community.

Inevitably, all unknowing (like you were once, too), I eventually found myself 47 minutes into 250 μg of Tim Scully's Orange Sunshine. The knowable world fell apart in front of what I had understood to be my mind.

Hours went by before I wanted to rise to my feet (I've never been fully erect since) and the first thing I did was to get Tim on the phone. "Tim," I throated, "six hours ago I took Scully's Orange Sunshine. I must see you for breakfast tomorrow."

"Tomorrow? Tomorrow? I can't make breakfast tomorrow, but I'm free for lunch."

That time I did the talking, but when he spoke I felt I understood him far better than before.

And the years rolled by again and in 1983 I got to publish those confessions, but, in reflection, I don't remember them as being particularly contrite.

Mistah Leary, He Dead

HUNTER S. THOMPSON

I will miss Tim Leary—not for his wisdom or his beauty or his warped lust for combat, or because of his wealth or his power or his drugs—but mainly because I won't hear his laughing voice on my midnight telephone anymore. Tim usually called around two. It was his habit—one of many that we shared—and he knew I would be awake.

Tim and I kept the same hours. He believed, as I do, that "after midnight, all things are possible."

Just last week he called me on the phone at 2:30 in the morning and said he was moving to a ranch in Nicaragua in a few days and would fax me the telephone number. Which he did. And I think he also faxed it to Dr. Kesey.

Indeed. There are many rooms in the mansion. And Tim was familiar with most of them. We will never know the range of his fiendish vision, or the many lives he was sucked into by his savage and unnatural passions.

Hunter S. Thompson has been a student of Dr. Leary's for many years, dating back to the Great Acid Wars of the middle Sixties when LSD-25 was still legal. He is the author of Hell's Angels, Fear and Loathing in Las Vegas, *and other classic American works.*

We sometimes disagreed, but in the end we made our peace. Tim was a Chieftain. He stomped on the terra, and he left his elegant hoof prints on all our lives.

He is forgotten now, but not gone. We will see him soon enough. Our tribe is now smaller by one. Our circle is one link shorter. Now there is one more name on the honor roll of pure warriors, who saw the great light and leaped for it.

The Harvard Crimson Story

AN INTERVIEW WITH ANDREW WEIL
BY ROBERT FORTE

RF: Dr. Weil, thanks for taking the time from your book tour to contribute to Tim's Festschrift. What better place to reflect on those days than here, perched on the cliffs of Big Sur? My first question is: Is it fair to say that psychedelic drugs helped to transform you from an overweight, cigar smoking, Harvard overachiever into one of the world's leading physicians—a bestselling author in the field of medicine?

AW: I was never really a cigar smoker. I used to hold them and didn't inhale them, still I would get enough smoke in to get acute nicotine poisoning more often than not. I took mescaline for the first time in the fall of 1960, my first year at Harvard, and had no particular reaction. I took it again a few weeks later, had a very profound experience. I didn't really know what to do with that, and so I think I stuffed it for a lot of my years at Harvard, and didn't really come back to experimenting with psychedelics until I was

---

Andrew Weil, M.D., is one of the leading physicians in the world today. Among his books are The Natural Mind, The Marriage of the Sun and Moon, From Chocolate to Morphine, *and the bestselller* Spontaneous Healing.

doing an internship in San Francisco. And yes, I would say they were very instrumental in my personal transformation, especially around the time I was twenty-eight years old. They started me on a road of experimentation in a lot of areas in my life; that I think got me to where I am today.

RF: Do you think that's why they are illegal?

AW: I think they are illegal because authorities sense their power to transform people and make them question a lot of the limiting beliefs that are prevalent in our society.

RF: That's a bigger reason than their biological or psychological dangers?

AW: Their biological dangers are insignificant. Physically, they're the safest of all the drugs that we know. The psychological dangers I think are real. I've certainly met people who are casualties of psychedelic use, and I think that's a serious concern. But I think the official response to them is all out of proportion to the realities of their risks, so there's got to be something else involved.

RF: Am I correct you've said before that the greatest drug problem in the country, probably in the Western world, is the drugs that are prescribed by the medical profession?

AW: No, I'd actually say that alcohol and tobacco, in terms of health hazards, are the greatest problems we've got; also I think there are a lot of drugs prescribed by the medical profession that cause a great deal of harm.

RF: Compared to psychedelic drugs, would you say that harm inflicted on our society from prescription medicines is greater or less than the psychedelic "problem"?

AW: That's really not a fair comparison. I think it's more appropriate to look at alcohol and tobacco—which are recreational drugs—than to look at prescription drugs. Of the psychoactive prescription drugs, I think the ones that are most thoughtlessly and widely prescribed are the benzodiazophines—valium and its relatives; they do a great deal of harm. They're highly addictive, they interfere with memory and intellectual function, and they're handed out like candy. That's the most important category of physician-caused drug abuse.

RF: You were there at Harvard, and you had a role in Tim's dismissal.

AW: I think my role was more instrumental in the case of Dick [Alpert]. Tim resigned on his own. One of the great misconceptions that's been frozen in history is that Leary was fired from Harvard. He wasn't. He left voluntarily. Richard Alpert was fired, and the investigative reporting that I did in the undergraduate newspaper certainly helped bring that about. That firing and the publicity about it and Leary was certainly the single factor that brought this whole phenomenon to the attention of American middle class culture. It was front-page news in the *New York Times*—the first time many Americans ever heard of these drugs. That was a major event in my life and in Alpert and Leary's lives as well.

RF: What happened?

AW: The undergraduate newspaper, *The Harvard Crimson*, printed a story. The university had wanted to get rid of Leary and Alpert, for a lot of reasons, and I think on some level they also really didn't want to be there under the kinds of rigidity that the university imposed. The university newspaper saw a great opportunity for investigative reporting and made a deal with the administration that if they came up with information that would help them get rid of them, that the university would act on it and give *The Crimson* the exclusive news rights. That was the basis of what happened.

RF: The university approached you?

AW: No, *The Crimson* initiated this. We went to the university, and the university said, "Yes, we'd love it." Because they felt they couldn't act; they didn't have grounds on which to dismiss them.

RF: You were the editor of *The Crimson*?

AW: I was *an* editor. I was on the editorial board. I wasn't the editor-in-chief.

RF: *You* initiated the program to expose them. What did you think you were exposing? What was your feeling about their scene?

AW: I think there was a lot going on around them that was questionable. There was a lot of wild stuff going on in their circle, whether they were directly involved with it or not. And I think the presence of that at the university created a certain amount of tension. They were a group who behaved and acted in ways as if they had something that nobody else did, some kind of secret knowledge. Leary especially kept talking about the academic "game," and that they were somehow outside of it, and that pressed buttons for a lot of people. So I think it was time for them to get out of the university; it would have happened in one way or another.

RF: Was the CIA involved?

AW: Not to my knowledge. When I first read books like *Storming Heaven* and *Acid Dreams*, most of that was news to me. I knew some general outlines of it, but I never knew any of the details.

RF: Well it's clear and on the record that LSD was used by the CIA and at Harvard. The first published LSD research in this country was done at Harvard by Robert Hyde. This work was paid for by the Human Ecology Fund, a CIA front. How do you feel about the way that all came down?

AW: Fine. I think it was supposed to happen. You know, it was a key thing in my life, too. For one thing, I don't think I would have gotten permission to do the marijuana studies that I did in my senior year of medical school unless I had done that. I got transcripts of the research committee that was debating whether to approve my research, and it was brought up that I was the person that had— I think the phrase was—"blown the whistle" on Alpert and Leary, and that influenced the committee to vote to allow me to do that. I also found myself a couple years after I left Harvard in a position that seemed to me very parallel to that of Alpert's, where I became the focus of a lot of institutional paranoia and I saw that my life had gone in a kind of parallel way. At that point I made an effort to get in touch with both of them and discuss what had happened.

RF: You said psychedelics were already a part of the Harvard undergraduate scene. You took mescaline there.

AW: Yes, but not very much, it was minor. At least in my circle, it was pretty novel and unusual to be able to do that. I didn't know any other people who independently had gotten hold of psychedelics when I was an undergraduate.

RF: So at the time you thought that you were doing everyone a favor by exposing the extracurricular stuff going on?

AW: Yes. One of the lessons I learned was how you advance in that world. A lot of my success at Harvard was due to that.

RF: It's hard to imagine that the Harvard administration could be so naive to not see that their action would be counterproductive to their concerns. This was the turning point. The beginning of the prohibition. Psychedelic drugs started to become forbidden and available only to outlaws. I wonder if they had been introduced to society some other "legitimate" way what would have happened?

AW: I don't think the university anticipated that at all. I don't think they saw it coming.

I'll tell you one my memories of Tim before I embarked on my venture with *The Crimson*. I met him first in the fall of 1960. I heard he was doing experiments with psilocybin and went in and told him I was interested. I wanted to take it. He said that they couldn't use undergraduates in their experiments, but he encouraged me to go out and try to find it on my own. I remember him telling me that this was the greatest thing he had ever come across, and he thought that within a couple of years there would be regular seminars in the university where people would take these drugs once a week and the remaining sessions would be for analyzing what had happened to them. I don't think he had any conception that this would cause antagonism or resistance. It was a really innocent belief he had, and I think that was the way he operated. He never imagined he would crystallize opposition.

RF: Even when he got arrested in Laredo, he thought he'd be

protected under our freedom of religion. Instead he got a twenty-year sentence for less than an ounce of low-grade pot.

AW: Right. You asked about how else they could have been introduced. Well, they could have been introduced through doctors, through psychiatrists, through shamans or shaman equivalents, through academics, through the underground. Those were all possibilities.

RF: For most of the past twelve years I've worked in one fashion or another to try to relegitimize the drugs for either medical, psychiatric, or religious studies within the mainstream structures that exist, and that's proved to be frustrating. As you were saying last night, these groups work on form and structure, and these drugs are destructuring. When I became interested in psychedelics I first thought of Leary's escapades as a problem that had to be overcome. After being frustrated for several years, I began to appreciate what he did, and to me his exuberance was a tactic that was absolutely necessary to get past the establishment; to propagate the drugs through the artistic, mystical, subversive, outlaw underground.

AW: Right. There are two comments about Leary that I have heard repeatedly from Harvard people over the years; and others, I suppose, but especially from Harvard people. One is that he did a greater disservice to the cause of psychedelic research than anyone in history, and the other one was that the poor man had really fried his brain. Neither of those seems to me to be valid. I have seen Leary over the years and he always looked to me very physically and mentally healthy. It was just amazing to me that these Harvard people could go around saying he'd fried his brain. The other one, in terms of discrediting psychedelic research, I don't know whether psychedelic research would ever have gotten going at American academic institutions. I think those drugs really push people's buttons, and it's too threatening, and I think maybe that's not the appropriate setting in which to study them.

RF: What do you think is the appropriate setting? Who do you think is best suited to use the drugs?

AW: Well, I think that we really need equivalents to shamans in our society. I'd love it if there were medical doctors who were qualified as shamans who could supervise and oversee that.

RF: What is a shaman in your language?

AW: Someone who has mastered out-of-the-body experiences, who knows how to mediate between the visible and invisible world, who's undertaken fairly rigorous training, on an individual level and with other people who are proficient at those things. But we don't have any normal mechanism of producing those people.

RF: Last night you described what you thought would be the next revolutionary breakthrough in Western medicine as having to do with the discovery and mapping of the energetic body—*kundalini* and things like that. I wonder if you think this is one such application of the psychedelics in Western medicine?

AW: Yes. I also think psychedelics can be healing tools. I've seen a lot of healing, not just of mental problems but of physical problems, from psychedelic experiences; they've got great potential in that regard. They're so nontoxic and safe if used in appropriate settings by people who are knowledgeable about them; it's a shame they are not available.

RF: For the healing of physical problems, not mental problems? Yet the healing is through a mental agency.

AW: Yes. I'm saying this because the research interest has mostly been from psychiatrists, but my interest has been at looking at the mind-body aspects, and seeing how a change at the level of consciousness initiated by psychedelics can produce dramatic changes in the physical body. But most people talk about psychedelic therapy, always looking at issues like addiction and alcoholism and depression, and you don't hear people talking about the other. It's just part of the whole mind-body separation problem that we perpetuate.

RF: I heard that some years ago Paula Hawkins, while running for office in Florida, tried to have you removed from your faculty position because of scientific statements you made about drugs.

AW: That's not quite accurate. When *Chocolate to Morphine* was first published in '83 there was a midterm election. It was right after Len Bias had died and the war on drugs got into high gear. I was on *The Donahue Show* by myself. Donahue was incredibly supportive of the book, and it was a great show. The questions were remarkable. Television stations really liked it. The show was shown again and again. In response to that, an organized effort againt the book was started by the National Federation of Parents for Drug-Free Youth, which Nancy Reagan and Paula Hawkins were the honorary chairpersons of. Paula Hawkins was running for reelection to the Senate and she made one of her main campaign themes getting the book banned from schools and libraries. She stood up on the floor of the Senate Judiciary Committee and waved the book around, passed copies out to members, and said that the worst thing about this book was that it was neutral, which I thought was interesting. It didn't say "no." She also waved the book around CBS Nightly News and actually got more publicity for it than the publisher did. Then the National Federation mounted an organized campaign to try to keep me from speaking publicly. There were several places where I had been asked to give lectures where the organizers were approached by representatives of this group who tried to intimidate them. One event was in Tucson, a statewide conference of drug abuse educators. I had been asked to be the keynote speaker. Right before the conference the organizer said that the National Federation had come to them in the person of a woman in Arizona (a politically powerful woman who had the ear of the governor) and said that I should be dropped as keynote speaker because I promoted drug use. They had a meeting and said no, they wanted me to remain as keynote speaker. She then brought in a woman who was her counterpart in California, and she said that she would use her clout with the governor's office to cut off funding to these state agencies unless they dropped me. They had another meeting and again said no, they would keep me as speaker. And then—and this especially bothered me—they called the White House, and within twenty-four hours the White House Drug Office FedExed a dossier on me that was about two inches thick, purporting to say that I was a proponent of drug use. That was the first I had heard of this thing. Then I found out this same document was being circulated to libraries and schools in an effort to get them to remove *Chocolate to Morphine*. I was working at that time as a health counselor at a popular spa, and they went to them. The owners of the spa told me that I couldn't work there anymore because I was politically undesirable. Then I went to my boss at the University of Arizona and said, "Look, this is happening and you should know that there's a possibility that these people are going to come around." They did not go to the university. Then Paula Hawkins lost the election. That was when something like 95 percent of Americans said that drug abuse was the greatest threat facing the nation, you know, and then a year later something like 1 percent said that it was. In fact it was totally manipulated by the media. At any rate, I have not—since she lost her bid for election—run into that kind of campaign anymore.

RF: How much of this backlash against drugs and drug abuse generally do you think is inspired by the fear of the transformative potential of LSD we saw in the sixties?

AW: I think that's there, but I think it's unconscious on the part of people doing it. I think it's a deep, unconscious motivation. LSD and its relatives are regarded in the same manner as heroin by the majority of Americans and treated that way under regulatory schemes. This is so irrational that the only way you can explain it is that it is deeply threatening on some unconscious level.

RF: A more effective drug policy would distinguish psychedelics from other recreational drugs. Psychedelics have been extremely beneficial to society in ways that aren't well known. Ralph Abraham for example suggests they were influential in the development of chaos theory in math and physics, and in the computer revolution. What about in your field? How have psychedelics impacted the growth of alternative, or, as you like to say, "integrative" medicine?

AW: A lot of the people I know in this movement have a history of using psychedelics in the past, whether or not they use them today. Those experiences were probably, as for me, important in their process of transformation that helped them come around to these points of view. I think that's simply true of many people in my generation.

Many of those people may not use psychedelics anymore, and may not have for a long time; nonetheless, they were important.

RF: Was it Aldous Huxley who said if the twentieth century is to remembered at all it will be remembered for the reemergence of psychedelic drugs?

AW: I think they are very powerful transformative forces and that the separation—however you want to call it, expulsion, separation—of Leary and Alpert from Harvard was the central event that disseminated them throughout the American culture.

RF: How do you think Tim will be remembered years from now?

AW: Certainly as a key figure of the 1960s and that whole movement. I think in any look at the countercultural picture, he's very central. I always give Leary and Alpert credit in my talks and writings for their insistence on the importance of set and setting. Although they didn't invent those concepts, they are certainly the ones that popularized them and insisted on their importance; and that has been a major theme of my work on drugs, and Norman Zinberg's. The terms "set" and "setting" go back a ways in psychology, but I don't know whether they were applied specifically to drug experiences before Leary.

One other thing I would say is today, when my main work is in the area of medicine, health, healing, I talk to very diverse audiences. I'm sure there are some people out there who are embarrassed by my previous history, my writings on drugs, and wish that wasn't in my past. I always point out that my current view of healing is just an expansion of the ideas that I developed working with drugs. The whole point of *The Natural Mind* is that drug highs originate within the nervous system and that the drugs act as triggers or releases if set and setting are conducive. My current view, that treatments activate or release innate healing responses if set and setting are conducive, is an expansion of that insight.

RF: They activate our capacity for the miraculous.

AW: Another memory I have of Leary is that the first time I met him, I liked him. He was a charming person and I remember him as being very twinkly and sort of leprechaun-like. He's an archetype of the Irish storyteller-enchanter, and there's something playful and mischievous about that. I think that's both been his asset and his problem. Very different personality than that of Dick Alpert.

RF: You weren't ever a student of Tim's; you just heard about him?

AW: Yes, I went over, met him, got to know people in that group. Then I experimented on my own independently.

RF: When did you have the idea to expose them?

AW: That came later. I met him in the fall of 1960. I took mescaline about a dozen times in 1960 and 1961. The newspaper campaign didn't start until late in 1962.

RF: Those are historic articles.

AW: There's a lot; there's also the magazine that I edited, called the *Harvard Review*. It was a new political magazine which I became editor-in-chief of for a year, and I devoted an issue to psychedelics. It had a manifesto by Alpert and Leary in it, and articles by Ralph Metzner and other key figures.

RF: I'm getting a different picture now. On the one hand, you initiated investigative reporting to expose them and have them removed from the university because you were unhappy with their activities, on the other you were enthusiastic enough about their manifesto to publicize it in your magazine.

AW: I think that reflects a split in me, personally more than anything else. I was the only person on *The Crimson* that had taken any of these drugs, so I think that reflected my own ambivalence, which I don't think was resolved until maybe ten years later.

RF: The rest of the staff at *The Crimson* was pretty much unaware of what was going on?

AW: Generally.

RF: But they were opposed to it?

AW: Yes. I don't think they were people who would have tried substances.

RF: Do you have any regrets about playing that role?

AW: No, not at all. I think that was the way it was supposed to be, and that was part of my growth and transformation, and you know, as I said, there was a point in my life when I really saw that I had gotten myself in a position that was very parallel to Alpert's at that time, and was quite amazed. I'm grateful for his example because I feel like he has—in a strange way—been a teacher of mine. We haven't had a lot of direct contact, but it's by his example.

RF: I see—Alpert's been a conduit for Eastern mysticism into Western psychology, and you've been for integrating Western medicine with discoveries from your cross-cultural travels.

AW: Right. Another thing was, during all those years, I was Richard Schultes's student. That's when I was studying botany, from '60 to '64—my undergraduate work. He's very down on Alpert and Leary.

RF: Well, he's very conservative generally about everything. He told me he thought the American Revolution was a mistake.

AW: Right. And yet has tried everything himself.

RF: He's tried everything but he's interested in them strictly for what he calls the "scientific" value, not the transformative aspects. Wasson was the same way, his interest was mainly in the historical, scholarly world, though he admitted, near the end of his life, this may have been a mistake; that had he approached them in a different way, "it could have been the source of a revolution on Wall Street."

AW: Of the three of them, I think Albert Hofmann is the most open and the most personally committed to the experience.

RF: Yes, but he insists that the best strategy is to propagate the drugs through the psychiatric profession.

AW: I think that would be disastrous. Psychiatry is the most authoritarian branch of the medical profession. You know, institutional psychiatrists are really the consciousness police, in a way. I found myself, when I was doing psychiatry rotations in my medical training, at incredible odds with those people over the issue of whether there were multiple realities. I mean that was simply not admissible. They say there is one reality and if you deviate from that, something's wrong with you and you have to come back.

I also remember Albert saying that the best news he'd seen coming out of America was a story in the *New York Times* that said LSD use was up among the American youth.

RF: It was either Oscar Janiger or Timothy who told me that in their early studies the highest incidence of "bad" trips was among psychiatrists. Second most was theologians.

AW: That wouldn't surprise me. Too bad, but it wouldn't surprise me.

RF: Religion and medicine are both exceedingly plagued by authoritarianism. This is the disease that psychedelic drugs can help to dispel, so there's bound to be resistance.

AW: I must also say even in the hippie communities that I visited, there was one part of me that always wanted to be part of that lifestyle, but the more I looked at it, the more it looked rigid to me. I saw a lot of sexism for example. The taking of a lot of these drugs does not necessarily equate with the breaking down of social roles and freedom.

RF: Taking the drugs generally induces a liminal state. What happens when you reenter is another thing. You can reimprint on another dysfunctional structure. Of course Tim first clarified this for everyone.

AW: Right. In *The Marriage of the Sun and Moon* I tried to show that anything destructuring brings the same kind of societal response— see the chapter I wrote on eclipses of the sun and why there's all this medical paranoia about them.

Here's a question I'm interested in. What's your take on MDMA? How threatening is it to the established order and why is

the LSD camp so down on MDMA? For instance, Terence thinks
MDMA is awful and that nobody should take it and I'm curious
about that, as to why that is. To me it seems MDMA is at least as
threatening . . .

RF: A lot of people have been profoundly affected by MDMA over
the years, proving its transformative potential. There's sort of a battle
between LSD and the MDMA camps as you say because people
form attachments to their drugs. Terence's perspective revolves
around tryptamines and he sometimes irrationally rejects other es-
teemed entheogens. In *Food of the Gods*, for example, he summarily
rejects Wasson's Amanita theory because he hasn't gotten off on it
in the five times he's tried.

As for MDMA, the establishment reacted irrationally exactly as
they did when LSD became popular. In the case of LSD, as is well
known, the government actively perpetrated a hoax in the name of
science that it caused chromosome damage. With MDMA it is brain
damage. I was there at the very first news conference at the University of Chicago when they announced the emergency scheduling of
MDMA based on research of Charles Schuster. Schuster had never
even seen MDMA at that point but he was the authority that provided the "reason" for the ban. The next year he was named head of
the National Institute of Drug Abuse. He told me he did the things
the government asked because they funded the U of C Drug Abuse
Research Unit.

As for the experience, if you think about it in terms of character, LSD will completely disintegrate your character for the time
being. With MDMA you will know that you have your character
on line, you'll feel a little more comfortable in it and you'll know its
not really you. It's more gradual, not as shocking and radical as
what I think Wasson called the "superior entheogens."

Notes About Dr. Timothy Leary

ROBERT WILLIAMS

Before forming an opinion about a person I usually like to first see through the eyes of the individual's adversaries and admirers and then I try to make my own judgment based upon my own personal observations. If you embrace the opinions of Timothy Leary's detractors you will hear diatribes about a renegade Harvard professor who in the sixties hooked his wagon to a liberal social phenomenon created by the chaos of an unpopular war. This, they say, compounded by racial civil unrest and an ever present breeding ground of drug culture rising to expose itself allowed him to grab the reigns as a drug messiah. Then you have the reverse side of the coin—the rather flamboyant image espoused by the Bohemian avant-garde that fancy Dr. Leary as the end-all, be-all, guruesque prophet of a golden age in which we will all sit down with the lion by still waters and convince Leo to eat trail mix.

From what I've read, along with personal experience from knowing him for some six years, I'd say that none of the above realistically applies.

Robert Williams is an artist whose work has appeared in many different galleries throughout the world since 1970.

Timothy Leary was gifted with a large number of attributes that many of us don't share. Besides being a man of letters and a student of history, Timothy was inescapably ensconced in politics and the human condition. But the characteristic that most dramatically separated Leary from other members of the hookah-puffing intelligentsia was his uncanny mental agility. In other words, the ability to process situations around him into abstract thought. Something along the lines of *Zen Flesh, Zen Bones*, where the last cherry you eat before the tigers eat you is always the sweetest. However, I wouldn't say that Timothy's thought patterns are classic Zen. His logic is infested with irony and spite, which dances on that delicate ground between reaction and emotion.

Always with an eye on things to come, he exercised his gift for communications through the computer. The future was Leary's mental football field and technocratic devices like computers were his offense.

Timothy was armed with a gregarious and affable personality. These social skills, coupled with a handsome and dashing appearance, enabled him to move in elite social circles where an average Joe would flounder. I think that Timothy Leary is right up there with Voltaire, Oscar Wilde, and John Dillinger.

The Unreachable Stars

ROBERT ANTON WILSON

Ezra Pound, when asked to contribute to a Festschrift for T. S. Eliot, sent in a typically terse response: "I can only repeat with the urgency of sixty years ago: READ HIM!" I lack Ez's capacity for concentration and brevity; and anyway I have expressed my opinion of the value of Dr. Timothy Leary's published works in a wide variety of books and articles, but I can repeat once more for this Festschrift: READ HIM! You will learn more from Dr. Leary's psychological and philosophical books than you can ever possibly learn from any other living author.

Of course, people who get their opinions from the major media "know" that Leary's works have nothing of value in them. In contrast to that conditioned (mechanical) reaction, I suggest:

1. Some of Dr. Leary's work has achieved general recognition throughout the psychological community. Specifically, the Leary

---

Robert Anton Wilson is the coauthor, with Robert Shea, of the underground classic The Illuminatus! *trilogy, which won the 1986 Prometheus Hall of Fame Award. His other writings include* Schrodinger's Cat *trilogy, called "the most scientific of all science fiction novels" by* New Scientist, *and several nonfiction works of futurist psychology and guerrilla ontology. His newest book is* Everything Is Under Control.

Interpersonal Test ranked as the number one (most used) psycho-logical test in the country a few years ago. I do not know if it still ranks that highly, but it still continues in wide usage; I frequently meet young people who have taken it at university or job applica-tions, and it still routinely gets administered to all convicts in the California penal system.

2. The work on Behavior Modification with LSD for which Dr. Leary has received unanimous condemnation among nonpsych-ologists and especially among the pundits of the mass media has not suffered universal criticism from those best qualified to judge—other psychologists. Many of them have said, off the record, that they suspect Leary will achieve vindication in a less hysterical age. On the record, when Dr. Leary got out of prison, he immediately received an invitation to give the keynote speech at the Association for Humanistic Psychology, strongly suggesting that those in his own area of psychology did not consider him in the same ballpark with Dr. Frankenstein or Dr. Strangelove, but rather saw him as a gifted researcher condemned by irrational prejudice. Like Galileo. Like Pasteur. Like Ben Franklin, whose lightning rods were once universally condemned as an insult to God.

3. The controversy about Dr. Leary's Behavior Mod work con-tinues and will continue because no more recent research has ei-ther totally confirmed or totally refuted him. This point I consider most important of all, and I will enlarge upon it. I may even relapse into boldface and capital letters. . . .

None of Dr. Leary's most important studies have either suf-fered refutation or enjoyed confirmation, because enacted law—statutes enacted after and because of Dr. Leary's research—makes it a crime for any other psychologists or psychiatrists to replicate such research. I know you've heard that the Inquisition ended in 1819, but in many areas of psychotherapy and psychopharmacol-ogy the U.S. government has taken up where the Vatican left off. Maybe you didn't get that. I feel sure, somehow, that Newt Gingrich didn't get it and doesn't want to get it. Let me say it again, in leaner English. ANY PSYCHOLOGIST OR PSYCHIATRIST WHO TRIES TO REPEAT DR. LEARY'S EXPERIMENTS WILL GET THROWN IN JAIL.

Dig? When postmodernists speak of "social forces shaping the scientific models" of a decade, of a generation or even of a longer time period, this does not merely refer to vague "prejudices" or "vested interests" or the notorious "conservatism of the head of the department"—although all of these play a role as social forces shaping scientific models. In some cases, "social forces" means something less diffuse and more Inquisitorial: the very terrifying threat of imprisonment in a prison system where mayhem, murder, rape, and corruption play a larger role than in any slum on the outside. Now I would say that counts as a quite concrete and clearcut example of how "social forces" have shaped the psychology of the past three decades.

Researchers don't do certain kinds of research because they don't want to get thrown in San Quentin, as happened to Dr. Leary.

Of course, a great deal of research relevant to Dr. Leary's work does exist, lost in the backward abyss of time like fossil bones— hundreds and hundreds of scientific papers. All these studies by other researchers appeared before the Holy Inquisition—pardon, the U.S. government—forbade such investigation. I have read most of it; I read it as it appeared in the 1950s and 1960s, because the subject fascinated me then as it does now. I assert that over 90 percent of these published papers tend to support Leary's basic ideas. Sometimes they disagree on details; sometimes they use their own jargon instead of his jargon; but they all tend to confirm his views on LSD as a very powerful behavior-changing agent with immense potential for therapy if used properly. Many also support his view that LSD used improperly, as in the infamous CIA experiments, can sabotage the brain so totally that "mind murder" seems the best word for such unethical experiments.

Do you think I exaggerate the degree of support for Leary (in research papers, not in theory or polemic)? Investigate the subject on your own; computers make such hunting for old articles easier than ever before. Find out what the evidence shows, as distinct from what "popular opinion" claims. Then see what you think of accepted opinions in general and the media that create and manipulate them.

As for my personal memories of Tim Leary, the man . . . So many years, so many memories . . .

1964: I came to Millbrook to interview Dr. Leary for a virtually unknown little magazine called *The Realist*, which has since become both famous and infamous. I found not the Harvard professor I expected but a youngish middle-aged man playing baseball on the lawn. When we sat down at the kitchen table to do the interview, I found the Harvard professor, the author of *The Interpersonal Diagnosis of Personality*, one of my favorite books on psychology, the man I expected. Later, when I asked a question about LSD, he replied, "Every trip has a point where the space game comes to an end, the time game comes to an end, and the Timothy Leary game comes to an end." I had had LSD maybe four score and seven times by then, but I had never found words to describe the peak as well as that sentence does.

1967, Chicago: I had a job with another famous/infamous magazine, *Playboy*, and Tim dropped by the office, and memory has so many tricks that I can't recall if his visit concerned an article by him or an interview with him. I remember telling him that I had found the letters LSD repeated several times in *Finnegans Wake* and asked what he thought of that. He replied that to Joyce LSD meant "pounds, shillings, pence," and this began my years of research of the duodecimal system in the *Wake*, culminating in my book *Coincidance* and my video "12 Eggs in a Box," finding Paleolithic origins for the zodiac, the twelve apostles, the twelve labors of Hercules, the l-s-d coinage that lasted from Babylon to the 1970s, and our system of trial by jury. Joyce had supplied the psychoarchaeological evidence, but Tim gave me the key to understand it.

1968, still Chicago: I turned on the TV news and there stood Tim in front of a cow. I soon identified the scene as the "farm" section of the Lincoln Park Zoo. Tim talked about the upcoming Democratic Convention and made some Pythonesque jokes about Leary's cow and the famous Chicago fire. I laughed like a loon, but the city authorities didn't have that kind of sense of humor. When the convention rolled around, the city had such heavy security (tanks, even!) that you could hardly tell it from Prague, under siege the very same week, as two corrupt governments—in communist Czechoslovakia and in capitalist USA—used excessive force to prevent their peoples from meddling in politics.

Tim's 1970 imprisonment for poor usage of the first amendment and his swashbuckling escape (which will someday make a great movie—what other great philosopher-rebel, except Bakunin, has broken out of jail so colorfully?) occurred far from me in space, but I followed the whole saga closely in the media.

In 1973, when they caught up with him and brought him back, I also had returned to These States and found a copy of his pamphlet *Neurologic* in a bookstore somewhere. I can't quite describe how that little book hit me, although I think of Cortez on that famous peak (in Darien?). I no longer consider *Neurologic* Dr. Leary's greatest work, because he has developed its thesis into several larger, more detailed and specific books. Nonetheless, in 1973 that small pamphlet came to me as the kind of Great Light that Copernicus represented to Giordano Bruno: what had previously seemed vague, even chaotic, suddenly fell into place as part of an organized system that made sense. Athough Leary did not mention all his sources, I saw that he had synthesized everything of value in most of the major psychological systems of our century with everything I had ever heard about the current research on brain function, and he made it all suddenly, beautifully, coherent.

If I had known at once what I learned later—that Tim had written this brilliant essay in pencil on the floor of a solitary confinement cell—I would have felt even more stunned. I felt stunned enough, anyway. I began a letter-writing campaign, informing all and sundry that we had our greatest scientist-philosopher locked up in a cage and would look like ignorant barbarians in a more civilized future. I accomplished nothing, of course. The United States that year did not want to hear a defense of the Mad Scientist of Millbrook. I did, however, hear from several of Tim's other friends and, eventually, I got his prison address. I started writing fan letters to him in prison. Soon I received an invitation to visit him.

My very first visit to Tim in Vacaville (I rememer mentally translating that as cow-town and feeling bemused) stands out in the halls of memory as the most intense learning experience of my life. I had expected to find a suffering martyr and to do my best to cheer him up. Instead, I found a buoyant and glowing young man (younger than when I first met him nine years before) who had transcended the prison experience so totally that *he* cheered *me* up.

I returned home thinking of Hamlet's "Nothing is but thinking makes it so," and Buddha's "All that we are is the result of all that we have thought," and all sorts of Christian Science and idealistic ideas that I had never taken seriously. Now I had to take them seriously—although I did not take them literally. Translating them into Dr. Leary's language, I realized that, whatever energies and signals get into our brain, we organize them, orchestrate them, and edit them in accord with a personal reality-tunnel. This framing of naked experience into customized, individualized reality-tunnels happens either unconsciously/mechanically, as in normal consciousness, or consciously/creatively, as in the Timothy Leary I met in my visits to Vacaville prison.

Before Tim got out of prison, he had written *Terra II* and *Exo-Psychology* (now rewritten as *Info-Psychology*) and expressed the future scenario, which he abbreviated as SMI²LE: Space Migration + Intelligence Increase + Life Extension. I had read a lot of futurist scenarios by then, and some (by Bucky Fuller and associates) I liked about as much as this, but absolutely none of them seemed more worthy of enthusiastic attention. We have the technology for space colonization already; if Tim's views on neurochemistry stand up, we have the technology for intelligence and consciousness-expansion; the technology for life extension has appeared more rapidly every year since Tim wrote those pioneering works. The ultimate consequence of Space Migration + Intelligence Increase + Life Extension = our evolution from neurotic terrestrial mortals to enlightened cosmic immortals. Does any rival scenario offer more than that? The fact that Tim devised all this while locked up as a felon never ceased to astound and confound me. The notion that we live in a rational, secularist time seemed more and more unbelievable. We live in the late Dark Ages, my friends, and Tim seems more than our Galileo. I regard him as our Leonardo. In those years, while they still had him caged, I thought often of the famous lines from *Man of La Mancha*:

> *And the world shall be better for this*
> *That one man, scorned and covered with scars,*
> *Still strove with his last ounce of courage*
> *To reach the unreachable stars.*

When Tim finally got out of prison, we appeared several times on panels together, both of us preaching the gospel of SMI²LE. In more recent years he has moved on, and mentions outer space less often, pushing cyberspace instead. It took me a while to catch up with him on this. I now see that if a large part of human neurological liberation awaits us in outer space, the part that we can get our hands on right now exists (and continues to grow rapidly) in cyberspace. I have found communities in cyberspace that have more freedom and more hope for us alive today than can possibly appear in space colonies in the next fifty years. (Speaking of the information ocean: only one computer game does not bore me quickly and continues to entertain and instruct me—Dr. Leary's "Mind Mirror." I cordially recommend it to all.)

I seem to have said little about Tim's wonderful humor here. I recall one incident that I think I remember in full. In Durango, where both of us spoke on future evolution a year or so ago, Tim lost his thread in midsentence—something that happens to all of us who lecture frequently. He stopped and said, "You know, I've found a new way to get high and stay spaced out for hours, and the government can't stop me. It's called senility. It has four major effects. First, increase in long-term memory—I can recall all of evolution. Second, decrease in short-term memory—when I get to the kitchen, I can't remember what I was going there for. I forget what the third is. And the fourth is—I don't give a fuck anymore." (In this humorless puritanical society, reports of that joke got around and some pundits declared triumphantly that LSD had made Dr. Leary senile in his seventies—as if many men who never tried acid didn't get Alzheimer's as early as their forties. And Tim does not show any symptoms of senility, in the judgment of those who know him. He only made a joke about senility. Oh, well . . . trying to correct the media about Leary reminds me of trying to correct them about Vietnam: every time a lie seems dead, they wait five years and recirculate it.)

Now, as everybody knows, Tim has prostate cancer. Some pundits will blame that on LSD, too, I suppose. As usual, Tim himself continues to astonish me; the last time we spoke on the phone he once again cheered me up. As you have heard, Dr. Leary intends to have his head cryonically frozen, gambling on the very good odds that future science will eventually reanimate him from the neural and genetic information there stored. He also intends to exit on the day he chooses, not on the day when medical science decides they can't drain any more money out of him by keeping him in misery in a hospital. So he will leave us—for a while—showing his usual trust in his own mind and his utter refusal to submit to any authority in which he does not believe, whether it call itself the State, the Church, the AMA, or that most terrifying of all deities, Public Opinion. He said recently that he will drop two hits of acid the day he goes into cryonic suspension. And out of a thousand people, roughly 999 will howl and scream that he shouldn't and he mustn't and it's all ungodly and un-American and blah-blah-blah. The one in a thousand who understands not just the courage of Tim's decision but its total radiant sanity represents the part of humanity upon whom all future evolution depends.*

*Since the above was written Tim has died. According to a film called *Timothy Leary Is Dead,* his head was preserved. According to all other reports, Tim changed his mind and did not have his head preserved. I don't know. But a month after his death, I received the following e-mail:

> Dear Robert,
> How are you doing? I'm doing fine over here, but it's not what I expected. Too crowded.
> Love,
> Timothy

Illusions

ROSEMARY WOODRUFF

On my third visit to Millbrook in the spring of 1965, Tim smiled at me over my gift of Woodruff-flavored May wine.

I thought he was kind. When we walked in the woods he showed me where he'd thrown his wedding ring into the pond where a man had drowned. Last year's leaves were brown under the shallow waters. I thought he was lonely.

When I met him again at an art gallery opening in early June, I'd taken LSD alone earlier in the day. I was wonderfully happy; happy to be solitary, complete within myself, peaceful yet exhilarated. A sweet sensation. That evening Tim spoke of psychedelic

---

Rosemary Woodruff Leary left St. Louis, Missouri, at seventeen as an air force officer's wife bound for an isolated desert base in Washington State. A year later she was a model in New York City. By 1964 she had been a television actress, interior decorator, jazz musician's wife, beatnik stewardess, and countless other personalities. After her marriage to Timothy Leary she became a stepmother, seminar instructor, light show artist, chatelaine for a sixty-four-room mansion, League for Spiritual Discovery guide, prisoner in the Poughkeepsie jail, and, after an arrest in Laguna Beach, California, a felon. After escaping to Algeria, she was a fugitive for twenty-four years. She now lives free and peacefully in northern California.

Rosemary and Tim

art and the techniques of "audio-olfactory-visual alterations of consciousness." He was didactic, oracular, self-aggrandizing, and very
amusing.

Afterward we walked to the corner for a drink.

"You remind me of someone I once loved."

"Let's see." From my pocket I took the small two-way mirror
an artist had given me, held it up between us.

"My hair, your smile, my nose, your eyes, what do you see?"

"Good match." He lit a cigarette.

"Perhaps." I lifted my glass to him.

He was exhilarating, like the first draft of pure oxygen after a
trip in the dentist's chair. There was that sense of having shared
something with him in some unremembered time, a most profound
experience. But I had to decline his invitation to Millbrook that
weekend. He was married to a beautiful, blonde, highly paid model.
And I had an eager musician. I liked his strong, Indian face, remembering it from another lifetime, loving. He was the epitome of
graceful dissipation. Dark rhythms starred his veins. Loving jazz
and elegance as I did, I loved him at first sight.

Escaping a summer of sadness, I was on my way to Millbrook

with Tim rather than to California with my family where I felt I ought to go. He fetched me in a borrowed Jeep. Running away from my home. One black eye, patched jeans, a ripped sneaker. I was shy, being saved that way.

"What have you been doing all summer?" he asked.

"Dying by degrees of heat and madness," I replied.

"I have a theory about death, would you like to hear it?"

"Sure."

"Ecstasy comes to everyone at that moment, the moment of death, and dying is a merging with the life process. What do you think?"

"I don't know, I really don't believe that death is a way out but lately I've found myself wishing this life would cease."

"So have I many a time. Let's make an agreement, shall we?"

"What's that smell?" The car was full of smoke and a knocking sound came from the engine.

"Open your window. I forgot the muffler's broken. This was the only car working." The cool dark air banished the fumes, but the knocking grew louder.

"What did you say?" I had to shout.

"Let's go together."

"Where?"

"Everywhere. Why didn't you come to Millbrook when I asked you to?"

"I didn't need rescuing then."

Blue eyes smiled companionably. "Now what would you like?" he asked me.

"Sensual enjoyment and mental excitement."

"What else?"

I looked at him, handsome profile, strong hands on the wheel. Keen flame-colored eyes, a man once dark, now silver-haired and fair. "To love you, I suppose."

Full moon in Aquarius, August midnight. We turned through the gates, across the bridge, under a tunnel of trees. The windows of the large white house were lit with red and blue, a castle with towers surrounded by countless acres of woods, lakes, gardens, and ruins. All the elements of myth and fancy were here and the master of it all, in a courtly way, opened the door. He led me up to the tower room. A slow smile. He left, descending the narrow stairs.

I woke to a soft summer day, sucking sweet white hoya blossoms from the window vine, forgetting my vow of solitude, remembering last night's long, slow waves of his desire that came hurtling up the stairs. I had felt him all through the night, footsteps pounding the maze of corridors, bare feet echoing the final rounds. My dreams were of a restless man in scarlet robes in the chamber below.

I wanted to know him if I could; he seemed wise.

It was a seminar weekend at Millbrook. Gurdjieff's techniques were the theme. The house was full of guests signed on for two days of lectures, light shows, "theories of expanding awareness," as the brochure said. There was also a television crew. In the afternoon Tim swiveled in the office chair, tossing metaphors to listeners at his feet.

"You lose your mind to use your head," he explained with a smile.

"How often do you coin such . . ." He stopped me with a look. How could I question him? I was the apprentice.

In the early evening with two dogs walking near us we paced the carriage drive through the overhanging maples to the gatehouse at the edge of the property. The medieval belltower of the gatehouse was the residence of Flo and Maynard Ferguson. She a wise woman, mother of five, and he a musician *extraordinaire*. I'd met them at Millbrook before and liked them immensely. Flo's humor and grace and Maynard's good nature and deserved reputation as one of the few consistently successful band leaders lent gaiety and glamour to the small community of Millbrook. With them we shared a bottle of wine and laughter and then decided, reluctantly, that we had to return to the main house for the evening lecture.

Tim and I stopped when we came to the small watchtower on the bridge to look out over the stillness of the lake. We kissed, hesitant at first, then knowingly. A sweet kiss. A promise. I wouldn't go to California.

The southwest room was a theater for the guests on Saturday night. Michael Hollingshead fed slides to the projectors, Ralph Metzner played musical tapes. Cross-legged on a rug before the baronial fireplace, Tim commanded the room's attention, directing guests and staff ranged around the walls. We all played parts. The plot was this: A spaceship, oxygen almost gone, five minutes to live, what would be the message home?

Some made jokes, a few confessed their sins. Most spoke of love and family, then it was time for Captain Tim. He cleared his throat. The fuses blew. The lights went out. The microphone was dead.

"We need some light here," he said testily. But everyone was too spaced to move.

I crossed the room and settled at his side. I had the sense of having made a perilous journey. Maynard and Flo made a welcoming gesture, arranging pillows so I could be near. I felt love and a desire to dedicate myself, also a bit of pride that I'd safely navigated the large room, feeling as I did the effects of the LSD that had been in the wine.

"Did you bring a candle?"

"No, but here's a match."

Then there was light from outside. Michael Hollingshead, whose fitful sense of humor could only be described as weird, was in a kilt with a strobe light flashing on while he did naughty leaps on the trampoline, a rather startling sight and fitting end to the disrupted lecture.

I was in bed before an open window and a midnight sky puzzling over Tim's alterations of Lao-tzu when he came into the tower room. I pointed to his poems scattered over the bed.

> *Gate of the soft mystery*
> *Constantly enduring*
> *Gate of the soft mystery*
> *Use her gently*
> *And without the touch of pain.*

"Why a 'touch of pain' and what do you mean, 'lose your mind?'"

"I'll tell you a story." He blew out the light. "Once there were three princes. Their father, the king, sent them on a quest. To answer the riddle of what every woman wants would prove which prince the best." His voice caressed me softly. I felt it slide across my skin. I felt it so intently, I almost missed the end. ". . . and this is what the witch replied: 'complete submission is the answer to a woman's pride.'"

I wondered. His surrender to the moment seemed so much more complete than mine; but pleasure was promised by his hand, voice, mind.

We painted crossed triangles on the chimney, put a gilded Buddha in a niche, restored a glass ruby to a plaster lion's eye, then had our first LSD session together. He brought all his experience of Lamas coughing deep in the Himalayas and a few other tapes. Dylan was my familiar friend he couldn't hear, whose words I sang in Tim's ear, "Awl I really want to doooo, is baby be friends with you!"

"The aim is to produce a psychedelic or ecstatic experience without using drugs. The methods involve an intense ten hour inundation of programmed stimuli . . . sensory, emotional and intellectual, artistic, philosophical . . . which reproduce and induce the LSD experience."

We were on the road. A caravan of cars full of equipment; Don Synder, Michael, Ralph, Tim, and me. We were a motley crew. We took over hotel rooms or donated apartments, covered the walls with paisley Indian cloth, set up projectors and lights, daily conducting twenty or more people through their nervous systems and ours. Eighty-year-old Vedantists, Reichians, Wiccans, Episcopalians, Amway salesmen, mystic housewives, wistful thinkers, a broad spectrum of occultists seeking epiphany. Ralph in measured monotone read relaxation rituals. Tim explained his theories of consciousness expansion, the need "to go out of your mind to use your head." I sat behind a projector, sliding high colors on the walls, listening to his voice gliding down long red tunnels. Acid red. Mesmerized, murmuring his poems with him. "Can you float through the universe of your body and not lose your way? Lose all, fusing?"

His voice was the thread I was attached to. Not the timbre but the tone of genial warmth and wealth of wit. The element of persuasiveness was faith amplified to public certainty of a chemically induced divinity; Irish charm gifted with the magic of the word, the word become flesh. I could not imagine loving anyone else. Everyone, compared to him, was boring.

Dear Mother,
I will write at length later. I wanted to send you a photograph and some literature concerning the foundation and assure you again of my happiness and good health. I am living on a beautiful estate with friends and I have never before enjoyed my life as much as I do now. Please write to me c/o Leary, Castalia Foundation, Millbrook, N.Y.
LOVE

He asked me to marry him. I said yes. But we would have to wait for his divorce. With his daughter, Susan, we went to New York City to bring my furniture and belongings back to Millbrook.

Ninth Street off Fifth Avenue had been my address for several years; the large room with the high ceiling and a fireplace was a refuge and a solace. I never thought to leave it; my only ambition had been to acquire the apartment next door and have that rarity, a floor-through flat. Everything in it had memory and meaning and I was comfortable in my own environment. I wondered if I'd be the same in the many-roomed mansion at Millbrook.

Susan returned to school. We were three in the huge echoing house. Jack Leary, Tim's sixteen-year-old son, handsome as a prince in a fairy tale, Timothy and I. I grew to love them in that brief quiet time, a space between the wars, long walks through the estate with the dogs, moony nights.

In our room on the third floor we would have dinner before a fire. After Jack left to do his homework, Tim would pace the room and I would watch him. He was so graceful, so likable. When he reached a point, he would turn and grin with pleasure at me. He reshaped the world according to his momentary vision which surrounded me like a bower, all flowers and laughing children. More flattering still was the assumption that I shared his views, understood his aims. I appreciated his wit. Instructing, bragging, flattering, and charming, what he didn't say didn't seem important. What was important was the response he elicited from me. I felt clever, graceful, chosen, and that I'd met my match. Besides, he needed me, the zenith of happiness no one else had ever, could ever, give him, the possibility of, he said, "perfect love."

Then he would listen to my tales, his eyes never leaving my face. Embraces of the eye and mind encouraged me to humor, making light of marriages, miscarriages, and mishaps of all the years before him. Uptown, downtown, nightclubs, hard-hearted owners, the decline of jazz, society gigs, waiting for the union check, paying dues, blues, brief flush of success, California, Hollywood movies . . . New York again . . . Ran away with a man twice my age, a composer of classical music. Silver-haired southern madman wrote symphonies all week, got drunk and lost on weekends. He turned me on to peyote and real poverty on the lower east side before it was fashionable or even Puerto Rican, all orthodox Jews and Ukranians. More jazz . . . Thank God I never got on to junk.

And then all the tales I cared to tell were told. The past was banished. Our lovemaking had a new depth of meaning. He wanted me to have his child. My hero. I loved him.

It snowed for days covering the hills and trees, adding height to the pillars before the garden, a pristine blanket of renewal. We dreamed of sun, warm sand, clear waters, a Christmas trip. The travel folders called Yucatan, Mexico, a land of hemp and honey. Jack, Susan, and someone to help with the driving would go with us.

Dear Family,
A week from today, Tim, Susan, Jackie, a boy named Rene to companion the kids, and I will start for Mexico. We'll all take turns driving a new Ford station wagon. We plan to go to Merida, Yucatan, and find a quiet place to stay for a few months. We should be back in Millbrook by the end of March. The house will need a lot of work to get it ready for our summer seminars.

My life is serene. The country is at all times beautiful. I enjoy the cold and rainy nights. I take long walks accompanied by two large dogs named Fang and Obie. We walk all over the estate. They've shown me the deer graveyard full of antlers and where they go to catch rabbits. I love and know this land so well.

There are lots of visitors on weekends. We had thirty people here for Thanksgiving. I cooked two turkeys, a ham and a haunch of venison. During the week I try to get the house in order and read and walk with Tim. Susan is away at school and in all these rooms there is just Tim, Jackie, me, two dogs, and four cats.

I'm really excited about the trip to Mexico. I'll send you postcards along the way.

LOVE

A long lazy drive to Nuevo Laredo. A bit of shame waited there. A familiar face and uniform greeted Tim on the Mexican side of the border—the police agent who escorted him to the plane in Mexico City years before. We were forbidden to enter. We had to go back to the American side. Mexico City would be consulted. Perhaps we could cross the next day if all was in order, the agent said. We walked a few yards to our luggage-crowded car. It was surrounded by Mexican police, idle, sunning themselves. I got in the back and hurriedly looked through our packed gear. Tim started the motor. I asked him to wait but he didn't hear.

I found what I was looking for and tried to open the window, but it was blocked by clothes and books. I turned to Rene, asked him to open the window. He was frozen in fear. We were a few hundred yards from American Customs.

Custom agents approached the car. "Do you have anything to declare?" They looked through our luggage and food. We were then stripped, searched: hair, ears, even ass. Charged with evasion of taxes, smuggling, transporting, we were jailed in Laredo, Texas, for less than half a lid of very weak grass.

The trial took place in February 1966. Tim was sentenced to thirty years and a forty thousand dollar fine.

No more quiet walks on moonlit nights. He was busy with

lawyers and press conferences, fighting the government, answering his critics, testifying to his revelations and to his certainty that LSD was the tool mankind needed to be free.

He perceived the world with the knowledge that psychology gave him and the unfettered imagination of an Irish hero, a combination that produced a fey charisma, a likable madness, an outrageous optimism. The magic of loving and being loved by such a man would keep me in thrall for many years.